Materials, Form
and Architecture

Materials, Form and Architecture

Richard Weston

Yale University Press

Published in North America by
Yale University Press
P.O. Box 209040
New Haven, CT 06520-9040
U.S.A.

First published in Great Britain in 2003 by
Laurence King Publishing Ltd, London

Library of Congress Control Number: 2003103217

ISBN: 0-300-09579-1

Project managed by Anne McDowall
Designed by SEA
Picture research by Helen Stallion

Printed in Singapore

Introduction

Glimpsed from a distance, these houses on a new estate on the edge of The Hague appear to be model suburban dwellings. Semi-detached, pitch-roofed and steep-gabled, with windows at the corners and doors in-between, they epitomize the European idea of house and might almost have been drawn by a child. Look again and you realize that they are anything but ordinary. Clad all over in an array of unexpected materials – green and blue polyurethane, profiled aluminium, wooden shingles, terracotta tiles – they suddenly look less like real buildings than life-size versions of hotels and houses assembled in profitable lines on a Monopoly board.

Multi-coloured groups of houses are hardly unfamiliar. The older streets of Copenhagen are famous for their varied pastel colour washes, which glow beguilingly in the gentle northern light, whereas further south on the Venetian island of Burano the housing is a riot of brilliant colours, sufficiently vivid to resist bleaching by the southern sun. And whilst we may admire the consistency and restraint with which, say, the traditional timber buildings of Sweden dot the agricultural landscape with pixels of red- and yellow-ochre, we are equally happy to enjoy a variety of colours applied to otherwise more or less identical timber buildings.

In all these examples, but unlike the Dutch estate, the colours are an applied finish, which can be changed at will. Part of our satisfaction in their variety may well lie in the belief, justified or not, that the diverse colours reflect the taste of the occupants – and as such, we might be tempted to reflect, are an apt expression of the structure and freedoms of democratic societies. The MVRDV houses of The Hague offer their residents no such choice. Their colours are integral to the cladding: you may choose to buy a green or blue model, but the colour can be changed only on what both owners and architects must hope will be a rather longer maintenance cycle than that of paint or wood-stain.

The strangeness of the Dutch houses has to do with much more than their apparently arbitrary variation of finish. Cut at will into the cardboard-thin walls, the windows seem larger than normal, and do not quite line up in the way that countless openings, arrayed neatly one above the other in load-bearing walls, have taught us to expect. Where roof and wall meet there is neither a gutter nor a fascia – rainwater, one assumes, is simply allowed to stream down the walls to join the surface run-off on paths and roads. The materials seal the box-like houses by wrapping all but seamlessly around junctions and corners, but then dangle short of the ground in a shameless and disconcerting display of their insubstantiality.

Although it is here made to appear strange, even slightly bizarre, the idea of covering a building with a single material is not especially unusual. In dry climates, traditional adobe buildings often fuse earth, walls and roof into a pale, dun-coloured unity, whilst the Greek island of Sifnos boasts tiny, white-all-over churches so dazzling and smooth they look as if they might be made of sugar icing. Such churches are, in fact, only unusually striking expressions of a Mediterranean tradition of whitewashing every surface of flat-roofed buildings – a tradition from which, as we shall see, Le Corbusier was to derive his 'Law of Ripolin' and vision of an all-embracing *polychromie architecturale*.

Precedents for this one-material-all-over approach are by no means confined to the vernacular. Countless modern factories and warehouses use the same profiled metal claddings on roofs and walls, and designers from Buckminster Fuller and Jean Prouvé to Future Systems have wrapped buildings with sheet metal or plastic, like pieces of large-scale industrial design. But the effects in both cases are quite different. No standard industrial shed is built with MVRDV's knowing avoidance of conventional flashings and trims to master joints and deflect rain, and the absence of these details is crucial to the slightly surreal effects they are after. And whilst exponents of the building-as-product school of design may

Housing estate near The Hague, designed by MVRDV.

achieve a similarly seamless form, they often do so by making their buildings look like a stylish hairdryer or bedside radio.

These houses are troubling for many architects because they challenge one of the central calls-to-arms of modern architecture: 'truth to materials'. In fact they issue a double challenge. Built using a recently developed form of construction known as 'rainscreen cladding', they ask us to contemplate what it means to be 'true' to materials when the all-important surfaces we see are entirely detached from the underlying construction. These houses could, in theory, be clad with any materials that will keep most of the rain off the insulation behind: why then, they ask house-builders and the buying public, are similarly built new houses in Holland still almost universally politely dressed with an expensive and needlessly heavy veneer of brick?

Like all architects of high ambition, MVRDV are embedded in the culture of their time, and to anyone familiar with the so-called 'Swiss Box' school of design – which we will explore in detail in Chapter 10 – this group of houses will not seem as bizarre as I have suggested. Indeed, it is but one of many contemporary projects in which a fascination with materials and the surfaces of buildings has displaced modern architects' familiar preoccupation with space and structure. Surfaces may now

be warped and folded using sophisticated computer-modelling packages, tattooed with decoration and arcane messages, or – as in these Dutch houses – finished with improbable materials in the service of aesthetic aspirations that owe more to fine-art practices such as Minimalism and Arte Povera than they do to the traditional disciplines of building. No longer merely the bounding surfaces of form and space, building envelopes are becoming the focus of attention in their own right: skin is the new space.

For all their radicalism, Modern architects were avowedly traditional in their commitment to the 'honest' expression of structure and materials – even if it was by no means always straightforwardly observed. In this respect their ideals represented, as Frank Lloyd Wright put it, 'a cause conservative'. Preferring to be identified as practitioners of the art of building, rather than with what they regarded as the bankrupt compositional methods of the Ecole des Beaux Arts, they eagerly embraced new materials, such as reinforced concrete, steel and large sheets of glass. Radically new kinds of space emerged, but until aspirations began to change in the 1950s the aim was always to make of them a new vernacular, a generally practised way of building, as expressive of the Machine Age as any of the great styles of the past were of the aspirations of their times.

Housing in Oslo.

Street on the Greek island of Paros.

Church on Sifnos.

Materials loom large in most discussions of contemporary architecture and it is difficult to attend a review of student work without hearing the word 'materiality' – even if, as often as not, all that is meant is 'materials'. The aim here is to reconnoitre this territory from the perspectives of history and ideas, and to explore ways of experiencing architecture as a material art. It is not a book about 'building materials', certainly not of the technical kind that find their way onto reading lists for courses in building construction, although it begins with a brief review of, and reflections on, the extraordinary range of materials with which people have built over time and around the planet. Two chapters examine ways in which relationships between materials and form have been discussed from antiquity to the present, the second being devoted specifically to the Modernist ideal of truth to materials. Six descriptive essays follow, illustrating different aspects of materials, before an extended discussion of expressions of materiality and transparency in recent and contemporary architecture.

Chapter 1
Materials for Building

Finely jointed but irregularly
coursed masonry on the site
of the pyramids at Giza
near Cairo.

It cannot have been so very different in Ur 5000 years ago: the same laboriously fashioned bricks… the same spaces around a courtyard; the same enclosure; the same sudden transition from light into darkness; the same coolness after heat; the same starry nights; the same fears, perhaps; the same sleep.
Aldo van Eyck[1]

Architects, theorists and historians have long been fascinated by the origins of architecture in the practical business of building, and so it comes as no surprise that the most celebrated history of architecture in the English language, written by Sir Banister Fletcher and first published in 1896, begins as follows: 'Architecture, with all its varying phases and complex developments, must have had a simple origin in the primitive efforts of mankind to provide protection against inclement weather, wild beasts, and human enemies.'[2] Although he devoted only three of more than 800 pages to describing three such 'rough structures'– caves, provided by nature and emulated by carving of stone or earth, or in masonry construction; huts, modelled on natural arbours; and tents, developed from the habit of lying under animal skins or fleeces – the reader is clearly intended to understand that these derivations from 'natural prototypes' anticipated the essence of much that was to follow.

The evidence for Banister Fletcher's speculations came less from archaeological findings about the past than from a long tradition in the architectural literature about the prior claims of his three archetypes.[3] A century later, the precise origins of building remain obscure. It seems unlikely that the hunter-gatherers who roamed Europe in the late Stone Age could have survived without constructing temporary shelters, and rings of stones dating back to before 12,000 BC may well have formed the bases of huts made from wooden poles, or perhaps tents of animal skins, but sure confirmation of such ephemeral features is hard to find.

Origins, real or mythical, retain their fascination, and few buildings loom as large in the history of architecture as that ubiquitous theoretical dwelling, the 'primitive hut'.[4] The lineage begins with the only architectural treatise that has survived from the ancient world, written in the first century BC by a Roman whose name, like that of Banister Fletcher, is also synonymous with a book: Marcus Vitruvius Pollio. The first shelters, in Vitruvius's view, involved setting up forked posts, putting flexible twigs or branches between them and then finishing the wall with mud – an early form

'The Cave', one of three archetypal dwellings illustrated by the historian Sir Banister Fletcher.

A primitive hut made of saplings, as visualized by the French architect and theorist, Viollet-le-Duc.

The most famous image of a primitive hut, from the Abbé Laugier's *Essai sur l'architecture*.

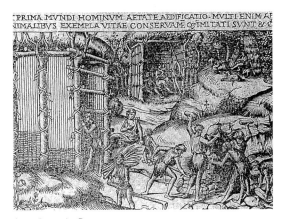

PRIMA MVNDI HOMINVM AETATE AEDIFICATIO MVLTI ENIM A
NIMALIBVS EXEMPLA VITAE CONSERVAME QÝ IMITATI SVNT &

According to the Roman architect Vitruvius, the 'first builders' wove their walls using twigs.

of composite construction, now generally known as wattle and daub, which was widely practised in pre-industrial societies and is still in use today. As an alternative, he describes walls 'built out of dried clods, framed with wood, and covered with reeds and leaves to keep out rain and heat', for which, again, it would not be hard to find contemporary counterparts.[5]

Like the great nineteenth-century French theorist Eugène-Emmanuel Viollet-le-Duc, whose putative 'First Building' was formed by binding together suitably spaced saplings,[6] Vitruvius's speculations were based on real huts he had seen in the Crimea, in Turkey, and near Marseilles. A form of construction using similar principles to that which Viollet-le-Duc illustrated has come to tragic prominence in recent years. The vast marshes between the confluence of the Tigris and Euphrates north of Basra have long been home to various tribes of Marsh Arabs. The local qasab reed grows to six metres (20 feet) in height and is used by the marsh-dwellers to create extraordinary dwellings, the largest of which – the guesthouses – can reach 36 metres (118 feet) in length. As a result of the Iran-Iraq war, and of continuing efforts to drain the marshes, this unique way of life may soon come to an end.

Unlike Vitruvius and Viollet-le-Duc, the 'architect' of the most famous of all primitive huts, the Abbé Laugier, opted for a purely theoretical approach. His celebrated design owes much of its fame to a memorable engraving, not published until the second edition of his influential *Essai sur l'architecture*,[7] which showed a female personification of Architecture directing a young child's attention to four trees lashed together to support a suspiciously roof-like triangular framework of branches. You do not need to read the accompanying description to realize that this is, so to speak, an attempt to de-construct a Greek temple rather than to re-construct a credible primordial shelter.

The reed-built houses of the Marsh Arabs in Iraq echo rudimentary ancient forms of construction.

The gable of the shrine at Ise
in Japan (top) is echoed by
these traditional structures
in Oman (above).

Post-and-beam store on the
Swedish island of Gotland –
almost identical in form
to the Ise shrine.

Rebuilt every 20 years,
the Shinto shrine at Ise
in Japan is thought to date
back some 1500 years.

We will return to Laugier and his primitive hut in the next chapter. But for our immediate purposes, what these conjectures about early forms of building reveal is just how conservative and tradition-bound a business building has for the most part been, at least when compared to many other aspects of human endeavour. The means of production have changed out of all recognition, new materials such as steel and reinforced concrete been introduced, and old ones such as glass produced in sizes and quantities previously unimaginable. But many of the fundamental materials for building – wood, baked and compressed earth, stone and metals – were all used by ancient civilizations, and often on a scale every bit as impressive as any later achievements. And when new materials have been introduced, they have generally been used in emulation of familiar modes of building: in this respect, at least, Laugier's ideas were soundly grounded.

In the stories of architecture's origins, the building materials are all unprocessed: materials found in nature – such as saplings, reeds, or fieldstone – are variously joined and stacked, not worked. Although log construction strikes many modern observers as the most primitive form of timber building, it is largely confined to the coniferous belt of the northern temperate zone, where straight trees are plentiful, and was undoubtedly preceded by simple forms of post-and-beam construction.[8] Stability was achieved by sinking the timber posts into holes, but at the risk of the timber rotting at its junction with the ground – a surprisingly tricky constructional problem to resolve whilst retaining strength. Despite this major weakness, and despite the fact that the Romans had solved it with a form of cill-and-column construction, timber barns continued to be built in this relatively rudimentary way into the seventeenth century in Germany. Japanese *minka* (rural houses) likewise persisted with traditional posts for a century and more.[9]

The history of building provides few clearer examples of the way in which constructional logic can lead to similar forms than the comparison of European thatch-roofed post-and-beam stores, such as those found on the Swedish island of Gotland,[10] with the Ise shrine in Japan. The latter was itself based on the storehouse, or *kura*, developed by the Yayoi people who dominated Japan during the Bronze and Iron Ages. Aesthetically, the Ise shrine is incomparably more refined than the buildings on Gotland, but in all essentials the constructional forms are identical.

Column and beam systems brought different structural challenges, chief amongst which was providing sufficient lateral restraint. In Europe this was generally achieved by various forms of triangulation, but in earthquake-prone Japan the resulting stiffness would have brought its own problems, and structures were designed to be 'solid and resilient'.[11] Joints of sometimes bewildering complexity were devised to maintain the continuity of the major structural members whilst allowing the whole structure to move slightly. Their construction placed formidable demands on the skill of the carpenters – in Japan, there was traditionally no distinction between carpentry and joinery.

A major issue in the design of even the most rudimentary timber structures is coping with the differential movements caused by the fact that, with changing moisture content, wood shrinks and swells very differently along its radial and longitudinal axes. Adequate seasoning can reduce but not entirely eliminate the problem, and in Russia log cabins were traditionally built with green wood and then 'aired', before being taken apart and reassembled with moss between the joints to ensure airtightness. The skill of Norwegian carpenters can be gauged from their ability to combine posts – or 'staves' as they were known locally – with log construction in the famous 'lofts', which were both symbols of, and stores for, the farming families' wealth, as well as – traditionally – home for newly-married couples on their wedding nights.

Norwegian loft, or store, built using large wooden 'staves' (posts) and cantilevered beams.

Traditional log-built store in the Finnish folk museum on the island of Seurasaari, near Helsinki.

In China and Japan, timber was the primary material of almost all the buildings of architectural merit. In Europe, by contrast, architecture – as opposed to everyday building – was dominated by masonry. The most daring uses of timber in the West often lurk unseen behind decorative ceilings. The Romans made impressive use of large timber trusses, and their example was imitated in the Renaissance, when spans of 20-26 metres (65-85 feet) became fairly routine. Sir Christopher Wren, for example, used 22 metre (72 feet) trusses in the roof of the Sheldonian Theatre in Oxford, and Andrea Palladio included in his *Quattro libri* the diagram of a fully triangulated, 30.5 metre (100 feet) span bridge built over the river Cimone in northern Italy.[12]

Medieval English carpenters worked many wonders above Gothic rib vaults, and in the major cathedrals, unlike parish churches or secular buildings, their skills were rarely on public view – the spectacular octagonal lantern above the crossing of Ely cathedral being a conspicuous exception. Their most impressive achievement was undoubtedly the hammerbeam roof of Westminster Hall. Erected in 1399 by the master carpenter Hugh Herland, it used a new form of composite construction to achieve unprecedented spans. This remarkable synthesis of mechanical innovation and aesthetic refinement has led John Harvey to claim it as 'the greatest single work of art of the whole of the European Middle Ages'.[13]

In the USA, where softwood was plentiful and labour short, the industrialization of timber production using steam- and water-powered mills – pioneered in England – proceeded apace. By the 1820s substantial quantities of standard sections were being produced, and the arrival of cheap, machine-made iron nails a decade later made possible a radically new form of construction: the balloon frame. This consisted of a regular grid of small-section timbers (typically 5 x 10 centimetres / 2 x 4 inches) to support the floor and roof joists, and was usually sheathed with diagonal boards for stability. Lightweight and versatile, the resulting timber box became the principal form of house construction in North America. The balloon frame was displaced by its variant, the single-storey platform frame, more than a century later, but small-section timber remained the dominant material in domestic construction.

Many of the most significant recent developments in timber for building have come from advances in glues. Large structural members can be laminated from standard softwood sections, and an array of plywoods and reconstituted boards are now available. These include the ubiquitous chipboard (fiberboard in the USA) and, more recently, medium-density fibreboard (MDF) – beloved of the DIY trade and television make-over shows, but now beset by health and environmental concerns arising from the fine dust produced when it is cut.

Although widely used in making boats and aircraft – the de Havilland Mosquito, one of the most successful aircraft of the Second World War, was made entirely of wood – plywood did not come into mainstream use in building until the 1950s. Its great advantage over normal timber is that by rotating successive veneers through ninety degrees it can take diaphragm stresses and offer greatly improved dimensional stability. Plywood is widespread in modern construction.

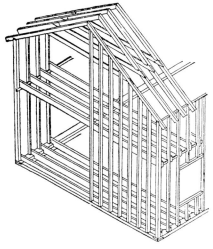

Balloonframe: made of machine-sawn timber sections, it became ubiquitous in the USA.

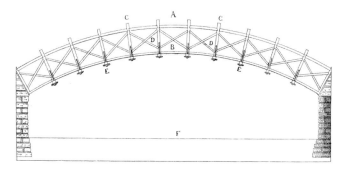

Timber bridge designed by Andrea Palladio and illustrated in his *Four Books on Architecture*.

Glue-laminated timber columns and trusses in Sverre Fehn's Hamar Bispegard Museum, Norway.

Hammerbeam roof of Westminster Hall, London: a tour-de-force of medieval carpentry.

Although suggesting masonry, the octagonal lantern of Ely Cathedral is made of timber.

It provides temporary shutters for concrete and is ideal as a structural sheathing in timber-frame construction, whilst waterproof glues, such as resorcinol formaldehyde, make possible a wide range of structural uses, most efficiently in 'stressed skins' – similar to its use in aircraft fuselages and wings. Birch-ply, produced in large quantities in Finland and Russia, is ideal as a finished material internally or externally, whilst cheaper grades produced from softwoods can be surfaced with a high-quality hardwood veneer to provide a more luxurious appearance.

The only building material that is more universal than timber is the earth itself. Variously excavated, rammed, dried or baked, earth has historically accounted for the bulk of the world's building production, and recent estimates suggest that between one third and one half of all people still live in some form of earthen dwelling.[14] Pliny the Elder records walls in Africa and Spain made by packing earth into a wooden frame, and the Great Wall of China is in part of rammed earth construction – or *pisé*, to use the now widely adopted French term.

The first crude bricks could well have been formed almost naturally, by hand-shaping cracked earth left by the mud deposited across the floodplains of the Nile, Tigris or Euphrates. Sun- and air-dried bricks, now widely referred to as adobe (a Spanish word deriving via Arabic from the Egyptian *thome*, meaning mud), have been used worldwide wherever the geology and climate were suitable. The earliest known permanent dwellings, excavated in the Middle East and dating from around 8300 BC, were circular constructions made with loaf-shaped mud bricks, whose upper surfaces were indented to key in the mud mortar: modern bricklayers would be in no doubt about how to lay them, and their form echoed the similarly built stone *trulli* of south-eastern Italy. The early Egyptian pyramids had brick cores, and by the seventh century BC the 90 metres (295 feet) tall Tower of Babel – inspiration for the Biblical story, and the world's first 'skyscraper' – was built of adobe and faced with fired bricks and asphalt mortar. And contrary to its popular image, ancient Athens was not a city of gleaming stone but dominated by dull mud brick: in keeping with the democratic spirit, even the courtyard homes of the wealthiest citizens seem to have been of the same 'humble' material.[15]

Top: Trullo in Italy: this dry-stone, corbel-vaulted form was also used by early mud-brick houses.

Above: Mud bricks laid out to dry in the sun – now known as 'adobe', and still widely used.

The Great Mosque at Djenné in Mali: mud-brick construction used at a monumental scale.

Building is rarely at the forefront of technological innovation, and the first artificially fired bricks, produced in Mesopotamia around 3000 BC, owe their production to the development of ceramic pottery. Cheaper, sun-dried bricks remained in general use, however, and were the commonest material in Rome right up until Imperial times, by when the State had acquired a virtual monopoly on the production of bricks in man-made kilns. Although fired bricks were eventually produced in vast quantities, Roman brickwork was generally covered by plaster or, on public buildings or the homes of the wealthier citizens, by a thin revetment of stone.

Kiln firing freed brick production from the constraints of being tied to a suitable climate, and the long history of artificially fired bricks challenges many of our assumptions about the sources of materials before industrialization. The craft of brick making spread with the Roman legions and took root throughout Europe wherever suitable clay deposits were available. The early medieval boom in religious building in England required vast quantities of bricks. Many were plundered from Roman remains but brickworks became increasingly common. When the port of Hull was founded in 1299, a municipal brickyard soon followed, making it the first English town built of brick. But for major public buildings – including the Tower of London – bricks were still often imported from Flanders.

As late as the sixteenth century in England, bricks were hardly ever used for the houses of anyone below the status of the higher gentry, except in a few areas in the east of the country.[16] When Sir Richard Weston came to build the revolutionary Sutton Place in Surrey, England – one of the great houses of the early Tudor period, and one of the few to have survived almost unchanged – the diaper-patterned walls combined glazed and plain bricks imported from France with structural and decorative terracotta. Adorning almost every possible feature from window and door surrounds to the turrets, the extensive use of terracotta, unprecedented in England, was almost certainly inspired by the Italian craftsmen Sir Richard employed. A similar mixing of native and imported materials and building traditions is encountered throughout most of Europe. In Spain, following the Moorish invasion, Islamic brick-building techniques mingled with those of Rome, and lived on long after the re-conquest, nowhere more spectacularly than in the vast Coca Castle, on which work began in 1453.

As a mark of distinction, Sutton Place used longer bricks than what was by then the standard 'modern' form. Invented around the mid twelfth century, probably in northern

Albi Cathedral in southern France: the finest brick-built religious building of the Middle Ages.

Church of St George in the pit, hewn directly from the rock at Lālibalā in Ethiopia (c.1300-1400).

Built of locally quarried stone, Queen Hatshepsut's temple at Thebes was called 'the sublime of the sublimes'.

Germany, this was shorter and thicker than the long, flat Roman type. A Dutch chronicle records 1238 as 'the third year of building in brick',[17] and the new form was widely employed for religious buildings throughout northern Europe. In Holland, brick dominated all other materials as nowhere else, and it has been claimed that as early as the sixteenth century the per capita Dutch output of bricks was double that in England at the start of the Industrial Revolution.

A seventeenth-century Dutch kiln could produce more than 600,000 bricks in a single firing, and a century later kilns capable of double this capacity are recorded. Only in the nineteenth century, when the mechanical extrusion and pressing of bricks replaced hand-moulding, and the continuous tunnel kiln was introduced, would the rate of production be dramatically increased. Used as ballast for the outgoing ships that sailed the empire of one of the world's great trading nations, Dutch bricks reached Africa, Asia and the Americas in substantial quantities, leading Richard Goldthwaite to suggest that, 'it is likely that no building-material industry has ever had a more widespread distribution of its products'.[18]

For all its versatility and weathering qualities, brick has generally been regarded as the poor relation of stone. Both Vitruvius and, following his lead in the fifteenth-century, Leon Battista Alberti, commended its use, but Renaissance architects generally emulated Roman precedents and faced their brick walls with plaster or stone. The latter was, of course, usually more costly and therefore carried greater prestige; but both, as we shall discuss in the next chapter, could offer the even surfaces required by the Classical emphasis on clarity of form. In their magisterial *Theory and Elements of Architecture*, published in 1926, Atkins and Bagenal point out that 'for every considerable building there is somewhere a quarry or a brickfield or a gap in a forest'. Although the extent of the international trade in materials since Roman times is far greater

than is often supposed, it is still true, as Atkins and Bagenal go on to observe, that 'the great schools of building coincide with various fine sources of material'.[19] The Florentine Renaissance might never have reached the peak it did were it not for the city's easy access, in the hills between Fiesole and Settignano, to the soft grey *pietra serena*, whose consistency and ease of working perfectly matched the new aesthetic ideals.[20] Similarly, the monumental architecture of Ancient Egypt would have been unthinkable without the country's natural resources.

Occupying a stretch of the Nile valley 700 miles (1100 kilometres) long, from the Mediterranean to a ridge of granite known as the 'first cataract', Ancient Egypt was rich in a remarkable variety of stones. The valley itself consisted of limestone to the north and sandstone to the south, whilst the eastern desert offered beds of alabaster. Further east still, in hills along the Red Sea, black granites, diorites and porphyries were quarried and transported to sites up and down the Nile via a canal dug to connect the great river to the Red Sea.

Building with dressed stone began, with all the suddenness of a lighting strike, around 2700 BC with the construction of the mortuary complex of King Djoser at Saqqara.[21]

Brickwork – as seen here on the Pantheon – lay behind the stone revetments of many Roman buildings.

Bricks are ubiquitous in Holland and, exported as ballast, spread world-wide in the seventeenth century.

Monumental architecture made of sun-dried bricks was flourishing by then, and most of the familiar features of Egyptian religious buildings – battered walls, free-standing screen walls, false doors in relief, and the different types of columns – were well established. Whereas the timber origins of the Greek Doric temple may be disputed by some, it is clear that the pre-existing Egyptian forms were translated directly into stone, and for a time even the stone-building methods themselves were also based directly on those developed using much smaller bricks.

In Egypt, the ability to work stone, combined with the organizational capacity of a powerful centralized government to marshal vast labour forces, made possible the development of buildings of a size that still boggles the imagination. The Great Pyramid of Cheops at Giza required 7.7 million tons of stone. It was erected using more than 2.5 million stones of up to 200 tons in weight, and at 147 metres (482 feet) high remained the tallest man-made structure on earth until the nineteenth century. An unfinished granite obelisk, which was found to have defects over halfway through the quarrying process, can still be seen near Aswan: if completed, it would have been more than 41 metres (135 feet) long and 1200 tons in weight. There is no reason to doubt the Egyptians' capacity to have completed its extraction and erection: two 30-metre (100-feet) obelisks at Karnak were quarried and positioned in a mere seven months, and in the Eighteenth Dynasty two statues each weighing 700 tons were moved 450 miles (720 kilometres) overland using, it is assumed, ropes and rollers – and an impressive labour force. The difficulty of working the intractable granite was prodigious, and being 'sent to the granite' was considered a harsh punishment for criminals.

Hugely impressive though they are, the pyramids we see today at Giza, on the edge of modern Cairo, have been almost completely stripped of their casings of polished limestone or rose-coloured granite and consequently give little idea of their original appearance. A small section of dressed limestone, lingering like snow on a mountain peak, has survived on the central, Chephren pyramid and confirms that, far from being rough 'rubble mountains', the pyramids were made as perfectly smooth planes. Dazzling in the desert sun and entirely devoid of the reliefs and inscriptions familiar on other Egyptian monuments, they were intended as materializations of the sun's rays. Achieving the precision required on this scale – the joints are less than half a millimetre thick – required surveying and masonry skills of the highest order. It is thought that the front edges of the stones were trimmed in situ using a saw – quite possibly just a sheet of copper and abrasive quartz sand. A special jointing technique, known as anathyrosis, was also used. As its name suggests, it was also later employed in Greece to obtain similarly fine stone joints and involved cutting an accurate contact band along the stones' front edges, whilst leaving their inner faces rough and slightly concave.

Features in relief, typical of Egyptian temples such as this at Saqqara, originated in brick construction.

Finely jointed but irregularly coursed masonry on the site of the pyramids at Giza near Cairo.

Top: The stepped pyramid of King Djoser at Saqqara in Egypt, built by the 'first architect', Imhotep.

Above: Pyramid of Chephren at Giza, fractionally smaller than the adjacent Great Pyramid of Cheops.

The Pyramid of Chephren is the only one of the group at Giza to retain part of its limestone casing – most was stripped to help build Cairo in the Middle Ages.

Consisting largely of limestone, the landscape of Greece did not offer the variety of stone enjoyed by Egyptian architects. But it had, as fourth-century BC Greek historian Xenophon noted, 'a plentiful supply of stone from which are made the fairest temples and altars, and the most beautiful statues for the gods'.[22] The most celebrated of all Greek stones, as fine as any in the world, was quarried from Mount Pentelikon: still worked today, it stands like a vast gabled temple in full view of Athens. Cut to knife-edge joints and arrises and perfectly finished, Pentelic marble – a metamorphosed form of limestone – enabled walls built stone by stone to appear as monolithic surfaces. Indeed, so tight was the 'molecular contact' between stones that some actually crystallized together. It could also be exquisitely carved for both architectural details and sculpture. Marble was reserved for the most important buildings, and a range of easily worked limestones, known collectively as 'poros', was used for general work on public buildings. As the name suggests, its surface was rough and full of cavities – ideal for keying in plaster, which, in emulation of the earlier practice of plastering important mud-brick-built buildings, encouraged the persistence of a tradition favouring jointless walls.

The Greeks developed a range of machines for lifting and moving large blocks of stone, which, as in Egypt, were shaped at the quarry before being transported to the building site, where only finishing work was required. They could move marble lintels capable of spanning 3.6 metres (12 feet) and more, and as this was wide enough for a chariot to pass under they were content, like the Egyptians, to consign the use of arches and vaults to stores and other utilitarian buildings. By Roman times, the transporting of stone had become a major international business. Marble was especially valued, and as the Romans wanted brighter, livelier types than the pale, earth-toned stones available locally, materials were brought from all over Italy as well as Greece and France.

The portico on the Pantheon, which was completed in 128 AD, consisted of eight 14-metre (46-feet) high unfluted granite columns, which were quarried and finished in Egypt. The giant monoliths were then brought by boat to Rome, where Corinthian capitals, carved from fine Greek Pentelic marble, were added.

The Romans did, however, have ready access to a stone that would become even more famous than that from Pentelikon: Carrara marble, quarried in the colony of Luna, at the mouth of the river Magra, which they founded in 155 BC. Vast amounts of stone were extracted and taken to Rome for the following 300 years. Carrara was the preferred stone of Renaissance sculptors and Michelangelo lived near the quarries for a while, dreaming of carving the peak of Crestola into a huge face and lighthouse. It is still extracted in huge quantities – the locals despairingly call it 'production by plunder'[23] – and transported around the world, mostly as thin slabs for cladding.

Until the eighteenth century, Carrara stone, like all limestones and marbles, was won by cleaving it along the weaker bedding planes – much as we see it portrayed in the background of Mantegna's 'Madonna of the Cave', painted in 1485. The use of explosives then became the norm, and by the late nineteenth century the resulting blocks were being cut with moving cables to which an abrasive slurry of sand and stone was applied; today huge diamond-coated wires are standard. Until the 1960s, 20-ton blocks of stone were still routinely moved around the quarry on sleds of strapped-together logs, much as they would have been in Roman times.

Top: The Parthenon's refinement was made possible by the Pentelic marble quarried near Athens.

Above: Lion Gate at Mycenae: massive stone lintels eliminated the need for arches.

The monumental, monolithic granite columns of the Pantheon in Rome were carved in Egypt.

Egyptian brick vaults, built c.1400 BC.

Carrara marble, seen here
on the Trevi fountain in Rome,
was the preferred stone
of Roman sculptors.

Components were carved
at the quarry, as seen in the
background of Mantegna's
'Madonna of the Caves'.

Lightened by coffering, concrete was used to build the greatest interior of Ancient Rome, the Pantheon.

Fallen fragment of concrete barrel vault from the Baths of Caracalla in the Roman Forum.

If Carrara provides yet another example of the continuity that is such a striking feature of the history of many materials, the structure of the Pantheon – whose 43.2-metre (142-feet) diameter dome was to remain the world's largest until the nineteenth century – offers a glimpse of things to come. In its construction, the Romans used an invented, not natural, material: concrete. Its development stems from the introduction of pozzolana, as it is known today, into the mortars used to bond bricks. Mined on the slopes of Mount Vesuvius, pozzolana forms a natural cement when mixed with lime, which the Romans obtained by burning travertine. For an aggregate the Romans used broken lumps of lightweight tufa and pepperino, and later brick-bats. The Pantheon's concrete walls were cast in permanent brick shutters, replete with the impressive relieving arches that in the twentieth century would inspire the American architect Louis Kahn, whilst the deeply coffered dome was struck from timber formwork, and the concrete left exposed.

The Romans were quick to exploit the potential of concrete, and many of their other major buildings, such as the great public baths, would have been inconceivable without it. But it was not taken up by later builders, and until the middle of the nineteenth century stone remained, overwhelmingly, the pre-eminent material for the most important architecture in Europe. The Pantheon also concealed another feature anticipating developments that only took hold with industrialization: its portico was supported by bronze roof trusses spanning nine metres (30 feet).

Save for steel, most of the metals now used in building have been worked for several thousands of years – hence the Iron and Bronze Ages – and the Romans themselves introduced lead for roofing which, as Palladio noted, was later generally used for 'magnificent palaces, churches, towers, and other publick edifices'.[24] Iron-chain suspension bridges were built in China during the early Ming dynasty (1368-1644) and imagined by Leonardo da Vinci, and Michelangelo and Sir Christopher Wren used large iron tension-chains to contain the outward thrusts of the domes of the cathedrals of St Peter in Rome and St Paul in London. But until the industrialization of production, the use of iron or other metals in the quantities required to make structural members was generally either prohibitively expensive or impracticable.

The large-scale production of iron began in England in the early eighteenth century, and began to find its way into building in the 1770s. The puddling process for making wrought iron was invented in 1784, and a skilled worker could make up to a ton a day. The rolling techniques that were later applied to steel soon followed, and were used initially for railway tracks, later for structural members. Iron was ideal for industrial structures such as cotton mills and warehouses, where it was used primarily in compression and combined with brick exterior walls to create multi-storey, fire-resistant constructions. By the mid nineteenth century, iron could be seen as 'not only the soul of every other manufacture, but the mainspring, perhaps, of civilized society'.[25]

Benyon, Bage and Marshall's flax-spinning mill in Shrewsbury, England: built in 1796, it was the world's first multi-storey, iron-framed building.

Concrete vaults, Baths of Caracalla, Rome.

As a structural material, however, iron was seriously weakened by excess carbon and other impurities, and in 1855 the Englishman Sir Henry Bessemer patented the simple but revolutionary idea of purifying the liquid pig iron by blowing air through it. Steel, hitherto made only in tiny quantities for such specialized uses as sword and knife blades, could now be produced industrially.

Refined by appropriating features from a method patented the following year by Robert Mushet, the Bessemer Conversion process laid the foundations of the modern steel industry. Used in compression, steel did not make economic sense in lightly loaded, low-rise buildings, but its strength made possible the development of the early high-rise buildings of Chicago, the first all-steel frame appearing in 1891 in the Ludington Building designed by William Le Baron Jenney. The 102-storey-high Empire State Building was steel framed, and in contrast to Europe, where reinforced concrete is still widely used, steel framing retains an almost complete monopoly on tall buildings in the USA.

The major disadvantages of steel in construction are its lack of fire resistance and vulnerability to rust, necessitating the use of galvanizing and/or suitable coating. Unlike wood, which catches fire and burns at a predictable rate (roughly 2.5 centimetres/1 inch per hour), steel rapidly loses strength above temperatures as low as 150°C (300°F). In buildings, steel was traditionally cased in brick, concrete or lightweight fire-resistant linings, but recently a range of intumescent coatings have been developed that can be applied like paint.

The properties of steel can also be readily modified to suit different needs. Repeated rolling of sheets or sections, or drawing of wires, greatly increases their strength by eliminating many of the microscopic 'Griffiths cracks', which result from misplaced atoms in the crystalline structure. The results can be dramatic: the best piano wires have a tensile strength of around 12 times normal steel. Increase the amount

of carbon and the tensile strength rises two- or three-fold, but with a corresponding increase in brittleness. Add nickel and chromium and stainless steel results, albeit at significantly greater costs. Although it lives up to its name in normal use, stainless steel tends to lose its corrosion resistance at high tensile loads – a little known problem, which could lead to a rash of structural failures a decade or two hence.[26] (The addition of large amounts of nickel produces yet another unexpected transformation: known as Invar steel, it has a thermal coefficient of virtually zero, making it dimensionally stable across a wide range of temperatures.)

A surprising alternative to conventional ways of dealing with rust is to add small amounts of copper, whose own oxidation when exposed to the atmosphere forms a protective layer. Trademarked in the early 1950s by the US Steel Corporation as COR-TEN and developed originally for constructing bridges, Cor-ten (or 'weathering steel' as it is now generically known) soon found favour amongst architects and sculptors – its first large-scale use in architecture was by Finnish-born American Eero Saarinen in 1964, on the headquarters for John Deere and Company.

Steel became the ubiquitous material of twentieth-century industry partly, as J. E. Gordon has pointed out, because it 'facilitates the dilution of skills'.[27] It eased the introduction of production lines, which required a minimum of craft skills, and it enabled many aspects of mechanical and structural design to be reduced to codified routines. In an increasingly homogenized world dominated by steel, managers and accountants soon supplanted engineers as the dominant figures in large-scale engineering and construction businesses.

The economical production of aluminium did not begin until the 1880s, in the USA. By the early 1890s the Aluminum Company of America (Alcoa) was producing around 320 kilos (700 pounds) per annum, and in 1912 it began to appear as foil for wrapping sweets. This was

Weathering steel, seen here on Anthony Gormley's 'Angel of the North', uses rust as a protective coat.

Contrary to expectations, the titanium cladding of the Bilbao Guggenheim Museum is showing signs of corrosion.

Retti candle shop built in Vienna in 1965 by Hans Hollein: aluminium did not come into extensive use in building until after 1950.

followed in the 1920s by household foils of the kind that would eventually find their way into building, bonded to insulation as waterproof membranes. The Wright Brothers' 1903 aeroplane included aluminium parts, and availability and cost confined the structural use of aluminium to aircraft until after the Second World War. In its wake, the number of smelters worldwide increased dramatically, from under 20 to around 140, making possible aluminium claddings and curtain-wall systems. Weight for weight, aluminium has a similar tensile strength to steel, but in lightly loaded compression structures is roughly twice as efficient.

In architecture, as opposed to purely utilitarian structures, the introduction of 'new' materials such as iron and steel provoked considerable opposition – something to which we will return in the following chapter. The earliest all-iron buildings were market halls – London's Hungerford Fish Market of 1835 being credited as the first – and greenhouses, such as the celebrated Palm House at Kew Gardens, London, designed by Decimus Burton in the 1840s. It fell to another greenhouse designer, the gardener Joseph Paxton, to conceive the definitive iron-and-glass structure: the Crystal Palace, centrepiece of the Great Exhibition of 1851. To meet the seemingly impossible six-month deadline, the result of dithering about

an appropriate design, Paxton designed the structure entirely of standardized parts – cast-iron columns, large sheets of glass, and riveted wrought-iron trusses. The strength of iron permitted a hitherto unprecedented lightness, and a century and a half later it remains, arguably, the most remarkable *tour de force* of industrialized building.

Two equally impressive metal structures appeared at the Paris Centennial exhibition of 1889. Eiffel's tower was built using wrought iron, not steel, which the *magicien de fer* – as he was known in France – still did not fully trust, whilst the great Galerie des Machines still holds the record for the largest clear-span steel structure. Designed by the architect Dutert and engineer Contamin, its vast three-hinged arches spanned 114 metres (374 feet) and touched the ground via pin joints as delicate as a ballerina on points. Too large to find a normal use, it was demolished in 1910.

The architecture of these great iron-and-steel structures was unthinkable without large sheets of glass. A seemingly magical product of heating silica, lime and an alkali such as soda or potash, glass had been made since the Bronze Age. Unlike metals and other materials made by heating solids until they liquefy and amalgamate, glass does not have a crystalline structure but retains the random molecular characteristics of a liquid. For most of its history it remained a luxury material, and in the ancient world was generally produced in opaque rather than transparent forms.[28] The first extensive use of glass in building, not surprisingly, was by the Romans. It appeared in pavements, as thin plates for cladding walls, in forcing frames in horticulture, even in drain pipes. It was also used in windows, although it never replaced mica, alabaster and shells for that purpose.

The Romans made flat glass either by casting or by blowing it in a cylinder and then flattening it out in the kiln – the resulting material being known as 'broad'. As with bricks, the Romans disseminated glass-making techniques

Gustave Eiffel, the 'Magician of Iron', had his greatest triumph with his tower built in Paris in 1889.

The Palm House at Kew, London – seen here before restoration – is a miracle of delicate construction.

widely, and it was in the valleys of the Seine and Rhine – encouraged by the more northerly climate, and the development of the skeletal Gothic style – that a substantial window-glass industry developed during the Middle Ages.

An alternative to cast and broad is the crown glass process. Used to make plates in Syria during the first three centuries AD, it involves spinning molten glass into thin disks up to a metre in diameter. The crown method was revived in Normandy in the fourteenth century and later extensively employed in Venice and in England. Thinner, more uniform and brilliant in clarity, crown glass's major disadvantage was the unsightly bull's eye left at its centre.

Cast glass has to be ground and polished to a finish, but can yield superb results. It was the approach taken by the Norman glass-maker Louis Lucas de Nehou, when he was put in charge of the Royal glassworks with the brief of finding a way to meet the demand for mirrors and for glass to be used in the coaches of the aristocracy. By 1691 de Nehou had effectively rediscovered and refined the process of making plate glass.

Industrial developments during the nineteenth and first half of the twentieth centuries saw no fundamentally new breakthroughs in glass-making, only the development of existing techniques on a much larger scale. Following the ending of the excise tax on glass in 1845, Dickens pointed out that in one week the Thames Plate Glass Works were turning out as much plate as all the glass-workers in the country put together before.[29] By the mid twentieth century, three complementary ways of making sheet glass were in use. Thin glass was made by drawing; thicker glass by casting; and patterned and wired glasses by rolling. Then in 1952, in England, Alastair Pilkington, an employee – but not relative – of the eponymous, Lancashire-based firm, had the simple but revolutionary idea of replacing the rigid bed by floating the molten glass onto a molten metal. Tin proved the most suitable, and a pilot plant was set up two years later.

By 1959 the new 'float glass' process was commercially viable and quickly all but replaced cast glass; by the mid 1980s float glass had also taken over the production of most thin glasses. The qualifications stem from the fact that producing float glass is rather like steering an oil tanker: the first generation of plants could not respond to specialized requirements, such as a particular colour, nor could the rate of production be controlled, cutting across the market logic of supply and demand. Float glass production requires massive capital investment and operates as a continuous process, with material flowing off the line at approximately 15 metres (50 feet) per minute day and night, year after year – until the plant has to be shut down after several years for major maintenance.

The great weakness of glass, it goes without saying, is its relative fragility. Although its compressive strength compares well with that of many stones, it can relatively easily shatter

Top: Large mirrors were a favourite device of Rococo architects; used to multiply space and light.

Above 'Early English' glass, made in 1907 for E. S. Prior's St Andrew's Church, Roker, England – a late masterpiece of the Arts and Crafts movement.

under impact or bending. Medieval texts mention 'unbreakable glass', the search for which certainly goes back at least to the Dark Ages: its production became, like the transformation of base metals into gold, a matter for alchemists.[30]

With the growing use of glass in roofs and motor vehicles, concerns about safety led to innovations of far-reaching potential. Pilkington Brothers began putting chicken wire in glass for use in roof-lights in 1896 – the first form of 'Georgian wired' – whilst for vehicles, laminated safety glasses were developed, initially with a transparent (or often, as time passed, not so transparent) plastic material such as celluloid bonded between two layers of glass.

The earliest forms of 'unbreakable glass' must have involved a form of tempering, achieved by quenching the glass in hot oil just after it had set. This solidifies the outer layers of glass immediately, leaving the still-liquid interior to cool and contract slowly, which in turn puts the surfaces into compression and the core into tension. The process was refined in the 1870s, but it was not until the 1930s that it could be applied to plate glass, with cold air jets used to effect the required rapid cooling. Modern toughened glasses have strengths up to eight or nine times that of normal glass, permitting – as we shall see in Chapter 10 – dramatic developments in the size and structural use of the material.

Enthusiasm for toughened glass was, for a while, tempered by an unexpected, and initially unexplained, series of building failures. The problem was first encountered in England in the late 1980s, when large sheets of toughened glass began shattering spontaneously. Structural analysis of the cladding systems involved gave no clue as to the possible cause, but it was eventually found to be due to nickel sulphide particles in the sand of the original mix. On south-facing elevations, in particular, the glass could heat up sufficiently for the molecules to change state, and in the process expand

dramatically – a transformation sufficient to precipitate the release of the internal stresses in the glass, 'exploding' it from within into myriad small pieces. Pilkington, one of the world's half dozen major glass companies, now estimates that only one in around 13,000 sheets of their glass[31] is affected by the nickel sulphide problem, but when used structurally glass is routinely 'heat soaked' in an oven at a temperature of around 1000°C (1800°F), to precipitate the shattering of any sheets affected by nickel sulphide inclusions.

In the history of modern architecture, glass is inseparable from its framing by steel and reinforced concrete. The development of modern concrete, the possibilities of which had been almost completely ignored since its invention by the Romans, began with the introduction of artificial cements far stronger than the lime mortars traditionally used to bond stones and bricks. Portland Cement, patented in 1824, was produced by burning lime and clay in a kiln, and it was not long before concrete was being cast in situ to make walls, and off-site to produce pre-cast blocks – which did not, however, begin to compete with bricks until a century later.

The idea of strengthening a mass material like mud with some form of reinforcing, such as straw or wooden laths, was hardly new, but the possibility of combining concrete with iron or steel depended upon the happy coincidence that all three materials have almost exactly the same coefficient of thermal expansion, ensuring that destructive cracking is prevented. In this case, the key developments came in France. In the 1850s the builder François Coignet began to experiment with reinforcing concrete slabs with small wrought-iron beams, and in 1867 the gardener Joseph Monier patented his idea for large concrete flowerpots reinforced with cages of iron wires, the basis of modern reinforced concrete.

Top: Laminated glazing to metro entrance in Rotterdam, with a core of shattered toughened glass.

Above: Space wrapped in glass: hall of Otto Wagner's Post Office Savings Bank in Vienna (1906).

Reinforced concrete ramps up to the roof-top test-track of the Fiat Factory, Turin, 1915-21.

As we have seen throughout this brief résumé, the history of building materials is full of 'technology transfers' from other, sometimes unexpected, fields. Monier's flowerpots were an improbable beginning to what was to prove one of the most far-reaching innovations in the history of building. François Hennebique wasted no time in applying the invention to building, making a crucial innovation by bending the reinforcing bars to enable the floor slab, beams and columns to function as a continuous structural unit. In the decade after 1900, the elastic theory of structures was developed in Germany, which permitted the systematic analysis of reinforced concrete: the techniques developed then have been refined but not replaced.

Cast as a 'liquid stone', reinforced concrete permitted a wide range of innovations, from exceptional spans to fluid – sometimes avowedly 'organic' – forms. Widely seen as the harbinger of a new style – explicitly so in Francis S. Onderdonk's 1928 book *The Ferro-Concrete Style* – its potential was to fascinate modern architects. But in the spirit of this chapter, which has stressed continuity rather than revolution, it is interesting to note that when, early in the twentieth century, the Hungarian architect Istvan Medgyaszay lectured on 'artistic solutions' using reinforced concrete, he suggested vernacular buildings of mud and timber as possible models.

The aesthetic ideals of Modern architecture were inextricably bound up with innovations made possible by steel, reinforced concrete and glass. At the start of a new century other concerns have begun to impose themselves, above all those surrounding the vexed, worldwide issues of global warming and the sustainability of resources. After food production, the building industry is the world's largest consumer of raw materials. It is also one of the most wasteful and polluting. Many extraction processes involve considerable amounts of waste – in the slate industry, for example, less than one per cent of the quarried material may find its way to building sites – and

despite efforts to reduce waste by-products and emissions, many of the production processes are inherently and massively polluting. Buildings in use also account for roughly half of the world's energy consumption.

In addition to their traditional interest in the structural/constructional and aesthetic qualities of materials, designers must now also consider their embodied energy (in production, transportation, and on site), potential for recycling, and renewability as a resource.[32] The issues involved in what it means to design sustainably are complex and well beyond the scope or focus of this book,[33] but in concluding this brief survey it is fascinating to note that some of the most advanced thinking on building materials is turning again for inspiration to the 'primitive huts' with which we began.

An image like that of a Marsh Arabs' reed house under construction (see page 13) can now be seen as a model of the kind of ecologically responsible construction to which our post-industrial civilization must aspire. Reed houses will hardly be filling the estates of the developed world, but seemingly 'primitive' materials, such as bamboo, pisé and straw bales – the latter first used as a building material out of desperation in nineteenth-century Nebraska – are finding serious new advocates, and not only on the fringes of alternative cultures. Anyone who has seen bamboo being used as scaffolding for high-rise buildings in Hong Kong – common practice until recently – will be aware of its remarkable structural properties. Very fast-growing and with an impressive strength-to-weight ratio, bamboo has long been put to impressive use by traditional cultures and has recently been the subject of serious research by, amongst others, the renowned Institute of Lightweight Structures founded by the late Frei Otto at Stuttgart University.[34]

In 1982 a large exhibition and conference devoted to earth-building was held in Paris: entitled 'A forgotten building practice for the future', it took place, ironically enough, in that

Earth-building as critique of modernity: 'House of Stories', Bleddfa, Wales, by Tono Mirai, 2001.

Reinforced concrete beams shaped to reflect the forces at work: concourse, Sydney Opera House.

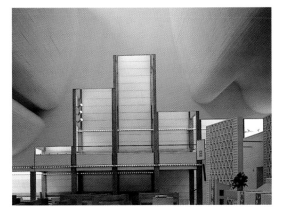

The 'cloud vaults'
of Jørn Utzon's church
at Bagsværd, Denmark,
use thin-shell concrete.

High-Tech palace of culture, the Pompidou Centre. Pisé construction is also the subject of extensive research, notably at the College of Architecture at Grenoble and its teaching wing CRATerre. It is also being used 'raw', on both aesthetic and environmental grounds, by increasing numbers of architects, amongst whom the Austrian Martin Rauch is a conspicuous pioneer.[35] Traditional methods of pisé construction are inherently slow, and to counter this David Easton, working in the USA, has developed a rapid system of construction that uses high-pressure compressed air to impact suitably selected soil against an open, one-sided formwork.[36]

There is, as yet, no large-scale industrial backing for pisé construction – it is hard to make big profits from such a universally available material as earth – but it has unquestionably moved from being an 'alternative' material to one with serious potential in an increasingly energy-conscious and polluted world. Rammed earth buildings need ten or 20 times less energy to build than concrete or brick ones, and, properly constructed, can greatly outlast those of traditional timber-frame construction. Suitable material is almost always available locally, generally on the site itself, and the resulting walls offer good insulation and regulate humidity naturally. And when the time comes, such buildings can, of course, be completely recycled into the earth of which they are made.

Until recently, building in wood might also have seemed to many architects almost as regressive as ramming earth to make walls. But the material's image has been changing out of all recognition, partly as a result of the effort to make greater use of renewable resources, partly due to technical developments, and partly because architects, freed of the burden of declaring their modernity by a simplistic adherence to the use of overtly 'industrial' materials, have again begun to explore its structural and aesthetic possibilities. Twentieth-century architecture was dominated by steel and the big-business values that came with it; the twenty-first century promises to be far more diverse, combining traditional, industrial and yet-to-be-invented materials in unexpected ways that make the most of their varied potentials rather than encourage the adoption of standardized solutions.

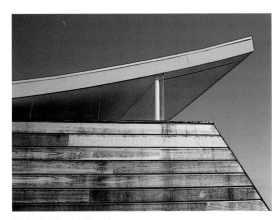

Cedar cladding, McDonald House, Stinson Beach, California, by Stanley Saitowitz, 1992.

Cane grid-shell model under test at Frei Otto's Institute of Lightweight Structures.

Chapter 2
Materials and Form

The fluidity of plastic form:
ceiling by Josep Jujol
in the Casa Milá, Barcelona,
designed by Antoni Gaudí.

Every work of art should reflect in its appearance the material as physical matter. … In this way we may speak of a wood style, a brick style, an ashlar style, and so forth.
  Gottfried Semper[1]

A walk along most beaches offers striking examples of two basic relationships between materials and form: carving and modelling. Eroded and smoothed by the action of seawater, pebbles and rocks assume varied yet characteristic shapes. In the example illustrated opposite, material has been slowly removed layer by layer, leaving raised areas where softer beds have been protected by a harder stone – much as in a vast landscape like the Grand Canyon. This process is the antithesis of the rippling waves left in sand between the tides. In the first case, resistant material has been carved; in the second, a plastic one modelled. With the rock, the resulting forms are clearly a product of the interaction between the material's inherent properties and the action of water, its erosive effects enhanced by the abrasion of particles of sand and loose stones. The sand, on the other hand, is a static, if short-lived, image of turbulent processes: the waving shapes are, to quote John Ruskin, 'the seal of the motion of the waters',[2] not something intrinsic to the sand – any comparable granular material would respond similarly.

Contemplating Michelangelo's unfinished 'Captive', one of four intended for the tomb of Pope Julius II, we feel ourselves granted unique access to the process of creation: the figure seems to be struggling to come to life before our eyes. Michelangelo must have seen it this way when he remarked that 'the greatest artist has no conception which a single block of marble does not potentially contain within its mass'.[3] We know that this cannot be literally true, but the sense that a sculpture was latent in the block remained a familiar conceit – as, for example, when Modernist sculptor Constantin Brancusi declared that 'the artist should know how to dig out the being that is within matter'.[4]

Whilst similar types of rock exposed to the action of water tend to resemble each other, clearly no other artist, given the same block, would 'uncover' the same form. In the next lines of his sonnet Michelangelo qualifies the idea by adding that 'only a hand obedient to the mind can penetrate to this image'. Reflecting on the interaction between the medium and the 'image', the Viennese architect Adolf Loos told a story about a stonemason who caught a salamander and decided to use it as the model for a gargoyle. When it was finished he proudly showed it to a painter, who laughed at the 'misshapen' result. The mason explained that his material and tools would not allow him to make an exact copy. Having worked in stone all his life, explained Loos, the mason inevitably 'begins to think stone and see stones'.[5] Looking at the deeply undercut leaves which crown the

Unfinished 'Captive'
for the tomb of Julius II
by Michelangelo
(Accademia, Florence).

Deeply undercut leaf motifs
on column capitals,
Wells Cathedral, England.

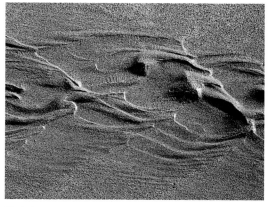

Plastic form: sand shaped
by the movement of water,
Pembrokeshire, Wales.

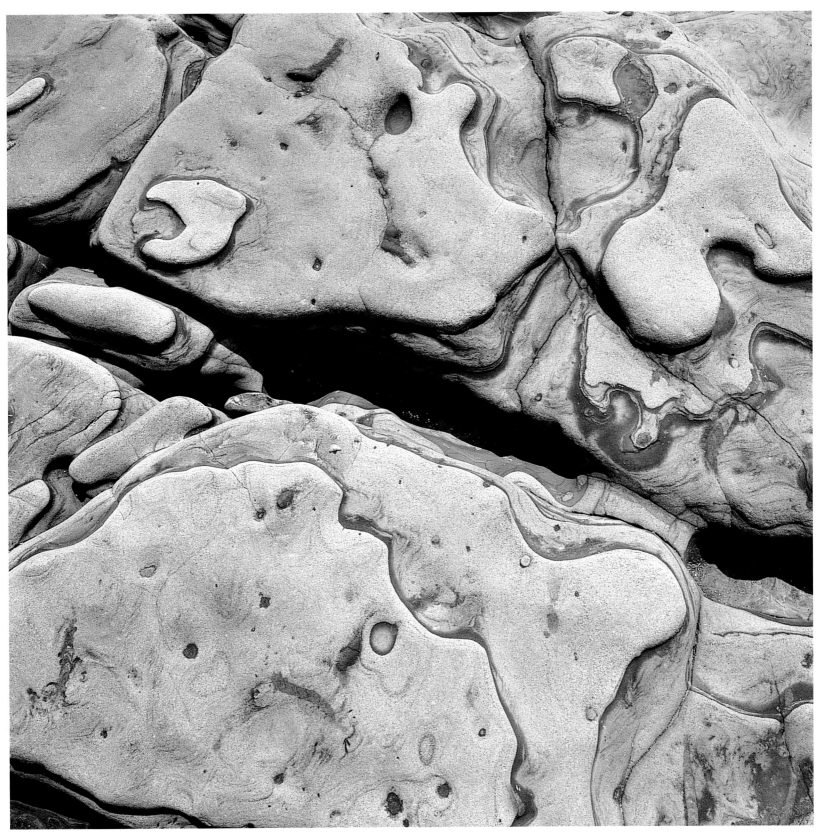

Carved form: sedimentary
rock eroded by the sea,
Point Lobos, California.

Wrought-iron balustrade in the Casa Bofarull, Barcelona, by Josep Jujol.

capitals on Wells Cathedral, England, we do not criticize them as unnaturally thick, or ponder how much more realistically they could have been represented in metal, but admire them as an elegant reconciliation between the demands of representation and the capacity, or 'nature', of stone.

All works of art and architecture involve a creative interplay between ideas and materials, to which both makers and critics have repeatedly been willing to assign ethical value. When we sense that a predetermined design has been arbitrarily imposed upon a resistant material, we may not only find the result aesthetically unsatisfactory but also be tempted to think that the material's 'nature' has been violated. The idea that materials have a particular 'nature' has an immediate appeal, but it requires only a moment's reflection to realize that it is far from straightforward. Few materials are used as found, and so the 'nature' of a building material is inseparable from the workmanship (or, nowadays, machine processes) by which it is prepared and used. And with materials such as metals, which can only be worked – cast, rolled, forged or pressed – and finished whilst hot, the only properties that can be expressed in the completed work, as David Pye has pointed out, 'are precisely those which the material has lost'.[6] The sinuous lines of Art

Nouveau ornament may seem to us a superb expression of the ductility of wrought iron – but only if we admire rather than try to reshape them.

Confronted with the wholesale imitation of traditional forms using industrially produced materials such as cast iron, many nineteenth-century architects decided that a commitment to working 'in the nature of materials' was essential to the search for a 'modern style'. These ideas will be explored in more detail in the next chapter, but here it is worth reflecting briefly on what might be meant by the 'nature' of a material such as stone. Consider the rusticated wall in Florence, below. Such deliberately rough construction goes back to the ancient Romans, although it is uncertain whether it was invented to emphasize a wall's strength; to lend it a 'rugged and threatening effect',[7] as Alberti argued; to save labour by leaving the exposed face more or less as found in the quarry; or to express the coarse-grained 'nature' of travertine. In contemplating the first use of rustication in the Renaissance,

Despite slightly reducing a wall's actual strength, rustication makes it appear hugely robust.

Rustication of the Pitti Palace, Florence: a monumental expression of stone's natural cleavage.

Machine-cut travertine framed by concrete: Kimbell Musuem, Texas, by Louis Kahn.

Stone in motion: the façade
of Borromini's church of San
Carlo alle Quattro Fontane, Rome.

Finely jointed ashlar
at Lansdowne Crescent
in Bath, England.

The rusticated base of the
Medici Palazzo in Florence
is surmounted by two storeys
of smooth ashlar.

The plastic forms of the stonework of the Casa Milá, Barcelona, could easily be mistaken for poured concrete.

by Brunelleschi on the Pitti Palace, Ruskin responded to it as an example of the latter, admiring the 'magnificence in the natural cleavage of the stone', which was so expressive of its 'brotherhood with the mountain heart from which it has been rent'.[8]

The lack of finish might seem to be suited to a rough-grained stone such as travertine, but does that make Louis Kahn's use of thin, machine-cut slabs of travertine's American equivalent on the Kimbell Museum in any meaningful sense 'unnatural' – especially as hand-wrought roughness could equally well be thought anachronistic? To build using massive stones in the middle of Texas in the twentieth century would have been wildly uneconomic, and it could even be argued that, rather like the 'thin slices' that biologists use to interrogate the inner workings of living organisms, the faces of Kahn's cladding are striking revelations of the micro-structure – the 'inner nature' – of the stone. This may be a different 'nature' to the rockiness celebrated by rustication, but is it any less valid? It certainly seems appropriate to a modern use of stone.

The almost seamless stonework of the upper floors of Lansdowne Crescent in Bath, England, is the architectural antithesis of rustication. The golden limestone here seems wonderfully – one is tempted to say 'artificially' – light. This feeling is created by the suppression of joints; by the crisp, gently incised ornament; and by the way the window reveals are painted white, suggesting that the stone is no more than the thinnest of skins stretched across the surface. Bath Stone has a fine, even grain and as such is ideal for constructing ashlar walls of regular blocks laid with thin mortar joints. Such a wall might therefore be said to be an apt expression of Bath Stone, although hardly to the exclusion of other ways of using it.

In each of our contrasting walls, the material expression can be understood only in a larger context embracing the place, the means available to handle and work stone, the social expectations and the designer's intentions. The rusticated wall in Florence is a vigorous declaration of support for the massive building – the Palazzo Medici – of which it forms the base. Its strength is emphasized by the shadows cast by the high southern sun, and might be interpreted as a statement of power in defence of the private wealth sheltering behind it. In Bath, the lightness and elegance seem as precisely tuned to the refined pleasures of a spa town as the delicate mouldings are to the soft English light.

Although the 'nature of materials' may elude easy definition, when faced with a wall like that which Borromini designed for the church of San Carlo alle Quattro Fontane in Rome, we feel that the familiar sense of 'wall' – of placing stone upon stone – has given way almost completely to a three-dimensional, sculptural vision. The wall may, as a matter of constructional fact, have been built by laying stone upon stone, but this plays little part in its formal expression. We marvel that stone can be rendered so responsive to design, transformed into such complex shapes, made to appear to undulate before our eyes, but we do not feel that the architect's intention is being realized so much *in and through* the medium of stone as *in spite of* its weight and resistance. The conception is masterfully imposed upon the material, and hard, intractable stone is treated almost as if it were plastic. It is almost easier to imagine these forms being produced by a process of casting than carving – a feeling even more emphatically conveyed by the undulating stone frontages of Antoni Gaudí's Casa Milá in Barcelona.

'When the walls parted and the column became': Doric temple at Metapontum in southern Italy.

'Stone comes forth': Parthenon, Athens.

To work with stone as Borromini and Gaudí did required, needless to say, a consummate understanding of the material. But neither example is likely to strike us as being an architecture *of* stone in the manner epitomized by the Greek Doric temple, which the English critic Adrian Stokes aptly described as 'an ideal quarry reconstructed on the hill'.[9] In a Greek temple, the philosopher Martin Heidegger suggests, we see materials 'come forth for the very first time … rock comes to bear and rest and so first becomes rock; metals come to glitter and shimmer; colours to glow'.[10]

Even for those who cannot share his belief that the task of art is to reveal the supposedly unchanging essence of the phenomenal world, Heidegger's observation still strikes at the heart of the matter. In a Greek temple, the materials are worked, assembled and presented in such a way that they ask us to pay attention to their individual qualities: in its presence, we feel that we see stone *as* stone – and as something marvellous. Arthur Schopenhauer also had Greek models in mind when he wrote that, 'it is absolutely necessary for an understanding and aesthetic enjoyment of a work of architecture to have direct knowledge through perception of its matter as regards its weight, rigidity, and cohesion'. To drive his point home he goes on to suggest that if we were 'told clearly that the building, the sight of which pleases us, consisted of entirely different materials of very unequal weight and consistency, but not distinguishable to the eye, the whole building would become as incapable of affording us pleasure as would a poem in an unknown language'.[11]

The suggestion that stone is somehow revealed as singularly 'stony' in Greek temples might appear to be undermined by the theory (discussed briefly in the last chapter) that their forms originated in timber, not stone, construction. This theory has never been without its detractors. To Adrian Stokes it was 'an entire mistake',[12] Le Corbusier considered it 'most false',[13] and for the great French architect-theorist Viollet-le-Duc, it was 'a thing essentially monstrous'.[14] Even Gottfried Semper, who, as we shall see, believed passionately in the mimetic origins of architecture, initially questioned it as an example of 'materialistic thinking', which overlooked 'the most important influences on art'.[15]

The wooden origins of Greek temples may never be proved conclusively, but the evidence is persuasive. Within the system of Classical aesthetics, however, credible evidence was not the real issue: it was a matter of theoretical necessity that architecture, in common with the other arts, be considered a form of imitation or 'mimesis'. Central to the aesthetic theory of Aristotle, this idea later became identified with

These early Doric columns at Paestum in Italy visibly swell under the load of the entablature and roof.

Columns and capitals at Paestum.

the simplistic formulation 'art imitates nature'. Aristotle, however, had something much subtler in mind, involving a process of idealization of a given model, which in the case of architecture was the construction of basic forms of shelter that were as close to a natural model as could be found – hence the fascination with the 'primitive hut'.

The process of mimesis necessarily involved a change of material because, as the French Classicist Quatremère de Quincy explained, 'the pleasure of imitation is proportionate to the distance which, in every art or imitative mode . . . separates the elements of the model from those of the image'.[16] Seen in this light, exquisitely refined stone imitations of comparatively crude timber originals make perfect sense. The quality of the stone architecture does not depend on how literally the wooden model has been copied, but on how successfully it has been reinterpreted in terms of the expressive possibilities of the new material. The basic constructional configuration of a Doric temple may be inherited from timber structures, but the formal refinements of the fluted columns, which seem to swell under the imposed load, are so 'deeply thought out in regard to light and materials' that they give 'almost the feeling of a natural growth' – to use the words of Le Corbusier.[17] Such refinements,

so apt to the process of carving, all but make the columns unthinkable in any material other than stone.

It is hardly surprising that the Greek Doric system came to be seen as the paradigm of *tectonic* expression, a theme recently analyzed with characteristic insight by Kenneth Frampton.[18] Derived from *tekton*, the Greek word for carpenter or builder, the term 'tectonic' came into use in the mid nineteenth century and quickly assumed the wider meaning of a complete building system, which bound all the elements into an aesthetic unity or form. This usage derived, above all, from a widely influential account of Greek architecture by Karl Bötticher – *Die Tektonik der Hellenen* – which was published in three volumes between 1843 and 1852.

The evidence for the derivation of Greek stone construction (right) from timber prototypes (above) is persuasive, but the idea has been the subject of repeated, and heated, debate.

The delicate tracery, painted stone and richly stained glass of the Sainte Chapelle in Paris epitomize the Gothic dematerialization of form by light and colour.

View through trefoil arch into the chapter house at Wells Cathedral, England.

Although the idea of the tectonic was formulated in response to Greek architecture, it was generalized to signify an approach based on the 'rational' expression of structure and construction, for which the Gothic cathedrals could offer an equally potent paradigm. The development of these ideas in the nineteenth century will be explored in the next chapter: here we will look briefly at the Gothic style from a radically different perspective, as an example of the antithesis of the tectonic – the dematerialization of form.[19]

Like Greek architecture, the development of Gothic was dependent upon the availability of superlative materials – mostly limestones and marbles – and on masonry techniques that enabled individual stones of complex shape to be cut on the ground and then set, with breathtaking precision, into the vaults above. What mattered above all to the Gothic masons was stone's load-bearing properties. The development of Gothic structure, with its concentration of loads into points and lines of support, exploited combinations of different stones. In place of the apparently monolithic columns of the Classical system, composite constructions emerged, designed both to accommodate and express the play of forces. In Salisbury Cathedral, England, for example, the nave piers consist of clusters of four marble shafts, which are stiffened by brass rings at their joints and fitted into a central limestone pier.

Although Gothic buildings later served as models of logical structure, the expressive ends of the Gothic vision eventually led to forms that were anything but tectonic. Stone was used, as Frank Lloyd Wright wrote in 1928, 'as a negative material' with 'neither limitations respected nor stone nature reinterpreted'.[20] To a religion suspicious of the flesh and of a fallen, material world, the objective was to transcend physical limits – the 'nature' of material was to be infused with spirit, not celebrated for its sensuous qualities. Where the Greek temple suggests a responsive acceptance of gravity, a Gothic cathedral soars in defiance of it. Where the Greek temple offers the utmost clarity of form, the Gothic dissolves into a profusion of slender shafts and delicate traceries, fusing stone and coloured glass into an almost undifferentiated unity. Although not especially

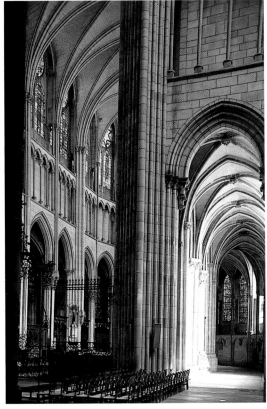

Divided into multiple shafts, Gothic columns soar up to launch the vaults across space (Auxerre Cathedral, France).

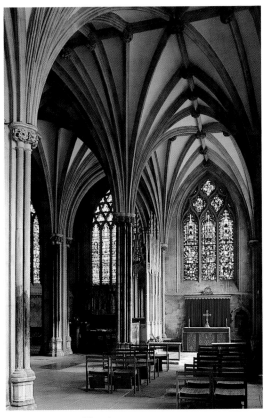

The transformation of form into myriad lines of force: east end of Wells Cathedral.

bright in absolute terms, Gothic interiors seem to be permeated by light, not – as in a Classical building – as a means of illuminating structure and form, but as a coloured 'material'. Palpable as stone, light permeates and transfigures the entire structure as a symbol of the divine grace that fills the universe.

The rib vaults overhead, simple and manifestly structural at first,[21] followed the same inexorable logic of dissolution. Multiplying in ever more complex patterns, the stone came to appear almost literally weightless, as if thrown across space like a woven canopy – or 'a cobweb lifted by the wind', to quote Ruskin's simile.[22] In Vladislav Hall in Prague Castle, completed in 1503 by the German master Benedikt Ried, the vault arches seem to hang between the wall piers, whilst a network of ribs, too fragile to be doing serious structural work, makes patterns across their surfaces. In the extreme development of the late Gothic style in Germany, looping-ribs became fully detached from the ceiling to float in space, or, as in the parish church in the town of Kötschach, broke free of the vault's structural lines altogether, creating the illusion of a trellis threaded with vines.

In the presence of a major Gothic building, we *know* that the construction is massively weighty and rests heavily on the earth, but it *appears* to soar and float. In this sense it admirably fulfils Heinrich Wölfflin's contention that the 'principal theme of architecture' is 'the opposition between matter and force of form', in which 'matter is the enemy … only insofar as we experience it as life-negating gravity'.[23] At its most extreme, the challenge to the inertia of stone creates a pervasive feeling of dematerialization, as if in early anticipation of Italo Calvino's conviction that in the new millennium an increasingly important task for art will be to 'remove weight from matter'.[24] The Gothic is, in fact, but one model of how Calvino's goal might be achieved in architecture: the impulse to dematerialization has been a recurring theme over the past two millennia,

in the service of contents as diverse as spiritual transcendence and the triumph of data over matter in our own Information Age.

In Byzantine churches, the desire to express a higher, spiritual reality was shared with the Gothic, but the architectural means differed radically. Ruskin's introduction to the interior of St Mark's in Venice evokes the atmosphere more vividly than any photograph:

Round the domes of its roof the light enters only through narrow apertures like large stars; and here and there a ray or two from some far away casement wanders into the darkness, and casts a narrow phosphoric stream upon the waves of marble that heave and fall in a thousand colours along the floor. What else there is of light is from torches, or silver lamps, burning ceaselessly in the recesses of the chapels; the roof sheeted with gold, and the polished walls covered with alabaster, give back at every curve and angle some feeble gleaming to the flames.[25]

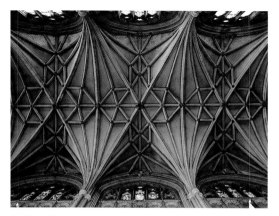

Gothic vaults and the abolition of apparent weight.

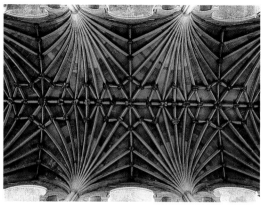

Norwich Cathedral, England.

Ely Cathedral, England.

Frauenkirche, Ingolstadt,
by Erhard Heydenreich:
intertwining ribs and redundant
column bosses hang free
in space in this demonstration
of Late Gothic virtuosity.

St Barbara, Kutna Hora,
by Benedikt Ried

Vladislav Hall, Prague Castle,
by Benedikt Ried.

Spatially, a Byzantine church is a model of volumetric clarity, but this can scarcely be sensed in the dim, uneven light. The physical limits of the space are rendered even more elusive by covering every surface with gold, iridescent mosaics and polished stones, so that light seems less to be reflected from the surfaces than to emerge from them, transforming the interior into a coloured atmosphere emblematic of the divine radiance. Or, as an inscription carved by a Byzantine architect in the Archbishopric Chapel in Ravenna has it: 'Light is either born here or, imprisoned, reigns here in freedom.'[26]

The Doge's Palace in Venice – which Ruskin considered 'a model of all perfection'[27] – offers a large-scale example of weight being removed from matter in the full glare of the sun. Supported by a vigorously pierced colonnade, the upper storeys are dressed from end to end in alternating blocks of rose- and white-coloured marble arrayed in a giant diaper pattern: it is a miracle of lightness, as evanescent as stone can get. The effect depends in part on the way the pattern is primary and takes no account of the varied openings, which are arbitrarily cut out of it, and in part on the extra width of the stones at the junctions of the large diamonds, leaving us uncertain as to whether this is an overall design or a sum of repeated parts. It is effective now,

despite the bleaching of the reds, and would doubtless have been doubly so when the stone was fresh and its colour augmented by paint.[28]

In Bavarian Rococo churches a brilliant, clear light, so different from Byzantine gloom and Gothic mystery, is marshalled to serve an equally pervasive dissolution of form. In essence, the spatial arrangement follows the familiar Renaissance basilican pattern: a vaulted nave is flanked by aisles, in which structural piers alternate with large windows placed centrally in each bay. But in mature Rococo churches, such as those of Die Wies and Zwiefalten, everything in the articulation of the interior works to undermine this stable image, so that, as Karsten Harries writes of Die Wies, the central space is surrounded 'with a visually indeterminate, light-filled mantle'.[29]

The bounding walls are modelled to conceal the sources of light, and windows that remain in view assume complex shapes, making them appear as ornaments of the wall rather than as structural openings in it. The columns are formed by intersecting round and square shafts, the alternation of sharp edges and curved passages making them responsive to the play of light and undermining a stable structural reading. The Classical 'signs' of structure, such as pilasters, are also treated decoratively, by visually detaching them, through

In Byzantine churches, light seems to emanate from the surfaces: St Mary Martorana, Palermo.

Squinch arch of St Mary Martorana: every surface is painted, or clad in gold or mosaic.

All feeling of weight removed: corner of the Doge's Palace, Venice.

changes of material, from the pediments they are supposed to support. Overhead, the vaults are carved away and hollowed out to produce 'a hallucinatory effect'.[30] The resulting tentlike lightness is, as Harries notes, especially effective, because the architects are playing with expectations grounded in our knowledge of heavy masonry construction.

If we do not know that Rococo ceilings are built of timber, lath and plaster, they will seem to us all the more virtuosic by appearing to push masonry to new, truly astonishing limits. This deception enhances the illusion of a seemingly weightless, immaterial construction: we do not know where heavy stone ends and lightweight plaster begins, and both become equally ethereal. A Rococo church such as this confounds Schopenhauer's strictures about deceptive construction: here we are delighted by 'a poem in an unknown language'.

Ringed with light, the interior of the abbey church of Zwiefalten achieves a tent-like lightness.

Top: The diaper-pattern of the Doge's Palace makes stone appear like a stretched fabric.

Above: By imitating stone with stucco, Rococo interiors, such as that of Die Wies, appear miraculously light.

Made of plaster and horse-hair, Egid Quirin Asam's 'Assumption of the Virgin' at Rohr defies gravity.

In the Church of the Three Crosses (1957) in Imatra, Finland, Alvar Aalto used Rococo tactics to produce a space that feels plastically modelled rather than constructed. The interior is defined by a double-skin wall, which allows him freedom to shape the space in response to light and patterns of use.[31] The wall's upper section leans in, emphasizing the feeling of enclosure and easing the transition to the ceiling, which takes on a similarly undulating form. In places, the inner and outer layers are completely detached and partially glazed, offering tantalizing glimpses of a structural system that is otherwise hidden from view. Windows and roof lights are endlessly varied, with no two repeating each other and several assuming complex shapes, which, as in Die Wies, make them seem part of the surface rather than cut into it. And all the surfaces, save for the floors, are painted white, reinforcing the overall plasticity.

Although the tactics of dematerialization are the antithesis of the banner of 'truth to materials', under which so many Modern architects marched, comparable impulses towards a 'spiritualization' of form were widespread in the immediate aftermath of the First World War. This is apparent in Germany, in the circle out of which that supposed paragon of rationality, the Bauhaus, emerged; amongst the Russian Suprematists, whose ideas remained on paper; and in the Dutch De Stijl group.[32]

For Bruno Taut and the other members of the Crystal Chain,[33] the aim of the New Architecture was 'the ultimate dematerialization of form'.[34] Hermann Finsterlin suggested that the controlled and rational spirit that cast architects as 'bondsmen of mere matter' would soon give way, to enable them to 'give swelling form to the living, breathing power of the soul… so that matter may learn to obey the soul'.[35] Glass was seen as the material *par excellence* in which this new spirit could be expressed, and a clear indication of the Crystal Chain's aspirations was given by Taut's temporary Glass Pavilion at the 1914 Cologne Exhibition. Renowned for

Like Die Wies (above), the interior of Alvar Aalto's Church of the Three Crosses at Imatra, Finland (top and right), exploits plastically modelled surfaces and indirect light to dematerialize the space.

its glass staircase, it also featured an interior suffused by light filtered through kaleidoscopic facets of coloured glass, of which the surviving black and white photographs give only the haziest impression.

Mies van der Rohe had close links with Taut's circle, and related aspirations can be discerned in the projects for Glass Skyscrapers that he exhibited in 1922. Although Mies's description emphasized how glass allows the structural essence of the building – the skeleton of columns and beams – to be clearly seen, the accompanying perspectives and elevation drawings gave no hint of this 'inner reality'. What Mies represented was only briefly alluded to in the text – 'the play of reflections' on the curved and facetted surfaces.[36] Mies's ideas on glass were almost certainly, as Fritz Neumeyer has shown, indebted to August Endell's 1908 book *Die Schönheit der grossen Stadt* (The Beauty of the Large City), and the glass towers are a fitting realization of Endell's description of a glass building, in which 'many small panels begin to reflect the sunset and the entire plane assumes a colourful, shimmering life'.[37]

Architects had been in love with reflections before, and the surge in the demand for mirrors in France – which, as we noted in the last chapter, was a stimulus to major advances in glass manufacture – was in part stimulated by Rococo designers' fascination with them as a means of destabilizing space and form. By placing itself entirely at the mercy of the ephemeral play of reflected light, the all-glass building could achieve a material dissolution, of which earlier architects could only dream.

Like their German contemporaries, the members of the De Stijl movement in Holland shared a utopian dream of a world transformed by, and ultimately into, art. Central to their vision was a new 'plastic reality', echoing the supposed hidden order of nature and represented by orthogonally arranged coloured planes. Describing their architectural aspirations, the movement's founder and propagandist, Theo van Doesburg, explained that buildings should be 'anti-cubic', composed of 'space cells' thrown 'centrifugally from the core' to present 'insofar as is possible from a constructional point of view – the task of the engineers! – a more or less floating aspect that, so to speak, works against the gravitational forces of nature'.[38]

Van Doesburg's article was published in 1924 to accompany the presentation of Gerrit Rietveld's Schröder House, which hinted at some of the qualities – and difficulties – of this new, gravity-defying architecture. Constructionally, the house is a messy hybrid of timber, steel, masonry and reinforced concrete, but visually it appears to be composed entirely

The abstract, coloured planes and open corners of Gerrit Rietveld's Schröder House, in Utrecht express the desire to escape the limitations of matter.

of coloured planes, which deliberately conceal how it works as a physical structure. Sixty years later a similar formal language was deployed by the Finnish architect Juha Leiviskä in designing a church at Myyrmäki on the northern outskirts of Helsinki. Here the interior is framed entirely by white planes. Immaterial and seemingly weightless, they multiply to baffle and reflect light, which streams in from screened sources all around. Leiviskä readily acknowledges his debt to the Rococo and, as in a church such as that at Neresheim, the proliferation of edges and surfaces renders the interior wonderfully responsive to light. Like its Bavarian exemplars, this is an architecture attuned to the local climate.

For all their fascination, these varied exercises in the denial of materiality and the dissolution of form might be thought peripheral to the mainstream of Western architecture. In point of fact their antithesis – the concern for expressing 'the nature of materials' – has played a far less significant role than might be imagined. When Doric architecture developed in Ancient Greece, the working of materials through craft was seen not simply as a necessary support for civilization, but as a model for the artistic and philosophical ideas that were its highest expression.[39] Theory did not precede and condition practice, but arose out of reflecting

on the 'well made thing' – in much the same way that Vitruvius advised architects to learn to write so that their buildings could live on through their commentaries.[40]

With the later separation of theory from practice came the conviction that has rippled on through architectural (and most other) theory ever since: the priority and superiority of the idea over its material manifestation. Aristotle and Plato, who differed about so much, were agreed on this, and their contention was admirably summed up more than two millennia later at the end of the eighteenth century by Immanuel Kant, when he argued that 'taste is swayed not by what gratifies a sensation but by what pleases merely by its form'. For 'form' read 'design' – *disegno* in Italian – and you have the familiar hierarchy of values by which Western art and architecture have been widely understood since the ancient world.

The emphasis on design was accompanied by a downgrading of 'secondary' aspects, such as materials and colour, which merely 'gratify a sensation'. For the most important of the Renaissance theorists, Leon Battista Alberti, this distinction was basic to his conception of architecture, as he made clear in the Prologue to his book *De re aedificatoria* (On the Art of Building): 'The building is a form of body, which like any other consists of lineaments and matter,

The planar composition of Juha Leiviskä's Myyrmäki Church is indebted to De Stijl and Rococo models.

Interior of the Rococo church at Neresheim, Germany.

Santa Maria Novella, Florence, by Leon Battista Alberti.

the one a product of thought, the other of Nature; the one requiring the mind and the power of reason, the other dependent on preparation and selection.' When Alberti discusses 'lineaments', they turn out to include history, the 'elements' of building, and the Vitruvian triad of *firmitas*, *utilitas* and *venustas* – structure, use and beauty (or 'commodity, firmness and delight' as they are more commonly known in English, thanks to Sir Henry Wootton[41]).

An illustration of how Alberti implemented his ideas is provided by his treatment of the 'lineaments' of a wall. Far from being a tectonic element with its own constructional logic, the physical, built wall is seen as a backdrop on which figures and ornaments can be drawn – *disegno* ('design') and drawing are almost interchangeable in Italian. On the west front of Santa Maria Novella in Florence the 'drawing' is made with a combination of white marble and green *verde di Prato*, whereas on the street-front of the Rucellai palace the Classical orders, colonnade, arches, and even what appear to be the individual stones themselves, are incised into the surface. The 'stones' we see are not, in fact, always the actual, more irregular units from which the wall is constructed, the latter having visible joints only where they coincide with the 'ideal' wall. The Rucellai palace fits well

with the Classical idea of mimesis – the design is an 'imitation' of an 'ideal' wall – but unlike a Doric temple, Alberti's was a graphic, designed architecture. It reflected a conceptual division between thinking and doing, echoed in a specialization of the roles of designers and craftsmen that was alien to Classical Greece, and as such anticipated the approach that would dominate subsequent teaching and practice, above all in the French Beaux Arts tradition.

In Alberti's system, beauty was regarded as inherent, 'suffused all through the body of that which may be called beautiful', whereas ornament, 'rather than being inherent, has the character of something attached or additional'.[42] Ornament and materials could enhance form by giving character and presence, but they were not integral to its conception. When the Abbé Laugier waged war on Baroque and Rococo excesses, he echoed Alberti's view, arguing –

Regulated by geometric figures and 'ideal' proportions, the façade of Alberti's Santa Maria Novella epitomizes the Renaissance concern with architecture as an art of design.

On Alberti's Rucellai Palace, Florence, the joints of the 'stones' we see (top) – elements of the building's 'design' – do not always correspond with the actual stones of which the wall is constructed (above).

in his *Observations sur l'architecture* – that a well-proportioned building will always produce a positive effect, independent of the richness of its materials or ornamentation.[43]

The revaluation of Renaissance art in the light of Modernist aesthetic ideas reinforced the emphasis on such 'timeless' values, leading to renewed interest in the more 'abstract' work of artists – such as Giotto, Masaccio and Piero della Francesca – who had been less highly valued, and sometimes completely ignored, by preceding generations. Similarly, most recent architectural histories, exemplified by Rudolf Wittkower's classic 1949 study entitled *Architectural Principles in the Age of Humanism*,[44] have emphasized proportional control and clarity of form and space – what Richard Krautheimer has called Alberti's 'highly exclusive purism'[45] – as the exemplary Renaissance virtues.

From Alberti to our latter-day Minimalists, belief in the pre-eminence of the values of design and purity of form has frequently been asserted through buildings of deliberate austerity, for which 'white' could be said to be the ideal 'material'. The prejudice against colour is longstanding. Plato condemned dyes as designed to deceive and a means by which women trick men, whilst later, in Rome, Pliny and Seneca argued that corrupting, florid colours were alien and came from the East. The ideal male body was seen as monochrome, whereas the female was unstable, prone to blushing and blanching.[46]

The devotion to white, 'cleansed of all foreign elements', to quote Walter Pater,[47] became almost a religion for the late eighteenth century's most passionate advocate of Classical values, Johann Joachim Winckelmann.[48] To justify his belief that the whiter a body, the more beautiful it is, he offered a surprisingly scientific-sounding explanation: because white reflected the greatest number of rays of light, it was the most easily perceived 'colour', and therefore the best at disclosing the qualities of pure form. For Neoclassicists like Winckelmann, Greek monuments replaced Roman art and architecture – with its love of ornate stones – as the epitome of Classical ideals. And nothing, to Winckelmann, seemed whiter than the bare bones of Greek statues and temples, unchanging beneath the southern sun.

Surface richness was never without its advocates, however, and even Alberti's approach was not as ascetic as it has sometimes been made to appear. Although he believed that nothing in a 'temple' (the Classically minded architect's preferred term for church) should distract the faithful, he nonetheless commended the use of inlaid marble or glass. And for most Renaissance practitioners and patrons it is clear that whilst what was termed *ornato* – meaning beautiful, precious or magnificent, and typically expressed through surface polish, embellishment and refinement – might be lower down the aesthetic scale than 'formal purism', it was a more generally desired objective.[49]

In a comprehensive re-assessment of the period, Hellmut Wohl notes that 'as we read through Renaissance writings on art, it is not uncommon to find greater responsiveness to the aesthetic properties of materials, especially of coloured marble and mosaics, than to works of painting and sculpture'.[50] The appeal of fine

Clarity of form and space: the interior of Palladio's church of Santo Spirito, Venice.

The casts at the Canova plaster-cast gallery in Possagno exemplify the Neoclassical passion for white.

Alberti commended inlaid
marble floors as an enrichment
of churches: Santo Spirito,
Venice, by Palladio.

stones was almost universal, and in early Renaissance wall paintings, beginning with Giotto's cycle in the Arena Chapel in Padua, the representation of coloured stone takes up a surprisingly large amount of available wall space.[51]

This passion for beautiful materials received its most exotic expression in the sensuous, not to say erotic, text entitled *Hypnerotomachia Poliphili* (known in English as 'The Strife of Love in a Dream'). Generally attributed to Francesco Colonna – although it has repeatedly been argued that it was, in fact, written secretly by Alberti[52] – the book relates the efforts of Poliphilo to win the love of Polia. As his name implies, the protagonist's love was not easily contained, and he is equally passionate about architecture and antiquity. In his dream he constructs and visits imaginary palaces, temples and theatres, and the woodcuts illustrating them are complemented by long, ecstatic descriptions of their material delights.

In the residence of Queen Eleuterylida, for example, Poliphilo passes through a court with a floor paved 'like a chess-board, alternately of coral-coloured jasper and of bright green with sanguine spots'. Surrounding this was 'a noble interlaced design of jaspers, prases [a leek-green quartz], chalcedonies, agates, and other conspicuous kinds of precious stone'. The seats are of 'red and yellow sandalwood' upholstered

with 'green velvet', and the surrounding walls were 'all covered with plates of pure, lustrous gold'. And so the description goes on, for four pages in all, taking in lapis lazuli, vermilion, amethysts, garnets, emeralds…[53]

Although written during the Renaissance and illustrated with Classical buildings, these descriptions are rooted in the medieval love of surface elaboration, on which Ruskin dwelt with similar devotion, suggesting that the Renaissance passion for *ornato* had much to do with the preceding idea of *ornatus*. To the medieval mind, this connoted God's transformation of formless chaos into a living world, and richly coloured stones were seen as figures – representatives – of the divine majesty. In a famous homily delivered in 1140, Pseudo-Dionysius the Areopagite likened coloured marbles in a pavement to flowers in a springtime meadow, but whereas the natural growths wilt and die away, the chapel 'shines eternally with its immortal flowers'.[54]

It is understandable that histories emphasize the discontinuities between the medieval and Renaissance periods, but it is well to remember that medieval religious thought was also deeply touched by Classical philosophy,[55] and that craft traditions could hardly be transformed overnight. To take one example: worshippers in many of Rome's early Renaissance churches walked on floors whose designs were indebted to the richly ornamented Cosmati pavements which developed and flourished in the late Middle Ages – probably the very type that were metaphorically in flower in the vision of Pseudo-Dionysius.[56] The idea, suggested by a late-fourteenth-century Dominican preacher, that we can see such coloured stones as figures of God's love, might not have been echoed so readily in the Renaissance, when aesthetic preferences were more often argued by reference to Classical authorities, but artists and patrons alike took pleasure in the sensuous appeal of decorative stones during both periods.

In the Middle Ages, richly coloured pavements, such as this in Venice, were likened to flowering meadows.

The rediscovery and survey of Greek architecture during the late eighteenth century, which had been a major catalyst for the Neoclassical movement, was followed in the early nineteenth century by several new waves of archaeological investigation by English, French and German scholars. Their findings were to shake the foundations of the Neoclassical aesthetic. In 1815 Quatremère de Quincy sent ripples around Europe by publishing a book containing reconstructions of the colossal lost statues of Zeus and Athena by the great sculptor Phidias. Coloured and studded with gold and ivory, they could hardly have been further from Winckelmann's beloved white! Further field work soon found incontrovertible evidence that, far from being paragons of whiteness, Greek temples showed clear traces of applied colour, confirming hints in surviving Classical texts, which had been conveniently ignored or explained away as referring only to small details, not to entire surfaces.

Following excavations in Selinus on Sicily, the Paris-based German architect Jacques-Ignace Hittorff made drawings of a conjectural reconstruction of a small temple resplendent in polychrome dress. It sparked an enormous controversy, which became so acrimonious it was dubbed 'the polychrome war'.[57] A century later, Frank Lloyd Wright could still rage that 'the Greeks abused stone shamefully – did not understand its nature at all except as something to be painted or gilded out of existence'.[58] But for the colour-loving Ruskin, it was a matter of regret that the 'temples whose azure and purple once flamed above the Grecian promontories' now 'stand in their faded whiteness, like snow which the sunset has left cold.'[59]

Successive generations of Beaux Arts students offered increasingly vivid – and, it has to be said, increasingly improbable – renderings of the suddenly colourful ancient world. This might all have been of little more than academic interest were it not for the fact that the issue of colour struck at the heart of a looming crisis

Top: The discovery that Greek temples were coloured prompted a radical revaluation of Classical aesthetics.

Above: Bindesbøll's Thorvaldsen Museum, Copenhagen, 1839-47: a major contribution to the debate about polychromy.

in European architecture, which can conveniently, if somewhat simplistically, be summed up as the divide between those to whom architecture remained primarily a matter of style and 'design', and the new breed of Functionalists who viewed it as the rational art of building, which needed to find new forms for new materials.

By far the most far-reaching ideas to come out of the debates about polychromy were developed by a young German architect who had been drawn to Hittorff's circle in Paris: Gottfried Semper. He entered the polychrome war in 1834 with an essay in which he at first seems to side with the functionalist position.[60] 'Art knows only one master – the need', he declares, aligning himself firmly with those progressive voices that believed architects must come to terms with the products of industry. The passage is worth quoting at length:

The thorough study of the natural sciences has led to most important discoveries. Brick, wood, metal, iron and zinc in particular, have replaced ashlar and marble. It would be inappropriate to continue imitating these last two materials – even more so to give them a false appearance... Let the material speak for itself; let it step undisguised in the shape and proportions found most suitable by experience and science. Brick should appear as brick, wood as wood, iron as iron, each according to its own statical laws.

The Greeks, Semper points out, also built structures in which 'wood, iron, and bronze formed an essential part', and they built them 'according to the statical laws peculiar to these materials, unrelated to stone'. The remainder of the essay argues the case for believing Greek temples to have been coloured. As the earliest examples were built of an unattractive grey stone (the Poros we met in the last chapter), they had to be stuccoed and then coloured. Later versions, made of the 'fine white' Pentelic marble, were obliged to follow this canonic

model, albeit without the need for stucco before painting. Under strong sun, Semper added, the brilliant marble would have been uncomfortably bright to the eyes, and this was ameliorated by colouring: the 'golden crust' we see and admire now was not, as had been supposed, 'the sediment of time' but of 'antique paint'.

By the time of his next book, *The Four Elements of Architecture*, published in 1851, Semper's position had moved on significantly. Materials should certainly be chosen and used 'according to the laws conditioned by nature', but their 'form and character' should be 'dependent on the ideas embodied in them, and not on the material'. After criticizing the 'materialistic way of thinking' deriving from Vitruvius's account of the wooden origins of Greek temples, Semper offers his own version of the 'primitive hut': in his later *magnum opus* entitled *Der Stil in den technischen und tektonischen Künsten, oder praktische Ästhetik* (Style in the Technical and Structural Arts, or Practical Aesthetics – 1861-63), he illustrates it with a bamboo structure from the West Indies seen at the Great Exhibition of 1851. The essential elements of this construction are the raised floor, central fireplace, the roof carried on columns, and the plaited matting. In *The Four Elements of Architecture*, these are theorized more universally as the sacred flame, the roof, the enclosure, and the mound.

Semper's four functional/constructional elements are in turn identified with four basic 'technical skills': ceramics and metalwork around the hearth; water and masonry, associated with the mound; carpentry for the roof and its accessories; and finally – in a new paragraph, to explain his seemingly idiosyncratic choice – the role of providing enclosure is assigned to the 'wall fitter' or 'weaver of mats and carpets'. This idea is of capital importance, not only to his theory of architecture, but also to his later explanation of style in all the arts and crafts. Wickerwork, he says, 'was the essence of the wall', and he might have reproduced

The Thorvaldsen Museum's richly coloured walls are an ideal foil to the work of the Neoclassical sculptor after whom it is named.

An architecture of colour: marble
'joints' and plaster 'stones'
of the Thorvaldsen Museum.

by way of support the version of the primitive
hut illustrated in the first Italian edition of
Vitruvius, published in 1521 (see page 13).[61]
Originally belonging to the construction of the
mound or platform, masonry was 'an intruder'
into the 'wall-fitter's domain', and so even where
solid walls became necessary for reasons
of climate, security or stability, they were seen
as 'only the inner, invisible structure hidden
behind the true and legitimate representatives
of the wall, the colourful woven carpets'.[62]

It is difficult to overstate the importance
Semper attached to weaving. In *Der Stil*, textiles
occupy almost as much space as the other
three arts combined, and he argues that the
crafts of weaving and dyeing, not painting, were
the original basis of pattern-making. He likens
the *cladding* of a building to the *dressing* of the
body, for both of which he used the same
German word – *Bekleidung*, which has no exact
equivalent in English. Consideration of fabrics,
and the ways they are joined using different
types of seam, leads him to formulate two basic
rules, which he extends to all made things:
firstly, make a virtue out of necessity; and
secondly, the material and process of fabrication
must be allowed to condition the result.

It was only by the Roman period, Semper
pointed out, that walling materials themselves
came to be seen as decorative; prior to that
'even the most noble . . . were given a coat
of paint'. Polychromy, far from being an
aberration or an embarrassing survival from the
Greeks' primitive past, was both a recollection
of the temples' origins and a means of focussing
our attention on the visible surface of the wall.
Colour was the 'subtlest, most bodiless coating'
and therefore 'the most perfect to do away with
reality, for while it dressed the material it was
itself immaterial'.[63]

Semper's emphasis on colour challenged
the academic hierarchy, which valued form over
'secondary' qualities: colour, argued Semper,
precedes form and 'brings the eye back again
to the natural way of seeing, which it lost under

the sway of that mode of abstraction that knows precisely how to separate the visible and inseparable qualities of bodies, the colour from the form'.[64] In this, intentionally or not, he seems to echo the seventeenth-century architect-theorist Claude Perrault, who distinguished between *positive*, and universally understood, beauties – such as that of rich materials – and *arbitrary* qualities – such as the Classical Orders or refinements of proportional design – which are a matter of 'will and custom'.[65]

In Semper's hands, archaeological discoveries that might have proved to be of purely antiquarian interest become the grounds for a radical inversion of the generally accepted conception of architecture. Drawing on the far-reaching distinction made by Bötticher between a work of art's 'core-form' and its 'art-form',[66] Semper contended that the 'truth' of a building did not reside in its construction (core-form), but in an appropriate surface dressing (art-form). The 'true' wall is what we see, not the inner construction we cannot see, because the surface 'dressing' is free to refer back to the wall's origins as woven fabrics that defined space, whereas masonry construction confuses this *spatial* role with that of *structural* support. By using 'real' materials instead of paint, the Romans had inverted the Greek conviction that 'inner content should conform to outer beauty'[67]

– and not the other way round, as the proponents of the art of building we consider in the next chapter believed.

Although he enjoyed a long and successful career in practice, Semper's work was never as radical as his ideas, and it fell to later generations of architects, such as Otto Wagner and Adolf Loos, to explore their implications. Consider, for example, Wagner's apartment building, known as the 'Majolicahouse', in Vienna. The decorative flower and tendril motifs move freely across the surface, all but ignoring the regular rhythm of windows – much like the diaper-pattern on the Doge's Palace. The tiling transforms the wall surface into a lightweight fabric, which seems almost literally to hang from the bronze lions' heads placed, like giant studs, between the top-floor windows. There could be no more vivid evocation of Semper's ideas on cladding and the priority of textiles, and in the 'dressing' of his best known building – the Post Office Savings Bank in Vienna – Wagner is just as clearly Semperian.

The Bank's upper floors are clad with marble, the lower two with Swedish granite, and the entire façade is punctuated by a regular grid of fixing bolts – or rather, aluminium covers marking the bolts. The bolts appear to be holding the slabs in place, but were only needed to retain them whilst the mortar set. The bolt-heads could have been concealed but,

The façade of Otto Wagner's Post Office Savings Bank in Vienna (top) is dotted with a grid of aluminium caps (above) that cover the bolts used to hold the thin-stone cladding in place whilst the mortar set.

Wagner's 'Majolicahouse' in Vienna exemplifies the idea of the façade as a 'dressed' fabric.

as Wagner pointed out, viewers familiar with the bolts and rivets of iron structures would understand them as fixings, making clear that the building is covered with thin slabs of stone. In *Modern Architecture* – 'A guidebook for his students to this field of art', as Wagner sub-titled it – Wagner saw the use of thin panels of stone conspicuously 'bolted' to the façade as an essential feature of 'a modern way of building', not least because by dramatically reducing the thickness of stone required it enabled the finest materials to be afforded – a prediction admirably fulfilled (albeit in ways he could hardly have imagined) in the corporate palaces built throughout the developed world in the later decades of the twentieth century.[68]

In Semper's terms, the necessity of the bolts during construction was turned into a virtue by using them to ensure that the process of fabrication both conditions, and is legible in, the final form.[69] The use of such visible fixings was hardly new: explaining the 'honesty' of the revetment of St Mark's in Venice, Ruskin pointed out that 'every slab of facial marble s fastened to the next by a confessed rivet', and that the cladding follows the form of the masonry behind so closely – 'like a coat of mail' – that no 'deceit' could be suspected.[70]

No one, arguably, learnt more from Semper than Adolf Loos. He confessed his debt in an essay entitled *The Principle of Cladding*,[71] in which he argued that each material has its own *formensprache* ('language of forms'), and then went on to formulate his 'principle of cladding'. The latter, following Semper, requires that 'we must work in such a way that a confusion of the material clad with its cladding is impossible'. This precluded painting cheap wood to resemble a fine one, such as mahogany – an almost ubiquitous practice in Vienna, he noted sarcastically. And, one might add, it would also have precluded the even more curious and once fashionable Venetian practice of painting perfectly good brick- and stonework to resemble themselves.[72]

Loos was particularly insistent about the idea that a material has its own 'language of forms'. It was a way of countering his contemporaries' passion for simulating one material with another, and might appear to bring him close to the idea that a material has a universally valid intrinsic 'nature'. In fact his thinking is better understood as contextual rather than functional. For Loos the 'nature' – and hence meaning – of a material is inseparable from its use in a particular place, building or interior. For the mixed-use building he designed in Vienna's Michaelerplatz, now known as the 'Looshaus' and completed in 1910, he chose a state-of-the-art, reinforced-concrete frame. This

'Looshaus' in the Michaelerplatz, Vienna, by Adolf Loos.

is revealed at the rear, where the structure is exposed and filled with gridded glass and ceramic tiles; there is even a totally glazed lift shaft, which may well be the earliest example of what would become a familiar trope of Modern architecture.[73]

A similar display of naked structure on the building's public frontages would, in Loos's eyes, have been entirely unacceptable. For the upper storeys, occupied by apartments, he chose lime wash: 'When plaster shows itself candidly as a covering for a brick wall,' he wrote, 'it has as little to be ashamed of in its humble origin as a Tyrolese with his leather trousers in the Hofburg.' The humble plaster looked back to the city's oldest building traditions, not forward to the Rationalism of the 1920s, as has sometimes been claimed. Rejecting the overblown ornament in favour at the time by reverting to an older tradition was Loos's way of being 'modern' – and entirely appropriate for such a 'timeless' use as dwelling. The plain wall proved far too austere for the city's planners, however, and embroiled Loos in the greatest public controversy of his career.[74]

The lower, public floors were designed for Goldman and Salatsch, a leading gentlemen's outfitters, and for an associated tailors' workshop and school. To Loos, fine tailoring – which meant English tailoring and those with

the good taste to emulate it[75] – represented the kind of continuity of craft upon which true style depends. In recognition of this, he wrapped the entire lower floors with large slabs of highly polished and figured Cipolin marble. The marble panels frame square-gridded oriel windows, made of glittering brass and modelled on English examples,[76] and the thin slabs of highly polished stone are set vertically to disassociate them entirely from traditional coursed masonry. The marble graining is carefully matched in the manner of wood veneers, creating 'butterfly' figures like giant Rorschach blots. No cladding ever seemed thinner or less structural, and even the monolithic columns were deployed for symbolic reasons: arriving too late from the quarry, they had to be hung from the frame above. The 'deceit' is not as problematic as it might appear, because the rich veining suggests an ornamental rather than structural use, and the columns' purpose was to make apparent the building's civic dignity, not suggest a false continuity with the Classical past.

Loos's most direct influence was on the Art Deco style, which took its name from the 'Exposition Internationale des Arts Décoratifs et Industriels Modernes' held in Paris in 1925, but in a provocative re-reading of the period, Mark Wigley has argued that Art Deco's most implacable enemy, Le Corbusier, also owed him

Above and right: Perfectly flat and richly coloured and figured, the green Cipolin marble facings of the Looshaus leave no doubt that they are a form of surface cladding, not solid construction.

a considerable debt. To coincide with the Paris exhibition, for which he designed the Pavillon de l'Esprit Nouveau, Le Corbusier published a book that offered an alternative account of the decorative arts. The arguments culminated in a chapter entitled 'A Coat of Whitewash: The Law of Ripolin'[77] – Ripolin was a well-known paint-maker, and to Le Corbusier whitewash represented a sign of 'high morality'.

Le Corbusier's passion for white grew out of the Purist aesthetic he developed with the painter Amédée Ozenfant, with its Platonic emphasis on the 'primary sensations' aroused by simple geometric forms. Like Alberti and the Neoclassicists before him, Le Corbusier viewed plain surfaces as the most effective means of exhibiting 'mathematical lyricism', which to him was the highest form of aesthetic order. He was also convinced that industrialized construction techniques, when fully developed, would yield the smooth 'factory finish' he sought. The reality of building in the 1920s, was, needless to say, rather different, and far from being the seamless products of new building technology, his Purist villas were ad hoc combinations of new and traditional materials, plastered over and painted white to appear homogeneous and machine-made. Although generally interpreted as temporary substitutes for a machine-age material of the future – reinforced concrete not

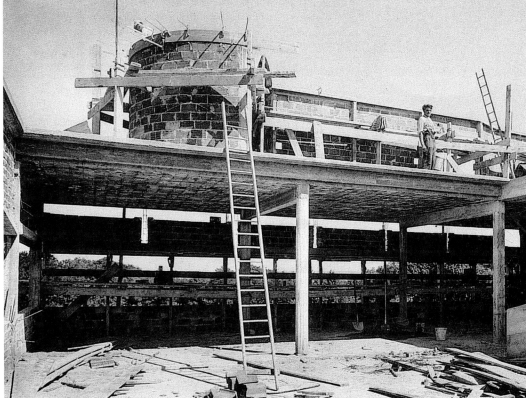

The construction process of the Villa Savoye was not as industrialized as its appearance was calculated to suggest: 'dressing' with white plaster was Le Corbusier's means of achieving machine-age purity of form.

At the workers' housing estate in Pessac (above), Le Corbusier used colour to transform the volumes into assemblies of planes, whereas in the Villa Savoye (opposite), the white surfaces emphasise the 'mathematical lyricism' of spaces and forms 'brought together in light'.

quite having lived up to expectations – the white surfaces, argues Wigley, were, in fact, a deliberately chosen *dressing* to create a 'pure image, a two-dimensional projection of modern life', which locates a truly modern architecture where it belongs, 'in the seemingly elusive space of communication'.[78]

Through its 'elimination of the equivocal', wrote Le Corbusier, whitewash encouraged the 'concentration of intention on its proper object'. And in architecture, as he had famously declared in his first book, *Vers une architecture* of 1923 (translated as *Towards a New Architecture* in 1927), the object was the 'masterly, correct and magnificent play of volumes brought together in light'.[79] In this, as in so much else, Le Corbusier was heir to one of the nineteenth century's most lasting legacies to the twentieth, the idea that the history of architecture was a history of different ways of shaping space. Rather than concentrate on tectonic expression, argued August Schmarsow in his 1893 essay 'The Essence of Architectural Creation', architects had much to gain by 'disregarding … its entire execution in durable material' so as to rediscover its 'time-honoured inner aspect' as 'the *reatress of space*'. Conceived thus, architecture embraced 'the art of building cities', road construction, agriculture and gardening, and formed 'a basic constituent in the history of *worldviews*':[80] Schmarsow's reading of history might almost have been a programme for the Modernists' all-embracing vision of a new worldview for the Machine Age, with space as its universal material and rational construction as its means.

Chapter 3
In the Nature
of Materials

At Säynätsalo Town Hall, Alvar
Aalto emphasized the individual
bricks by angling them slightly
in the bed and recessing the joints.

Wright saw the fluid forms
and bold cantilevers of the
Guggenheim Museum,
New York, as expressions
of the nature of concrete.

*Cultivate brick, the red or the yellowish-white.
Utilize all of its many possibilities. Use few or
no shaped bricks. Do not copy details, whether
Greek or Gothic. Make them yourself from the
material. Do not believe that stucco is a building
material, and smile when your professor says
that 'paint is also a material'. If you ever get
a chance to build a house of granite, remember
that it is a precious stone, and if ferro-concrete
becomes a building material do not rest until
a new style is found for it.*
    P. V. Jensen-Klint (1919)[1]

When the fourth edition of Otto Wagner's
book *Moderne Architektur* was published in
1914, it appeared under the title *Die Baukunst
unserer Zeit* (The Building Art of our Time).
To his contemporaries, the new wording was
an unequivocal sign that Wagner was aligning
himself with those who believed that the future
of architecture lay with the development of new
forms suited to new materials, not with the
re-working of historical styles. For Frank Lloyd
Wright, responding to the 'nature' of a new
material was both the best way to conquer
professional resistance to change and the
surest route to a new architecture: 'Every new
material', he declared, 'means a new form,
a new use if used according to its nature.'[2]
The belief that working 'in the nature
of materials' could be the hallmark of an
authentically modern architecture grew out
of nineteenth-century debates about style,
but its intellectual underpinnings lie much
further back. Both Galileo and Leonardo da Vinci
realized that physical structures could not simply
be scaled up and down in size, but that their
proportions had to change according to their size
and materials – as was the case, Galileo pointed
out, with animal skeletons.[3] The Classical view
that forms were independent of matter was
no longer tenable, and from the early eighteenth
century onwards scientists and engineers began
to devote increasing attention to understanding
and quantifying the properties of materials

to enable their performance to be calculated.

Claude Perrault's division between 'arbitrary' and 'positive' beauties addressed the challenges posed by the mechanical view of the world. He argued that the laws of mechanics, being absolute, offered the potential for 'positive' beauty, whereas preferences based on appearance and taste were necessarily arbitrary and open to disagreement.[4] The divide between the 'aesthetic' and 'mechanical' aspects of architecture was gradually institutionalized, nowhere more overtly than in France, where the 'fine art' of architecture was taught in the Ecole des Beaux Arts, whilst entirely separate institutions developed for building and engineering.[5]

The first recognizably modern statement of a functionalist position was made as early as the mid eighteenth century by Carlo Lodoli, a Venetian Carmelite monk, whose ideas are known only through the somewhat contradictory accounts of two disciples, Andrea Memmo and Francesco Algarotti. Both agreed, however, that Lodoli rejected all attempts to explain architecture as an art of imitation, and argued that it should be seen, as Memmo wrote, as 'an intellectual and practical science which aims to establish by reasoning the good custom and the proportions of artefacts, and to discover through experience the nature of the materials which compose it'.[6] Lodoli did not reject the use of ornament, but consigned it – like Perrault – to 'taste and usage'.[7]

The belief that the application of the laws of structure to the properties of materials would provide a new foundation for architectural form became central to the view of architecture as the art of building. When, in 1828, the German Heinrich Hübsch published an essay entitled 'In What Style Should We Build?', he argued that the nineteenth century needed to develop a style as appropriate for its age as the great styles of the past, with rational construction as the guide.[8]

An early indication of a direction such a search might take was given by Karl Friedrich Schinkel in the Bauakademie – or school of architecture – he completed in Berlin in 1836. In place of the full-blown essay in Classical style, which might have been expected, Schinkel provided a living demonstration of his belief that utility was the first determinant of any architecture. Instead of stone, he opted for brick, and throughout the building the dimensions were determined by the bonding pattern. The style was recognizably Classical, but every detail was re-thought in terms of the properties of brick. The cornices had notably shallow projections; all the mouldings were kept simple to avoid frost damage; and the segmental arches were reflected internally in shallow brick vaults tied with iron rods – as in the early English industrial buildings Schinkel admired.[9]

The most systematic development of the rationalist view was articulated in France by Viollet-le-Duc. Rejecting the mimetic origins of Greek architecture, he argued that its arrangements 'indicate stone throughout – quarried, worked, hoisted, and made manifest by reason of its nature and of the function that it fulfils'.[10] Roman architecture, by contrast, 'may be compared to a man clothed: there is the man, and there is the dress; the dress may be good or bad, rich or poor in material, well or ill cut, but it forms no part of the body'.[11] In the Gothic, however, body and dress were inseparable. Gothic construction is 'supple, free, and as inquiring as the modern spirit: its principles permit the use of all the materials given by nature or industry in virtue of their own qualities'.[12] A thorough knowledge of materials, believed Viollet, is 'the first condition of composition', and in designing this way architects would 'proceed as Nature herself does'[13] – a thought echoed throughout Frank Lloyd Wright's writings on materials.[14]

The constructional clarity of High Gothic buildings such as Rheims Cathedral (above) was a model for many nineteenth-century architects, such as Deane & Woodward (Oxford University Museum, top), who were seeking an architecture of iron and glass.

It is revealing that Viollet-le-Duc chose to present the most complete account of his ideas in the seemingly objective form of a Dictionary. Wright considered the *Dictionnaire raisonné*,[15] published in ten volumes between 1854 and 1868, 'the only really sensible book on architecture'.[16] Its subject was French architecture from the eleventh to the sixteenth century, and it eventually ran to ten volumes of more than 5000 pages and 3000 illustrations. Argument and illustrations were interwoven in an almost unprecedented way, and the latter included the first use of exploded views to explain buildings – inspired by the use of dissection in comparative anatomy and geology. Employing materials 'according to their qualities and properties', Viollet argued throughout, was essential to being 'true to the constructive processes' that are the basis of architecture.[17]

In the two-volume publication of Viollet-le-Duc's lectures – which Wright presented to his son John Lloyd with the commendation, 'in these volumes you will find all the architectural schooling you will ever need'[18] – he included projects to illustrate how iron and masonry could together create a modern Gothic. He was a less persuasive designer than theorist, however, and his models found few imitators. But he was widely read and hugely influential, and in the Amsterdam Stock Exchange, completed by Berlage in 1903, the vision of combining light- and heavyweight materials was finally given compelling form. The steel and wrought-iron trusses rest on corbelled pad-stones, from where the loads are distributed down projecting brick piers to stone columns. Between the lines of support, paired arches subdivide each bay, and at the ground floor a broad brick-relieving arch shelters two stone arches to provide both a beautifully judged change of scale and the tectonically necessary suggestion of greater strength. The result is, as Kenneth Frampton has written, 'as rich and inflected as the structure of a gothic cathedral'[19] – and, as Mies van der Rohe observed soon after its completion, 'truly modern'.[20]

Similar sentiments to those of Viollet about 'honest' construction had already been articulated in England by August Welby Northmore Pugin in his 1841 book *The True Principles of Pointed or Christian Architecture*. 'The two great rules for design', pronounced Pugin, 'are these: 1st, that there should be no features about a building which are not necessary for convenience, construction or propriety; 2nd, that all ornament should consist of the essential construction of the building.'[21] He went on to explain that 'the architects of the middle ages were the first who turned the natural properties of the various materials

Viollet-le-Duc's proposals for combining iron and masonry, such as this example from his *Discourses on Architecture* (above), were not as influential as his writings – but they find an echo in this recent building (right) by Peter Foggo in the City of London.

Berlage's Amsterdam Stock Exchange was deeply marked by Viollet-le-Duc's ideas on rational construction.

The cast-iron columns, steel I-beams and brick arches of Guimard's Ecole du Sacré-Cœur in Paris were designed as a tribute to the ideas of Viollet-le-Duc.

to their full account, and made their mechanism a vehicle for their art'.[22]

Although he vigorously denied any debt, John Ruskin's *Seven Lamps of Architecture*, published in 1849, owed much to Pugin's ideas.[23] Like Viollet and Pugin, Ruskin believed that there cannot be 'any good architecture which is not based on good building',[24] and he shared their passion for Gothic as the supremely 'truthful' form of construction. But whereas the Frenchman endeavoured to justify his decisions by reason alone, Ruskin's views were grounded in a moral framework inspired by his Evangelical faith. For Ruskin, industrial production was the work of the Devil, and cast or machine work that imitated craft (hand) production – what he called 'operative deceit'[25] – was one of the gravest and commonest sins of Victorian manufacture. 'To those who love architecture,' Ruskin declared, 'the life and accent of the hand are everything',[26] and as a consequence, 'true architecture does not admit iron as a constructive support'.[27]

The second volume of Ruskin's next book on architecture, *The Stones of Venice* – which he pointedly started writing on the same day as the Crystal Palace, epitome of everything he detested, opened to the public – has a long chapter entitled 'The Nature of Gothic'. It contains some of his most brilliant and influential ideas, and in 1892 was issued by William

Morris's Kelmscott Press as a small book in its own right: in his Preface, Morris declared it 'one of the very few necessary and inevitable utterances of the century'.[28] Although he was receptive to the structural rationality of Gothic, and critical of the undermining of structural logic in the late Gothic style we discussed in the last chapter, Ruskin concentrated on what he called its 'moral and imaginative' aspects, emphasizing qualities that eluded machine production and industrial materials.

For Ruskin, cast ornament, such as that in the Bradley Building in Los Angeles (above), could never rival the touch of the hand exemplified by the free-carving of this figure at Wells Cathedral, England (right).

Convinced that 'no good work whatever can be perfect',[29] Ruskin advocated 'savageness' and extolled the virtues of rough workmanship. This was necessary to allow modestly talented craftsmen some freedom of expression, and resulted in hitherto disregarded aesthetic qualities – Ruskin's love of lack of finish came well before it was widely appreciated, following later exposure to Japanese arts and crafts. He saw 'changefulness' as another basic requirement, pointing out that medieval masons were 'capable of perpetual novelty'[30] – not something industrial processes were designed to deliver. And by advocating 'redundance' – an abundance of ornament deriving from 'a magnificent enthusiasm'[31] – he sought to challenge what he saw as the corrupt logic of a market economy and the arrogance of Classical design. 'No architecture,' Ruskin declared, 'is so haughty as that which is simple; which refuses to address the eye, except in a few clear and forceful lines; which implies, in offering so little to our regards, that all it has offered is perfect.'[32]

Ruskin was widely read, and even the future Le Corbusier's early education in Switzerland was deeply marked by this 'paradoxical prophet, laboured, complex, contradictory' who 'shook our young minds profoundly.'[33] In England, Ruskin influenced successive generations of Arts and Crafts practitioners, thanks in part to the eager advocacy of the leading light of the movement, William Morris. Although a pattern designer of genius, Morris favoured simplicity in architecture. By building in a 'common sense and unpretentious way, with the good material of the countryside', he argued, new buildings could become 'a growth of the soil'.[34] Morris regarded plainly-built medieval structures as ideal models for new public buildings, and none more so than Great Coxwell Barn in Gloucestershire, 'unapproachable in its dignity, as beautiful as a cathedral, yet with no ostentation of the builder's art'.[35] The material facts of the barn's construction offered all the 'style' that was required.

The anti-industrial ideas of Pugin, Ruskin and Morris contributed to a climate in which few architects were disposed to explore the potential of new materials: the most original English architecture of the late nineteenth century was domestic, and conventionally built. The prolific Gothicist, Giles Gilbert Scott, declared in his *Remarks on Secular and Domestic Architecture* that it was 'self-evident' that 'the triumph of modern metallic construction opens out a perfectly new field for architectural development',[36] but beyond its radical innovations in utilitarian buildings – and with the singular exception of the Crystal Palace –

Gothic 'savageness': illustration from John Ruskin's book *The Seven Lamps of Architecture*.

The medieval tithe barn at Great Coxwell, Gloucestershire, was amongst William Morris's favourite buildings.

England contributed little to the development of an *architecture* of iron.

Viollet-le-Duc, by contrast, was certain that the key to progress lay in coming to terms with industrial materials. Ask the Romans to build with cast and wrought iron and large sheets of glass, he suggested, and they would not have known where to begin, whereas 'the modern genius … is something else again: if we asked a typical modern man to build us a room with a twenty-metre opening out of cardboard … we can be fairly sure that he would ultimately construct the desired room'[37] – as Shigeru Ban demonstrated at the 'Hanover Expo 2000'.

For advocates of the art of building, iron was *the* harbinger of the long-awaited 'style of our time'. Its potential was manifest in the market halls, greenhouses and railway stations designed by engineers, and whilst these might not quite be 'architecture', they were undeniably impressive. John Nash dared to use visible iron columns in the Red Drawing Room at Brighton Pavilion as early as 1818, but the first full exposure of an iron structure in a public building came in Paris in 1850, in the Bibliothèque Ste Geneviève by Henri Labrouste. The barrel-vault form was conventional, and the structure highly ornamented, but it was still a provocative challenge to convention.

Top: Cardboard-tube-structured hall at the 'Hanover Expo 2000' by Shigeru Ban.

Above: Railway stations such as St Pancras, London, were amongst the early triumphs of iron construction.

Beyond questions of propriety, to most observers iron structures still posed a fundamental aesthetic problem: the rational use of the material demanded a slenderness that could not be assimilated into the Classical system of form and proportion, based, as it was, on a solid 'body' of stone. The German architect Ludwig Bohnstedt could accept that iron would figure in new developments, but doubted if it would lead to a new style. 'Our traditional laws of style', he wrote, 'are rooted precisely in our experiences with a solid material – with stone – and have been made to harmonize with it; those laws determine the fulfilment of all demands, which up to now *only stone* has been able to satisfy.'[38] These stylistic difficulties were compounded, as the German theorist and architect Adolf Göller pointed out, by the fact that iron structures also contradicted our bodily experience of gravity. The idea of *Einfühlung* – empathy – had emerged as a key concept in German aesthetic theory and art history,[39] enabling Göller to argue that we perceive iron columns to be flimsy, just as we perceive a stork's legs to be too thin, because 'we imagine ourselves standing on such legs and feel ourselves in a very precarious equilibrium'.[40]

Attempting to counter such arguments, one of iron's early advocates in Germany, Edvard Metzger, wrote that whilst he could understand that 'iron construction is an abomination to the sculpturally minded architect', nevertheless the 'slim and graceful contours, striving upward, strong or delicate according to circumstance', which iron permitted, promised a new kind of beauty.[41] In a lecture the following year, even Karl Bötticher declared iron the material of the future, suggesting that the Greek and Gothic styles had nearly 'run their course' and that the foundations of a 'third style' were being laid.[42]

In 1849, an exceptionally prescient article on *Architecture Métallurgique* predicted the vital role glass would play in iron architecture. Houses would appear translucent, with 'wide openings of thick, single- or double-glazed glass panes, either frosted or translucent, [allowing] a magical splendour to stream in during the daytime, stream out at night'.[43] The full realization of this vision would await the frameless glass walls of the late twentieth century, and in conventionally habitable buildings nothing approaching it appeared until the completion of steel-framed structures in Chicago, such as Burnham and Root's Reliance Building (1890-95), where the plate glass windows form continuous ribbons and occupy an astonishing proportion of the total wall area.

'Magical splendour' might well have been used to describe the most overwhelming demonstration of the potential of iron and glass, Paxton's Crystal Palace. The crowds certainly marvelled, but few architects or critics could come to terms with it as architecture. Amongst those who did, the most evocative descriptions were by the German Lothar Bucher, who declared it 'a revolution … from which a new style will date', and eulogized the 'incomparable and fairylike' character of a space defined by 'a delicate network of lines', which, devoid of 'the play of shadows … dissolved into a distant background where all materiality is blended into the atmosphere'.[44] The sense of dematerialization was enhanced by the polychrome colour scheme devised by Owen Jones: red, yellow, blue and white pigments were systematically applied to the iron structure to emphasize the projection and recession of different members.[45] To one contemporary reviewer, the resulting 'perceptible atmosphere' appeared so 'natural' that it was 'difficult to distinguish where art begins and nature finishes'.[46]

Top: Paxton's Crystal Palace of 1851 remains one of the most compelling examples of glass architecture.

Above: The continuous windows of the Reliance Building, Chicago, mark it out as an exceptional early skyscraper.

Crescent House, Wiltshire,
England, by Ken Shuttleworth:
fulfilment of a century-old dream
of a light-filled glass architecture.

The Eiffel Tower's open structure was seen by a later generation as a paradigm of spatial continuity.

Although the Crystal Palace could be visited well into the new century, after being moved to a new site at Sydenham in Kent,[47] the most influential triumphs of iron construction came with the Eiffel Tower and the Galerie des Machines at the Paris Centennial exhibition in 1889. As with the Crystal Palace, later accounts emphasized the structural qualities of Eiffel's masterpiece, neglecting to note that it, too, was given a polychrome treatment to exaggerate its height[48] – the gradation upwards from dark to light is visible in Seurat's painting of the tower.[49] Reflecting on the exhibition, Cornelius Gurlitt wrote in Berlin that 'iron has conquered us and forced us to see it as beautiful, for it is rational and the product of a creative idea'.[50]

By 1902, in a polemic entitled *Style-Architecture and Building-Art*, Hermann Muthesius declared railway stations the 'offspring of a new time and new aesthetic' that 'belong to the realm of art as much as the church and the museum'.[51] For Muthesius, 'treating a material in a way contrary to its nature is hardly in accord with the spirit of a time such as ours, which is characterised by very practical and sober thought'.[52] The German word translated as 'practical' is the almost untranslatable *sachlich*, which – as the noun *Sachlichkeit* – would become the watchword of successive generations of progressive German artists and designers.[53] Muthesius attributed the aesthetic pleasure induced by structures such as railway stations solely to their direct fulfilment of a practical purpose – a thoroughgoing 'functionalism' – but in the 1913 issue of the *Deutscher Werkbund* yearbook he argued to the contrary that 'utility in and of itself has nothing to do with beauty'.[54] Nevertheless, the challenge was not, as many nineteenth-century architects had supposed, for the architect to beautify the engineer's structure, but to find a synthesis of architecture and engineering driven by a shared sense of form.

The aesthetic values of an architecture of iron or steel were gradually codified in the first

decade of the new century. Heinrich Pudor wrote about an 'airy' skeletal architecture;[55] Joseph August Lux proclaimed the birth of 'engineering aesthetics', with 'dematerialization' as the supreme law of iron construction;[56] and Alfred Gotthold Meyer[57] laid the foundations upon which Sigfried Giedion drew in establishing his influential accounts of the lineage of Modern architecture.[58] The first, published in 1928, was entitled *Bauen in Frankreich, Bauen in Eisen, Bauen in Eisenbeton* (Building in France, Building in Iron, Building in Ferro-Concrete) and featured a machine-age cover by László Moholy-Nagy, with bold lettering over a negative image of one of the engineering wonders of the early twentieth century: the transporter bridge at Marseilles. Inspired by the book, Walter Benjamin declared that it was through the 'functional nature' of iron that 'the constructive principle began its domination of architecture'.[59]

Giedion's tone in *Building in France* allowed no room for equivocation: because, in the West, the very concept of architecture was linked to stone and massiveness, architects' fundamental ideas would have to change to prevent their discipline becoming irrelevant. The new architecture would be 'as open as possible', thanks to iron's capacity to 'condense high potential stress into the most minimal dimensions… Iron opens the spaces. The wall can become a transparent glass skin.'[60] The Eiffel Tower offered a new 'sensation of being enveloped by a floating airspace', whilst the Galerie des Machines achieved 'an elastic counterpoise' in which enormous forces were held in equilibrium, so that 'CONSTRUCTION BECOMES EXPRESSION. *CONSTRUCTION BECOMES FORM.*'[61]

By the time Giedion's book was published, architects representing an otherwise diverse range of approaches were agreed that working with constructional directness 'in the nature of [new] materials' was the way to innovate. The new culture of materials pervaded Modern art and design. At the Bauhaus, Johannes Itten's influential 'Basic Course' required students to 'experience and to demonstrate the character of materials. Contrasts such as smooth-rough, hard-soft, light-heavy had not only to be seen, but also felt.'[62] Reflecting on what he saw during the Bauhaus's open week in 1923, Giedion urged designers to 'listen to the material and uncover the hidden life of the amorphous'.[63] And when Itten was replaced by László Moholy-Nagy, the message was the same: he entitled his second 'Bauhaus Book', *Von Material zu Architektur*.[64] For Mies van der Rohe, the discipline of 'working from material through purposive to creative work' was the means 'to create order out of the godforsaken confusion of our time'.[65]

Top: Cover of Sigfried Giedion's influential 1928 book, *Bauen in Frankreich*.

Above: The Pompidou Centre, Paris, epitomizes what Giedion called the 'constructive principle'.

Otto Wagner's Post Office Savings Bank: glass-block floor, glazed roof and riveted steel structure.

Asked to respond to a question about the need for 'a more intimate collaboration between the architect and other technicians', Le Corbusier observed that 'I have always had the weight of stone and bricks in my arms, the astonishing resistance of wood in my eyes, the miraculous properties of steel in my mind. … Which is to say that similar spaces or thickness had different potentialities, depending on whether they are to be made of stone, brick, wood, or steel; that each material has a characteristic emotional, no less than physical, force; and, all in all, that architectural design should always stay close to matter or materials.'[66]

Amongst sculptors, carving acquired an ethical dimension: 'Stone carving', wrote Eric Gill, 'isn't just doing things in stone and turning things into stone, a sort of petrifying process; stone carving is conceiving things in stone and conceiving them as made by carving.' Constantin Brancusi declared that 'direct cutting is the true road to sculpture',[67] and in the various versions of 'The Kiss' his reverence for the block was such that he was determined to take away the minimum stone necessary to represent an embracing couple – Brancusi later described the direct carving of this sculpture as his 'Road to Damascus' experience.[68] Echoing Michelangelo's feeling about form lying latent in the block, Ernst Ludwig Kirchner, a member of the Blue Rider

The Villa Savoye exemplifies Le Corbusier's early advocacy of 'homogeneous and artificial' materials.

Top: In 'The Kiss', Brancusi retained the integrity of the block from which the work was carved.

Above: Fluid form: 'light guns' and S-shaped wall of the chapel at Le Corbusier's La Tourette monastery near Lyons.

group, extended the idea to wood, declaring, 'there is a figure in every trunk. One must only peel it out.'[69]

As if to confirm that the future of architecture was equally tied to the inherent expressive potential of materials, Mies van der Rohe followed his designs for glass towers with theoretical projects for houses in brick and concrete, and for a concrete office building. The 'dashing weightlessness of new ferroconcrete structure', he wrote in 1924, indicates 'how our form and expression differ from those of earlier times'.[70] In *Vers une architecture*, Le Corbusier was scathing about 'the old-world timber beam', in which 'there may be lurking some treacherous knot' and argued that 'natural materials, which are infinitely variable in composition, must be replaced by fixed ones' – by which he meant 'homogeneous and artificial ones', such as steel, reinforced concrete and glass.[71]

The openness that steel- or reinforced-concrete-frame construction made possible was inseparable from glass and in 1929, in one of the first books devoted to its use in modern architecture, Arthur Korn wrote that 'glass is noticeable yet not quite visible. It is the great membrane, full of mystery, delicate yet tough… It is evident that a material of such qualities requires the building itself to be remodelled, conceived in a revolutionary way.'[72] None of the projects featured in Korn's book would have been out of place in Hitchcock and Johnson's account of The International Style, which appeared three years later.[73] But behind the euphoric tone of Korn's short introduction lay the utopian ideas of Bruno Taut and the Expressionist 'Crystal Chain', in particular of Paul Scheerbart, extracts of whose aphoristic *Glasarchitektur* (Glass Architecture) of 1914 had appeared on Taut's Glass Pavilion.

Scheerbart was a poet and novelist, not an architect, and he saw the opening up of rooms to 'the light of the sun, the moon, and the stars … through every possible wall' as a way to 'bring us a new culture'. His enemy was 'brick culture', which hemmed people in, unlike the open 'glass environment', which will 'transform mankind'.[74] The iconography of glass on which Taut, Scheerbart and other members of the Crystal Chain drew has been traced to accounts of Solomon's Temple in the Bible and the Koran, and was steeped in the medieval aesthetic tradition, which equated 'beautiful' with 'lucid', 'luminous' and 'clear' – with the Gothic cathedral as its supreme expression.[75] Asked to contribute to the prospectus of the Association of German Mirrorglass Factories, Mies van der Rohe identified himself with this tradition by concluding that the 'purity' of modern materials reflected 'the luminosity of original beauty'[76] – an echo of 'the profound words of St Augustine' that he quoted throughout his life: 'Beauty is the radiance of truth.'[77]

House for Heidi Weber, Zürich, by Le Corbusier: a vivid new expression of steel construction.

Writing about Bruno Taut's Glass Pavilion, Adolf Behne suggested that the 'longing for purity and clarity, for glowing lightness, crystalline exactness, for immaterial lightness, infinite liveliness, found in glass a means of fulfilment'.[78] Four years later, in the aftermath of war, Behne argued that 'building with glass … would be the surest way of transforming the European into a human being'.[79] These sentiments found their most extravagant expression in Taut's *Alpine Architecture*: published in 1919, it envisaged ornamenting the mountains and lakes with glass structures, to be lit at night by coloured beacons.[80]

These visionary dreams from what might appear to be the periphery of Modernism fed directly into mainstream thought. The search for the all-glass building became an aesthetic goal in its own right, to which various contents and meanings were freely attached. Politically, for example, supposedly 'open' government has repeatedly been equated with transparent architecture – from Mussolini's description of Fascism as 'a house of glass', exemplified by the openness of Terragni's Casa del Fascio in Como, to Norman Foster's glass-domed refurbishment of the Reichstag in Berlin.

When Walter Gropius referred to the newly completed Bauhaus building as an example of the kind of 'glass architecture' that was 'just a poetic utopia not long ago', but 'now becomes reality unconstrained',[81] he had Scheerbart in mind, as surely did Theo van Doesburg in describing his design for Léonce Rosenberg's studio as being 'like an empty crystal'.[82] Scheerbart might even have played a part in the multi-layered glass *mur neutralisant* of the Salvation Army Hostel, which Le Corbusier completed in Paris in 1931 – a similar system is described as the fourth point of Scheerbart's *Glass Architecture*.[83]

Intended to eliminate the effects of solar gain by passing cooled air through the wall, Le Corbusier's 'neutralizing wall' was doomed to failure when budget cuts led to the omission of the inner layer of glass and refrigeration plant. But it still yielded a slick glass skin of great sophistication, one of several realized in Europe by the early 1930s. The plate-glass façades of Mendelsohn's Petersdorff store in Wroclaw anticipated a pattern that would become almost universal for shops, whilst the glass and metal cladding of the Van Nelle cigarette factory on the edge of Rotterdam, and of the Boots Factory at Beeston near Nottingham, featured curtain walls of the kind that would later become ubiquitous on office buildings.

Frank Lloyd Wright shared the Europeans' passion for glass, and in 1928 wrote about it as the 'most precious of the architect's new materials'[84] because it could change the traditional relationship to nature. Two years later, in a lecture at Princeton, he pointed out that tradition had 'left no orders about this material as a means of perfect visibility: hence the sense of glass as crystal has not, as poetry, entered yet into architecture… Shadows were the "brush work" of the ancient architect. Let the modern one now work with light, light diffused, light reflected – light for its own sake, shadows gratuitous.'[85]

Mussolini's description of Fascism as a 'house of glass' was emulated in Terragni's Casa del Fascio.

Emblem of democracy: glass dome of Norman Foster's refurbishment of the Reichstag in Berlin.

An early glass curtain wall:
the Boots Factory, Beeston,
England, by the engineer
Sir Owen Williams.

The slick surface of the extension
to the Musée des Beaux Arts
in Lille typifies glass walls
of the 1990s.

Above and right: Curtain walls
by Mies van der Rohe, Federal
Center, Chicago.

At Fallingwater (built at Bear Run in north-eastern Pennsylvania in 1935), as in many of Wright's later houses, the link to nature was emphasized by running the glazing directly into the wall and by butting glass to glass to dissolve the sense of enclosure at corners. Given Wright's hatred of the modern city, such openness would have been unthinkable for the Johnson Wax headquarters in Racine, Wisconsin. He therefore opted to 'destroy the box' by replacing the solid corner between wall and ceiling with a system of glass tubes that could be bent to form streamlined corners. The same system was later deployed as translucent ribbons wrapped in bands around the laboratory tower. Visually, the glass-tube glazing was a beguiling invention, but technically it proved fraught. In the days before flexible sealants, the caulking in the joints cracked under thermal stresses, enhancing Wright's reputation as a master of leaks, and leading to much of the glass being replaced with plastic sheeting shaped to resemble the tubes.

Aesthetically, the parameters of glass explored later in the twentieth century were largely determined in the years either side of the First World War, but technically it saw more innovations than any other building material. Variously coated, tinted and laminated, its properties could be tuned to give better environmental performance, or to virtually eliminate the need for cleaning. Special glasses can now be turned from transparent to opaque by the transmission of an electric current, made to retain images 'drawn' on them with a light pen, or permanently etched *internally* using a laser. By the 1970s, new structural glazing systems eliminated framing, and by the 1990s glass was being used as a loadbearing structural material: its compressive strength is similar to that of stone.[86]

With a manufactured material whose properties are as malleable as those of glass, it is meaningless to speak of a fixed 'nature', especially when its 'natural' state might be thought of as that of invisibility. Given that the ideal of transparency is often more theoretical than actual, it is surprising that others did not follow Mies van der Rohe's example and explore the aesthetic potential of reflections or – as in the Barcelona Pavilion – use faintly tinted glass as a means of asserting its physical presence. (It goes without saying that the subtleties of Mies's work had nothing in common with the vulgarities later associated with both mirror and tinted solar control glasses.)

In the Barcelona Pavilion, transparent and slightly tinted glass combine with highly polished surfaces.

Top: Spatial continuity: bedroom in Frank Lloyd Wright's 'Fallingwater'.

Above: In the Johnson Wax Administration Building, Wright dissolved the solid corners with pyrex tubes.

The Johnson Wax laboratory tower is clad almost entirely in bands of glass tubes.

Glass-tube barrel vault
of elevated walkway at Wright's
Johnson Wax complex: when
the caulking between the tubes
failed, they were covered with
acrylic sheeting.

Reinforced concrete posed comparable, if very different, expressive challenges to glass. Inspired by the analogy with primitive forms of adobe building suggested by Istvan Medgyaszay, to which we referred in the first chapter, Pudor likened it to a 'scientific form' of mud construction and concluded – he was writing in 1910 – that 'we are searching for the soul of this material today'. For Frank Lloyd Wright, concrete had 'neither song nor story' and generally amounted to 'an artificial stone at best, or a petrified sand heap at worst'.[86] With its hidden armature of reinforcement, reinforced concrete approaches the strength of steel, but with the added potential that the reinforcing can be designed to produce structural continuity, potentially making concrete structures more like natural organisms, such as shells, than constructions assembled from discrete members.

To the Italian engineer Pier Luigi Nervi, concrete was 'the best structural material yet devised by mankind. Almost by magic, we have been able to create "melted" stones of any desired shape.'[88] But to many architects, especially those seeking to express its 'nature', this very flexibility was problematic. Because solid concrete was produced by pouring it in a fluid state into a mould or form, it shared with clay that lack of resistance that many Modernist sculptors detested. 'Kneading wax, or mixing

clay, disgusts me', wrote Paul Dardé. 'They offer no resistance, they take any form, they are easy and sloppy.' Wright was similarly dismissive of Louis Sullivan's love of terracotta: 'All materials were only one material to him in which to weave the stuff of his dreams. Terracotta was that one material.'[89]

Adrian Stokes had this problem in mind when he referred to Le Corbusier's 'lightning concrete', with which he could make 'a room of any shape'.[90] Extending the distinction between carving and modelling to all art, Stokes argued that in the modelling process, the material 'has no "rights" of its own' and the forms consequently seem to be 'without restraint'. They may be 'the perfect embodiment of conception' but that conception is not continually adjusted to the material, and is therefore aesthetically less satisfying.[91]

The difficulty of attuning forms to the 'nature' of concrete is compounded by the fact that as a cast material its surface speaks more about the formwork into which it is placed than it does about the concrete as it pours from the mixer. The walls – as opposed to the cantilevered roof planes – of one of the first concrete buildings to enter the history of architecture, Wright's Unity Temple in Oak Park near Chicago, could just as well have been built in masonry. Wright referred to them as 'great

This bridge in Lucien Kroll's medical faculty complex near Brussels (top) and Morris Lapidus's Marin Center in Chicago (above) illustrate the fluidity possible with reinforced concrete.

Wright's Unity Temple in Oak Park was amongst the first public buildings made of concrete.

concrete blocks',[92] but recognized that their character was attributable more to the formwork than to the concrete.

Like glass, concrete's properties – structural and visual – can also be substantially changed by using different mixtures and types of cement, sand, aggregates and additives. With reinforced concrete, the configuration of the hidden bars and meshes effectively dictates the structural 'nature' of the material. Concrete itself is isotropic – that is, it has the same properties in all directions – but it is often given a specific 'grain' by being reinforced predominantly along one axis.

When, in 1928, Vischer and Hilbersheimer published a book entitled *Concrete as a Determinant of Form*, it featured a row of four cooling towers on its cover and discussed large-scale structures by engineers such as Eugène Freyssinet. With more conventional buildings, however, it was less clear how to exploit its potential. An independent frame was a prerequisite of the 'free plan', but the choice of structural material was essentially pragmatic. In Europe, reinforced concrete was generally preferred, whereas in the USA similar designs, such as Richard Neutra's Lovell Health House, were frequently built using steel and timber. To Mies van der Rohe, the frame was always seen more as an 'idea' than as a functionally determined physical structure reflecting the actual play of forces. Visible cross-bracing to resist wind loads was rejected on principle, and differences in loading suppressed – as Louis Kahn pointed out when commenting on the Seagram Building: 'The columns which are on top should be dancing like fairies, [and] the columns which are below should be groaning like mad, and not have the same dimensions.'[93]

In *Vers une architecture*, Le Corbusier wrote optimistically about the builder's yard becoming a factory, and of houses 'made in a mould by pouring in liquid concrete from above, completed in one day as you would fill a bottle'.[94] But when, two years later, he came to deploy the Ingersoll-Rand Company's 'concrete cannon' to test these ideas on workers' housing at Pessac,[95] the resulting finish was so uneven and gloomy that he elaborated a new system of 'architectural polychromy' to cover it. The aim may have been a direct expression of concrete construction, but the reality was the kind of 'dressing' that owed more to the example of Loos and Semper, than to the constructional rationalism of Viollet-le-Duc.[96]

Giedion interpreted Le Corbusier's achievements of the 1920s, stemming from the invention of the Dom-Ino frame in 1914, as the creation of an 'eternally open house'. At Pessac, he pointed out, 'the solid volume is opened up wherever possible by cubes of air, strip windows, immediate transition to the sky … air flows through them! … There arises – as with certain lighting conditions in snowy landscapes – that dematerialization of solid demarcation that distinguishes neither rise nor fall and that gradually produces the feeling of walking in clouds.'[97] As in the 'dematerialized' iron structures of the nineteenth century, the power of reinforced concrete for Giedion lay not in its physical presence, but in its ability to eliminate solidity, to create voids that, unlike most previous forms of construction, suggested no tectonic expression – hidden reinforcing could provide the necessary strength, and openings could seemingly be cut as easily, and as arbitrarily, as in cardboard. Contemporary criticism of the houses as being 'as thin as paper' was precisely to the point – but in a positive, not negative sense, in Giedion's eyes.

For Giedion, Le Corbusier's Pessac houses were models of the openness made possible by concrete.

Several houses at Pessac are linked by vaults, which dissolve their mass and capture the surroundings.

Concrete did not come into its own as an exposed material until after 1945, when Le Corbusier led the way by giving up the pretence that it could deliver a smooth, 'machine-age' finish. Its true 'nature', he now decided, was rough – and as such ideal for affirming the heroic affinity with nature that would be a hallmark of his post-war work. The *béton brut* (raw concrete) of the Unité d'Habitation in Marseilles, and later of the monastery of La Tourette near Lyons, celebrated the textural richness to be derived from casting in rough, boarded shutters – hence the Unité's rapid appropriation as an example of 'Brutalism',[98] and as a precursor of what Udo Kultermann and others would later promote as the new face of a world architecture.[99] The rough, textural qualities are akin to the 'savageness' Ruskin extolled, and their importance aesthetically can be sensed by comparing Le Corbusier's buildings in France and India with the smoother, but visually less alive, surfaces delivered by American contractors on Harvard University's Carpenter Center.

Few twentieth-century architects tried to design more rigorously or poetically 'in the nature of materials' than Louis Kahn. For Kahn, knowing the nature of a material – not merely 'knowing about it'[100] – was essential to getting close to 'the original inspiration to express' through art. Characteristically, he never attempted to define 'nature' too specifically, and, in the case of concrete, his buildings are more about the way the material is formed than about some mythical inner nature. At the Salk Institute he specified teak-faced plywood shutters and detailed them meticulously to leave traces of the casting process and thereby create a subtle constructional ornament – 'ornament', Kahn declared, 'is the adoration of the joint'.[101] Junctions in the formwork are marked in the finished surface by thin, crumbling lines, which project slightly and cast sharp shadows under the high Californian sun, whilst a regular grid of small, recessed holes is left by the ducts for the bolts used to keep the forms flat and rigid while the concrete set.

Carpenter Center at Harvard University by Le Corbusier.

The rough surfaces of La Tourette are visually more powerful than the 'better'-built Carpenter Center.

Above and opposite: For Louis Kahn, constructional ornament began with the 'adoration of the joint' – an idea vividly illustrated by the detailing of the concrete at the Salk Institute in La Jolla, California.

Kahn employed a similar expression on the concrete walls that form the base of the Kimbell Museum in Texas. But for the columns and vaults of the structure above he sought as nearly homogeneous a finish as possible. Internally, the joints in the shutters for the long vaults – actually bent beams spanning longitudinally – are visible but suppressed, ensuring that they read as seamless, continuous structural members. For the Assembly Building in Dacca, Bangladesh, Kahn responded to the more modest resources, and difficulties of quality control, by accepting that whilst the concrete itself might be less refined than that at the Salk Institute, it could be 'ennobled' by marking the joints between pours with strips of marble. The process echoed his advice to architects 'to draw as we build, from the bottom up', and to stop their pencils 'to make a mark at the joints of pouring or erecting'.[102]

The continuity possible with reinforced concrete was not easily exploited, because such structures are statically indeterminate and only became calculable with the advent of computer-based 'finite element' models. Reflecting on the limits of calculations in 1955, Nervi regretted that 'some of the highest qualities of the human mind, such as intuition and direct apprehension … have been overwhelmed by abstract and impersonal mathematical formulas', adding that 'in the distant past intuition allowed the execution of works which cannot be analyzed today by the most modern theoretical methods'.[103]

In Dacca, Louis Kahn ennobled rough concrete by marking joints between pours with marble.

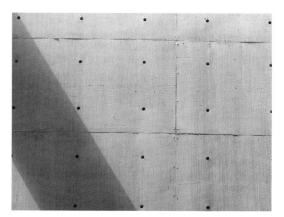

The concrete walls of Tadao Ando's Koshino House are dematerialized by raking sunlight.

The reinforced concrete canopy leading up to the guest house at Fallingwater appears to float in space.

Given his advocacy of nature as a model for design, it is hardly surprising that Frank Lloyd Wright was fascinated by the idea of continuity. He regarded the cantilever as 'the most romantic of all structural possibilities'[104] and at Fallingwater projected floors and terraces dramatically in all directions. The upstands are continuous with the slabs, but it is by no means clear whether or not they strengthen the structure by stiffening the slab, or simply add an additional load.[105] An even more striking example of what Wright called the 'new aesthetic' of continuity, however, is provided by the folded-plane canopy, which connects the main house to the guest wing.[106] Supported only along its outer edge by slender steel columns, and thinner than modern codes of practice would allow, it seems literally to defy gravity and float in space.

The plant-like columns of Wright's Johnson Wax Administration Building rise and taper gently outwards to meet the circular crowns that branch from the shaft. They were so novel that their strength had to be proved by a physical test, during which Wright famously sat under the test column as it was stacked with sandbags to more than ten times the design load![107] Wright's most ambitious large-scale expression of structural continuity, however, was the helix of the Guggenheim Museum, New York, where

the inherent difficulty of achieving seamlessly continuous forms with necessarily discontinuous formwork and successive pours revealed itself in intermittent surface irregularities.

Bricks might appear to be free of the difficulties affecting the handling of concrete, but for the first generation of Modern architects they were problematic for other reasons. Not only were they redolent of the handicraft traditions of the past, but also their texture was more suited to the expression of solidity and weight, not of surface and lightness. The only major Modern architect to build in brick during the 1920s was Mies van der Rohe. Emulating Schinkel's example, he dimensioned his walls according to the brick bonding pattern: 'What logic in its bonding, what liveliness in the play of patterns. What richness in the simplest wall surface. But what discipline this material imposes',[108] he later observed, explaining the virtues of bricks to his students at the Illinois Institute of Technology. Although it can scarcely be seen in small reproductions, every brick was drawn on the plan as well as the perspective of the Brick Country House project of 1923, and the same rigour is apparent in the three brick houses he built in the mid 1920s. The detailing is also notable for the suppression of elements – such as lintels – that might distract from the material itself, pointing to an attitude rather different to

The flowing spiral of the Guggenheim Museum illustrates the freedom possible with concrete.

The Guggenheim Museum exemplifies what Wright called the 'new aesthetic of continuity'.

Wright's ideal of organic form is well illustrated by the plant-like columns of the Johnson Wax Building.

that of those who believed form should be derived directly from the expression of a rational structure.

After the Second World War, with the completion of Le Corbusier's Jaoul Houses in Paris and Alvar Aalto's Baker House at Massachusetts Institute of Technology and town hall in Säynätsalo, Finland (see next page), brick was rehabilitated as a viably 'modern' material. In keeping with his new, brut aesthetic, Le Corbusier's houses projected a peasant-like roughness on a site next to that most civilized of urban parks, the Bois de Boulogne in Paris, whilst at Säynätsalo, Aalto looked back to one of the major monuments of National Romanticism, Ragnar Östberg's Stockholm City Hall. For Louis Kahn, finding the 'correct' expression for bricks involved a rhetorical, and oft-repeated conversation with the material:

When you are designing in brick, you must ask brick what it wants or what it can do. Brick will say. I like an arch. *You say,* But arches are difficult to make, they cost more money. I think you could use concrete across your opening equally well. *But the brick says,* I know you're right, but if you ask me what I like, I like an arch.[109]

Kahn believed it was possible to have such a conversation with any material, and that treating a material as 'living', and respecting its 'rights', was the best way to find an effective expression of its unique qualities.[110] In the case of brick it yielded powerful results. At the library for Phillips Academy in Exeter, New Hampshire, Kahn wrapped an almost free-standing brick ring around a concrete-framed inner structure. The brick piers are tied together by almost flat brick arches, and their width diminishes as they rise, enabling the area of glass to increase as the loads reduce: 'structure', Kahn observed, 'is the maker of light'.[111] In point of structural fact, the loads are taken by piers at right angles to the 'loadbearing' wall, and the arches are considerably deeper than the loads require. The wall we see is a representation of structure, and to clarify the constructional facts Kahn breaks open the corners to reveal the walls as screen-like planes.

The rough walls of Le Corbusier's Jaoul Houses in Paris helped to reclaim brick as a *modern* material.

Louis Kahn wrapped the concrete interior of Phillips Academy library (New Hampshire) with brick piers, which taper in response to the load (above). The corners (top) reveal the apparently thick construction to be screen-like planes.

At the Indian Institute of Management in Ahmedabad, Kahn articulated the walls by developing a composite structure of shallow brick arches and reinforced concrete ties, which are manifestly too slender to act as lintels. To cope with earthquake loads, he also used large double-arches to form circular openings. The idea occurred to him when his structural engineer, August Kommendant, explained that the upward forces induced by an earthquake were similar to those generated downwards by gravity, and could be resisted using a similar structural form. Kahn was delighted when he discovered that much the same idea is described in Leonardo's notebooks,[112] but his double-arch circular openings were adopted by less scrupulous designers as an attractive 'motif'.

For Kahn, 'honouring' the potential of brick lay in exploiting its structural capabilities: to use it merely as a cladding was to diminish its 'nature'.[113] He would not have approved of, say, the factory-made panels that Renzo Piano now favours, even with the stack-bonding pattern as a sign that they are non-structural. Nor would he have countenanced Aalto's love of levitating large areas of brickwork – as, for example, at both the Jubilee Hall at Jyväskylä University and Säynätsalo Town Hall. Rather than expressing brickwork's structural potential, Aalto delighted in the textural qualities that could result from emphasizing the individuality of the bricks. At Säynätsalo he instructed the masons to lay them at slight angles to each other to add richness (see pages 68-9),[114] whilst for Baker House he chose a rough clinker brick and asked that even the most erratically formed ones should be used – some are literally banana-shaped and appear to be on the brink of falling out of the walls. Finally, around the courtyard walls of his own summerhouse on Muuratsalo he achieved extraordinary richness by arraying different combinations of brick and bond types, interspersed with areas of tile.

For Aalto, the essence of brick lay in the textural qualities that make it such a rich 'dressing'. Semper's term seems even more apt to describe the Templeton Carpet Factory in Glasgow in 1889. William Leiper's design, which owed much to the Doge's Palace in Venice, presented the factory as an almost literal representation of its products. Walls were rarely as explicitly 'woven' as Leiper's, but textile patterns readily come to mind in contemplating much High-Victorian polychromatic brickwork. Although prompted by the discovery of Greek polychromy, the fashion was also a response to the growing industrialization of brick manufacture, which led to greater uniformity and consequently a more lifeless surface. The results struck many contemporary observers as a transgression of acceptable norms, none more so than William Butterfield's Keble College, Oxford, which was quickly dubbed the 'holy zebra' style, and its 'startlingly contrasted colours' condemned as 'destroying all breadth and repose'.[115]

As one of the oldest of all building materials, brick might be thought unlikely to admit of conspicuous innovation. But in the hands of the elderly Sigurd Lewerentz at the churches of St Mark's, in the Stockholm suburb of Björkhagen, and of St Peter's, in Klippan in the south of Sweden, we see it reborn.[116] By normal modern standards, the brickwork of St Mark's seems bizarre: the mortar is not so much a means of cementing brick to brick in thin beds, as a matrix in which the individual bricks seem to float – a textural effect that forms, as intended, an uncanny link to the trunks of the surrounding birch trees.

The circular openings of the Institute of Management, Ahmedabad, resist gravity and earthquakes.

The walls of Aalto's summerhouse on Muuratsalo island, Finland, are a showcase of brick types and textures.

Aalto expressed the gently curving wall of Jyväskylä University's Festival Hall as a floating surface.

On MIT's Baker House (above and above right), Aalto insisted that even the most irregular clinker bricks be used.

Above: Victorian polychromatic brickwork: Keble College, Oxford, by William Butterfield (left), and Templeton Carpet factory, Glasgow, by William Leiper (right).

At Klippan, the walls appear more conventional until you notice the idiosyncrasies necessitated by Lewerentz's refusal to sanction the cutting of a single brick, and by his determination to articulate the wall expressively. Vertical joints widen dramatically, some sections are made of bricks stacked horizontally or on end, strange swellings project under undisclosed internal pressures, and window and door frames are set on the face of the wall, not within their openings. Despite their conspicuous originality, the walls seem more ancient than modern: Lewerentz's drawings show every brick, but the final setting-out and many of the details were only resolved on site, where he spent as much time as in his studio.

Inside, the sense of containment by bricks is overwhelming. You walk on brick floors, between walls of brick, beneath brick vaults, which span between steel joists, swelling gently like ocean waves, and you finally sit facing a brick altar. No frames mediate the openings, which are cut abruptly into the thick walls with no hint of an arch or other means of support, and the primary beams likewise disappear into dark voids with no visible pad-stone to receive the load. And what photographs cannot convey is the almost preternatural darkness, which binds the fabric into an all-enveloping unity.

In the presence of Lewerentz's late churches one is tempted to echo Heidegger's words about Greek temples and suggest that here brick 'comes forth for the very first time'. A building such as Kahn's Exeter Library offers a compelling demonstration of what brick can *do*, whereas Lewerentz – like Mies in his early houses – is determined to show us what brick *is*. For Kahn, as for most Modern architects, working 'in the nature of materials' meant immersing them in an appropriate functional, usually structural, role. Lewerentz's aim was different: by emphasizing the 'nature' of bricks that we can directly perceive – their size, colour and texture – rather than their more abstract structural properties, he aimed to *build*, not merely design, an *atmosphere* conducive to worship. And in handling bricks in this way he anticipated a major preoccupation of recent years: the *materiality* of materials.

The frames of Lewerentz's St Mark's Church in Stockholm are placed outside the openings, on the wall face.

Lewerentz's refusal to cut bricks at St Peter's, Klippan, defies conventional standards of bricklaying.

Paved, walled and ceiled with bricks, the interior of St Mark's becomes like a brick cave.

Lewerentz's brickwork in Klippan
emphasizes the material rather
than structural qualities of bricks.

Chapter 4
Place

Built place: a recently
refurbished street
in central Copenhagen.

The object to which a type of thought like Ruskin's applies, and from which it is inseparable, is not immaterial, it is distributed here and there over the surface of the earth. One must go and look for it where it is found, at Pisa, Florence, Venice, in the National Gallery, at Rouen, and in the mountains of Switzerland.
Marcel Proust[1]

Despite the rhetoric about working 'in the nature of materials', the high ground of Modern architecture was commanded by a dematerialized vision of space and time as the basis of an international style for the Machine Age. In the wake of the Second World War, however, the virtues of the local and specific were reasserted over the universal and generic. Central to this critique was the concept of 'place'. Concrete and time-bound, heterogeneous and particular, our feeling for place – 'space humanised' as the Dutch architect Aldo van Eyck defined it – is grounded in our bodily experience of the world. It is therefore inescapably material: 'Like a good pot of stew or a complex musical chord,' writes anthropologist Keith Basso, 'the character of the thing emerges from the qualities of its ingredients.'[2]

The appeal of Corbusian *béton brut* and the renewed interest in the textural delights of brickwork and other traditional materials reflected this re-engagement with the tangible, the embodied, the manifestly material. Aalto's town hall at Säynätsalo may be a masterly piece of architectural composition, but it is as a *built place*, inseparable from its forest setting and made of brick, that it impresses itself most forcibly on the memory – plastered and painted white, its impact would be entirely different. Surprisingly, the burgeoning literature[3] about place pays little attention to the crucial role materials can play in promoting the visual and tactile qualities, which loom large in our sensory experiences. It could be thought that their role is too obvious or prosaic to merit comment,

or it might reflect a bias implicit in the Classical origins of 'sense of place' or *genius loci*.

The idea of *genius loci* was adopted from the Greeks, to whom 'place' evoked the unchanging qualities or 'essence' of a location, associated with a local spirit or deity. Rather like the pure 'Forms' Plato posited as existing in a higher realm of ideas, the spirit of place was seen as lurking behind appearances, and could be revealed by penetrating beyond them.[4] When, in the eighteenth century, the poet Alexander Pope advised English landscape-garden designers to 'consult the genius of the place in all',[5] it was precisely this act of mental excavation he had in mind – something akin to what we now refer to rather more prosaically as 'site analysis'.

The idea that an unchanging reality lies embedded beyond appearances is so prevalent in Western thought that it can make paying attention to the often fugitive surface of things seem intellectually inferior. And yet in locations that seem to embody most powerfully the conventional idea of 'sense of place', it is very often the pervasive presence of a single, readily available local material – or something as literally 'superficial' as applied colours – that are their most striking feature. 'It is surprising', the painter John Piper has observed, 'how little guide-book writers tell us about the colour

The raised courtyard of Aalto's Säynätsalo Town Hall exemplifies the post-war interest in 'place'.

Varied colour washes are a recurring factor in the sense of place of many central European towns.

Arlington Row, Bibury, appears to be, as William Morris wrote, 'a growth of the soil'.

The red soils of Tuscany are ideal preparation for enjoying its towns.

of towns and villages. They describe the shape of everything – hills, valleys and approaches, the plan of a place, the kind of architecture – but almost never the colour of the buildings.'

When the materials of places are quarried or made locally they are often interpreted as suggesting that feeling of belonging, or 'dwelling', that many writers on place regard as one of its key qualities.[6] Even if we cannot see limestone formations actually exposed in a Cotswold village like Bibury – which William Morris considered the most beautiful in England[7] – our experience of the surrounding countryside still enables us to perceive a group of seventeenth-century cottages such as Arlington Row, built with the local stone, as – to use Morris's words – 'a growth of the soil'.[8] Weathering enhances this impression, but a similar feeling of 'rootedness' was also the aim of the advice Sir Joshua Reynolds gave on choosing the colour to paint a house: 'If you would fix upon the best colour … turn up a stone or pluck up a handful of grass by the roots, and see what is the colour of the soil where the house is to stand, and let that be your choice.'[9]

Central Italian towns, such as Florence and Siena, provide large-scale confirmation of Reynolds' prescription, because there is no better preparation for a visit to them than to approach through fields carpeted with the rich, red-brown soils of the region. The colour comes from the oxidation of iron, which in turn lends a marked red or orange colour to the roof tiles and bricks fired from the local clays. These colours not only blend with the soils from which they are derived, but also seem a perfect complement to the distinctive greens of the vegetation. This limited range of earth colours was traditionally broken only by stone: framing openings in walls, as lines that edge and structure paving, and on the façades of churches and other public buildings.

Reflecting on the feeling that 'no really Italian building seems ill at ease in Italy', Frank Lloyd Wright suggested that 'the secret of this ineffable charm would be sought in vain in the rarefied air of scholasticism or in the ateliers of any pedantic fine art. It all lies closer to the earth. Like a handful of moist, sweet earth itself. So simple that to modern minds trained in the intellectual gymnastics of "cultivated" taste it would seem unrelated to important purposes. So close to the heart it is that almost universally it is overlooked especially by the scholar.'[10] It would be possible to offer 'scholastic' justifications for Wright's assertions, and just as surely they could be analyzed to reveal the cultural biases that underpin them: happily, there is insufficient space for either to detain us here.

The roofscapes of Florence (above) and Siena (right) are inseparable from the land.

The most memorably coloured places frequently seem as well attuned to the quality of the local light as to the earth. It is difficult to imagine better colours to meet the deep blue southern sky than the earthy reds of central Italy, unless it is the brilliant white, which – to reduce heat gains from the sun – traditionally covered the buildings in many hot climates, including the Mediterranean 'villages in the sun', which Myron Goldfinger memorably presented as precursors of, and models for, Modern architecture.[11] The Romans seem to have painted their plastered walls predominantly a strong red, whilst the Venetian island of Burano is still decked out in a variety of reds, yellow ochres, blues and greens – all applied with sufficient intensity to resist being enfeebled by the intense light. The traditional colours manage to harmonize like the pigments of a painter's palette – and bear striking similarities to those Le Corbusier used in his Purist villas, later codified as harmonic 'colour keyboards' for the Swiss paint-maker Salubra.[12]

Despite the more demanding climate, the extensive use of applied colour washes is also common in northern Europe, but there the intensity of the hues is generally reduced – extensive areas of colour as intense as that in Burano would be oppressive. In some of the most memorably coloured urban ensembles, as for example in Stockholm and Copenhagen, the preference is for less saturated colours, which glow in the limpid, atmospheric light. As fruit of the passion for Greek polychromy, the Thorvaldsen Museum in Copenhagen might be regarded as an exotic import. Seen in its urban context, however, it is difficult not to view its rich coloration as much as a distillation of the city's pastel-coloured eighteenth- and nineteenth-century streets as an importation of southern traditions.[13]

Nowhere, arguably, are colour and surface so important or so refined an element of place as in Venice. The site was hardly encouraging – uninhabited marshes, chosen for defensive reasons, remote from potential enemies – and offered no local materials. Medieval Venice was largely a city of wood and plaster standing on a forest of timber piles, but by the early Renaissance

White villages, such as that on the Greek island of Naxos, were seen as models for Modernist abstraction.

The Jugendstil district of Helsinki is characterised by endlessly varied colour washes.

Top: The intense colours of the Venetian island of Burano are a match for the southern light.

Above: Colour-washed houses on the outskirts of Stockholm.

Copenhagen has long been famed for the subtle colours of its eighteenth-century streets.

The polychrome Thorvaldsen Museum seems, in context, like a distillation of the colours of Copenhagen.

it had been re-built with red bricks from Mestre, coarse-grained yellow ones from Treviso, white Istrian stone and its ubiquitous complement, red Verona marble. As the city-state's empire grew in strength, the spoils of war and Crusade – columns and capitals and slabs of fine stones – returned in remarkable quantities, transforming the front of St Mark's with its marbles 'from all corners of the earth'[14] into a living emblem of the scope of Venetian power.

As in Amsterdam, the cost of building the canals made canal-frontages expensive, leading to narrow, deep plans with correspondingly large windows to help natural light reach into the depths of the rooms. Walls were made thin for lightness, and this is exaggerated by the strength of the exposed foundations and heavy mouldings at the base, the erratic distribution of windows, unusually small mouldings, and the weakening of shadows by light reflected upwards from the ubiquitous water. If we remember Venice as a city of stone, and most people surely do, this is because long, thin oblongs – *listons* – of the white Istrian stone are everywhere, framing façades and openings and edging pavements. On many of the finer buildings, the Istrian stone is complemented by inlays of thin coloured marbles and other decorative stones. For Ruskin, this 'incrustation of brick with more precious materials' was the key to the character of Venetian architecture. Practically, incrustation can be explained as a consequence of the city's remoteness from quarries, whilst aesthetically the emphasis on surface effects it encouraged – above all, on colour – creates an all-pervasive 'floating lightness'.[15] You see it on the grand scale in the Doge's Palace, where the diaper-patterned cladding seems like a fabric stretched between its spiral corner mouldings, whilst above, pierced crenellations, delicate as lacework, dissolve the building and capture the sky.

When Ruskin, in one of his finest bravura passages, described the Venetian lagoon as 'that green pavement which every breeze broke into new fantasies of rich tesselation',[16] he had in mind the polychrome pavements of interlocked geometric shapes of marble, which seem to express the precarious stability of Venetian 'ground'. Seen at their most extensive in St Mark's, and at their best preserved in Santa Maria e Donato, the cathedral church of the

Top: White Istrian marble frames vertical and horizontal surfaces in Venice.

Above: Venetian buildings, such as these on the Grand Canal, seem to rise weightless from the water.

Incrustation of brick with more precious materials: the recently restored Ca' d'Oro in Venice.

The delicacy of Venetian building is emphasized by the solidity of water-resisting foundations.

Venetian buildings like Santa Maria dei Miracoli (above and right), the most richly decorated Renaissance church in the city, are compositions of colour as much as of form.

The upper stages of the Doge's Palace epitomize the Venetian elimination of weight.

The stone revetments of St Mark's in Venice transform its surfaces into a paper-thin montage.

island of Murano – where, Ruskin, noted, every fragment was variegated[17] – they are but one example of the way everything in Venice seems to partake of the evanescent play of light on water. So pervasive is the feeling of liquidity that Adrian Stokes ventured to read the 'gradual swelling of circular shape' in the façade of San Zaccaria as suggesting the 'lengthening disks upon water where a stone is flung'.[18]

With the invention of terrazzo – *pavimenti alla veneziana* – around 1500, floors appeared to be coated with a thin film of water. Made with scattered fragments of marble, variously coloured and shaped and suspended in a mortar bed, terrazzo is abraded to a perfectly smooth finish to yield a highly reflective and visually elusive surface. In the shop Carlo Scarpa designed for Olivetti, close to a corner of Piazza san Marco, you walk on a floor that is an inventive cross between the much finer-grained terrazzo and traditional mosaic. Tesserae of small, irregular squares of reflective glass paste are set in parallel bands in a bed of light-coloured cement mortar. The uneven sizes and edges of the squares are vital to the overall quality, as the intrusive effect of machine-cut stones in repairs to mosaic pavements confirms.[19] The banding creates an easily discerned 'warp' in one direction, whilst in the other the irregularity and wide spacing of the tesserae prevent a regular rhythm, like that of perpends in brickwork, being established. Instead, eager to see pattern in apparent disorder, the eye tends to read an irregular, undulating 'weft'.[20] This hint of waves is brought dramatically to life during the frequent *acqua alta* floods when, as Tudy Sammartini reports, the water transforms the floor 'into a gently rippling mirror reminiscent of certain experimental paintings by Paul Klee'.[21]

In the gallery of the Querini Stampalia Foundation, Scarpa turned the necessity of coping with floods to expressive ends. In the main hall, which doubles as a small gallery, the floor is compartmented by lines of smooth concrete and then filled with variable-width rectangles of concrete, whose surface has been washed to reveal an aggregate of fine pebbles. Both materials turn up at right angles to form the lower section of the flanking walls, where they are edged with a strip of Istrian stone. Above, protected from all but the worst floods, the walls are clad with thin slabs of travertine, cut across the grain to give a richly textured surface.

With characteristic vision, Ruskin likened the richly variegated floors of Venetian churches (above) to the 'rich tesselation' of reflections in the city's canals (top).

In the Olivetti shop in St Mark's Square (above), Carlo Scarpa reinvents terrazzo using irregularly shaped squares of glass paste (right).

In the Querini Stampalia
Foundation, Scarpa turned
the inevitability of floods
to expressive ends.

Dazzling white in the unpolluted atmosphere, the wooden churches are integral to New England's sense of place.

Top: Like most traditional Dutch towns, Delft presents an almost continuous cityscape of brick.

Above: Rising to cross bridges, brick is ubiquitous in central Amsterdam.

Unlike many modern Dutch architects, the Portuguese Alvaro Siza chose to build in brick in The Hague.

For the ceiling, Scarpa chose a glossy white plaster, made using an almost forgotten technique known as *stucco alla veneziana*. This began with the laborious application by hand of a *sottofondo*, or base coat, containing a moisture-absorbent *calce* of hydrated lime and sand or a *cotto* derived from discarded clay brick and roof tiles. In the exquisite variant known as *marmorino*, marble powder is mixed with the topcoat: properly applied by hand it yields a marble-like hardness, which is complemented by a reflective sheen imparted using a hot iron.[22] The technique using *cotto* is ideal in Venice because it can absorb large amounts of water from humid air, whilst visually the reflective surface is exceptionally responsive to light.

Although few cities now offer as coherent a feeling of place across so large an area as Venice, the use of local materials and distinctive building traditions can extend to an entire region or country. The image of New England is inseparable from its white-painted timber churches and houses, seen sharp against the blue sky and vivid greens of the landscape – even if such things are less frequently encountered, and less unvarying, than memory suggests. Similarly, across the length and breadth of pre-industrial Japan, many of the roofs – the dominant element of traditional houses and temples alike – were made of the same grey clay. Smooth, unvarying in colour or texture, like the mud of tidal flats, its presence was ubiquitous. It was partly because of its links to Japanese tradition that Team Zoo chose to pave the mile-long Yoga Promenade in Tokyo using specially designed paviors and other components made of the same clay – returning it to the earth, so to speak.

The distinctiveness of Dutch cities like Delft, Leiden and Amsterdam manifestly owes much to the surviving networks of canals, along which the familiar narrow-fronted, tall-windowed buildings are ranged below a skyline of jostling gables. But it would be immeasurably less potent were it not for the matrix of brickwork, which binds house to house and, just as important, walls to pavements. Invited to build in The Hague in 1985, the Portuguese architect Alvaro Siza thought it obvious to use brick, albeit in ways that are quite clearly 'modern'. For many *Dutch* architects, however, such a decision would have seemed a betrayal. They 'react strongly against the use of brick,' noted Siza, 'regarding white stucco as the touchstone of modernity and seeing other materials, like brick, as reactionary. It is as if we were back in the 1930s when the struggle between Nazi architecture and the avant-garde first emerged.'[23]

Architectural critics were generally quick to defend the use of render in historic contexts by Lucien Lafour and others of his generation who came to prominence in the 1980s,[24] and the determination to be seen as authentically 'modern' was made doubly urgent by their eagerness to distance themselves from the stylistically Post-Modern. But by matching the scale and rhythms of the street, and by using traditional windows rather than ribbons of glazing, their work had already assimilated many of the 'contextual' lessons of the broader postmodern critique of modern architecture. All that remained was to follow Siza's example and use brick. But that final step, for many architects, was a concession too far.

The determination to wear certain materials – white or coloured render, large areas of glazing, glass blocks – as badges of modernity arose in part from an understandable desire to reject the naivety of many planning authorities, whose insistence on the use of 'local' materials as a means of 'fitting in' to an existing context so often results in buildings of intrusive banality. But it also reflected the realization that mass-produced reconstructed 'stone' (concrete with an aggregate of natural stone), wire-cut bricks, or fibre-cement 'slates' are contemptible substitutes for traditional materials, completely lacking in the subtle variations of colour, texture and size that give life to traditionally constructed building surfaces. In part, the Machine Aesthetic

The grey-tiled roofs of Japan (above) were emulated by Team Zoo in paving Tokyo's Yoga Promenade (top).

was a response to the fact that Ruskinian changefulness and all that it implied was, even if desired, an impossible objective using industrial products.

The idea that architecture should be made by finding material – physical and thematic – close to hand, in a given place or locality, was antithetical both to the ambitions of the International Style and to the inexorable trend towards the universalization of building techniques and materials. It was, however, an option in Le Corbusier's work from as early as the Villa de Mandrot at Le Pradet in France, completed in 1931. And with Frank Lloyd Wright, the determination to make buildings that responded to the landscape of which they are a part was a leitmotif of his entire career.

The contrast between the 'international' and 'site-responsive' approaches is neatly summed up by the contrasting attitudes of Wright and Richard Neutra to the challenge of building in the desert. Asked to design a 'Desert House' for Edgar Kaufmann in Colorado, Neutra took the opportunity to demonstrate 'how modern technology enables the architect to extend the habitable area of the world'. The desert house, he added, 'cannot of course be "rooted" in a soil to "grow out of it" … It is frankly an artefact, a construct transported in many shop-fabricated parts over long distance into the midst of rugged aridity.'[25]

Neutra's remarks were doubtless intended as a criticism of his former employer, Wright, to whom 'rooting' a building in a place was almost a *sine qua non* of architecture. At Taliesin West, the 'desert encampment' near Phoenix, Arizona, to which Wright and the Taliesin Fellowship[26] migrated for the winter, this love of the landscape was melded with a fascination with the indigenous cultures of the American Southwest. Where Neutra's desert house was an air-conditioned invader, which could have sat comfortably on a large suburban plot, the planning and construction of Wright's place in the desert were, as Neil Levine has shown

in compelling detail, inseparable from the site's cultural history, topography and climate.[27]

Few modern buildings so vividly evoke Gottfried Semper's 'Four Elements' – hearth, timber roof, textile enclosure and earthwork – as Taliesin West.[28] The site is made habitable by a series of level earthworks framed by thick, earth-hugging walls. To build them, Wright set up wooden forms, against which, flat side out, he placed loose boulders and fractured pieces of rock gathered from the desert. Smaller stones were inserted to fill the gaps and then this loose assembly was bound together by a lean mix of concrete. The surface, like massively magnified terrazzo before grinding down, echoed the texture of the surrounding mountains, which Wright described as 'tattooed', 'spotted like the leopard's skin' or – in a reference to the traces of earlier inhabitation, which fascinated him – 'patterned like hieroglyphics'.[29]

To counterpoint the massiveness of the walls, Wright spread canvas roofs between deep redwood beams, with timber-framed opening flaps of canvas at the eaves and gables for ventilation. The roofs were meant to be regularly renewed as part of the Taliesin Fellowship's annual migration between Wisconsin and Arizona, and the result, Wright felt, 'afforded such agreeable diffusion of light within, was so enjoyable and sympathetic to the desert, that I now felt more than ever oppressed by the thought of the opaque solid overhead of the much too heavy midwestern [Prairie] houses'.[30]

Taliesin West was one of the supreme achievements of that life-long meditation on how to derive an architecture from its site, which began with the so-called Prairie Houses built before the First World War. Sited for the most part in suburban Chicago and far from a living prairie, the Prairie acted as a generic context, which, in Wright's view, demanded low, spreading forms. The spaces and massing stretched out from a focal fireplace; wall surfaces were framed by strong, horizontal lines made by base courses and copings; and the

The 'desert rock' walls (above) and canvas roofs (top) of Wright's 'desert encampment', Taliesin West, were direct responses to the site and climate.

The low walls and deeply-overhanging roofs of Wright's Robie House were a response to the region's prairies.

choice of materials and detailing reinforced this all-pervading horizontality. Wright favoured long, thin Roman bricks, and pointed the bedding courses in plain mortar, whilst suppressing the vertical joints with a coloured mortar; and in detailing timberwork, he insisted that every visible screw-head was carefully set to the horizontal.

At Fallingwater, the previously generic response became site specific: as Wright put it, the materials were chosen to 'sing their song' in response to what he called 'the music of the stream'.[31] Writing about 'the nature of stone' in *Architectural Record* seven years earlier, Wright had declared: 'The rock ledges of a stone-quarry are a story and a longing to me.'[32] At Fallingwater, the memory of the quarry is inscribed into the architecture. Wright found a local stone, which he had roughly squared and then laid – one is tempted to say 'stratified' – to echo the natural bedding of the sedimentary rocks, which form low cliffs along the stream. The effect was so important that he had the first masonry contractor replaced for failing to deliver what was required.

In complete contrast to the stone, the cantilevered reinforced-concrete floor trays and roof planes were made smooth, with rounded edges, and painted an autumnal light ochre colour – Wright originally intended to coat them with flecks of gold leaf to suggest the flash of light from water on dead leaves. The painted surfaces form a neutral ground receptive to the play of broken light and shadows beneath the tree canopy, visually lightening the two major 'floating' layers of the house. Sliding between piers/'cliffs' of stone, they echo the stepped descent of the stream below: the architecture is an abstraction of, and inseparable from, the materials of which it is made and the place it occupies.

Wright's response to the landscape is direct and elemental, and in Fallingwater and Taliesin West – both of which were built in total isolation from other buildings – the masonry walls are made to appear as 'natural' as possible. The site of Jørn Utzon's first house – Can Lis – on Majorca, which he began building in 1971, offers a similarly elemental encounter with cliff-top and ocean – 'nothing until Africa' as he likes to observe, pointing out to sea.[33] Despite this prodigious prospect, the context is almost suburban, on the fringes of the small town of Porto Petro. And so, rather than specify – or, like Wright, invent – his own palette of materials, or self-consciously emulate a craft-based vernacular, Utzon determined to use whatever materials were available from the local builders' merchants. They turned out to be stone blocks, quarried nearby; reinforced-concrete I-beams and

The stratified walls and dramatic cantilevers of Wright's Fallingwater echo the geology and topography of the site, from which the house is inseparable.

lintels; shallow-arched *bovedillas* clay tiles and stone slabs, to form, respectively, the ceiling and flat roof/suspended floor; clay pantiles for roofing; and, finally, ceramic tiles.

The house Utzon made using these materials bears no resemblance to the mediocre dwellings being built all over the island with them. And unlike them, it belongs so completely to the island and to the Mediterranean culture, which is its ultimate context, that it would scarcely have looked out of place in Crete 3000 years ago. In part this has to do with the artfully careless placing of the separate blocks, which recalls the seemingly random juxtapositions uncovered on archaeological sites, but mostly it is a matter of materials and detail and of the way they are marshalled to suggest an elemental synthesis of sun, stone, earth and sky.

Inspired by Lewerentz, frames are placed on the outside of the openings. For doors this necessitated gouging away some stone to make room for the hand to reach the latch – rubbing the back of your hand against the stone is a slight but still insistent memory of the place. Everywhere, Utzon delights in the traces of how things are made. Rather than countersink and plug nails in the timber, he wanted to see the tiny trailing lines left by weathering, which mark their presence. He also asked that the surfaces of the stone blocks should not be rubbed down

to eliminate the marks of the circular saw – in grazing sunlight the effect is remarkable, like traces of half-eroded inscriptions. The one exception to this constructional 'honesty' is critical: the deep openings, which frame views of the Mediterranean, are supported by hidden reinforcing, because expressed structure would have been intrusive: nothing, here, is allowed to distract from the confrontation with the horizon.

Architectural accounts of place – from the advocacy of 'townscape' to the phenomenological approach of Christian Norberg-Schulz (who discussed Can Lis at length[34]), not to mention the brief discussion in this chapter[35] – tend to treat it as if it were a quality that inheres in specific locations and can be discovered through insight and analysis. This is a convenient but dangerous shorthand. 'Sense of place' is necessarily a function of people's relationships with specific locations, not a property of them, and for many people it may well have as much to do with intangible memories, associations, scents or other qualities, which do not register visually or loom large on most architects' agendas. 'Place', as commonly understood in architecture, partakes too much of the inertia of the physical, and readily lapses into that sentimentality and preciousness that can attend so many well-intentioned efforts at environmental

Built with locally available materials, Utzon's Can Lis on Majorca feels both ancient and modern.

Courtyard at Can Lis: a stone framework for outdoor living.

Your hand touches stone as well as metal when opening the doors.

preservation. Seen as a gift from the past to be preserved, a concern with qualities of 'place' all too easily invites us to dismiss the messy realities of daily life.

A very different approach, 'totally neutralized … balancing between fondness and scorn, ideology and ignorance', to quote Lucy Lippard,[36] emerged in the 1960s in the USA. The first moves were made, independently, by artists and by geographers, such as J. B. Jackson.[37] Ed Ruscha's artist's books, starting with *Twenty-six Gasoline Stations* and followed by the equally deadpan *Every Building on Sunset Strip*, invited the viewer to pay serious attention to some of the most despised of everyday environments. Even more provocatively, in 'A Tour of the Monuments of Passaic, New Jersey', published in *Artforum*,[38] Robert Smithson deliberately echoed the form of English 'Picturesque' tours of the late eighteenth century, which began with William Gilpin's *Observations on the River Wye*.[39] But in place of pellucid streams and sounding cataracts, Smithson recorded waste discharge pipes and derelict land. For Smithson, 'the investigation of a specific site is a matter of extracting concepts out of existing sense-data through direct perceptions. …One does not impose, but rather expose the site. …The unknown areas of sites can best be explored by artists.'[40]

Top: Animated by sun in mid-afternoon, the living room at Can Lis is a 'machine for viewing' the Mediterranean.

Above: Utzon asked the masons not to rub down the saw-marks, to give the stone an integral 'ornament'.

Nail-heads are slightly sunk but exposed, to leave traces of how the door is made.

The revaluation of the ordinary and everyday formed a sub-theme of Robert Venturi's 1966 book *Complexity and Contradiction in Architecture* – with its advocacy of the 'ugly and ordinary' and (in)famous declaration that 'Main Street is almost all right'[41] – and then became the dominant message of *Learning from Las Vegas*, in which Venturi and his colleagues invited architects to look seriously at the commercial strip as an environment of communication. A good example of this revaluing of the 'ugly and ordinary' is provided by the three artist's studio-houses Frank Gehry built on Indiana Avenue in Venice, California in 1981. The visual chaos of bungalows, scrapyards and overhead power-lines, which confronted him there, was precisely the kind of context into which, in Japan, Tadao Ando was inserting his concrete 'bastions of resistance'.[42]

Rather than deliberately exclude the man-made context like Ando, however, Gehry opted to make it the springboard for architectural invention. The requirement for double-height studios meant that the houses were bound to loom large in the surroundings, and to reduce their apparent bulk, whilst relating to the existing buildings, the windows are conventionally framed in aluminium, but used at an exaggeratedly large size. Although identically built using a timber-frame structure, each house is sheathed in a distinctive material – sky-blue render, unpainted plywood and green asphalt shingles – which you sense might well have been found lying around the neighbourhood. The materials are ordinary and belong to the place, but Gehry's handling of them brings to mind abstract sculptures more than conventional buildings.

The preoccupation with context and willingness to pay close attention to the everyday world have become major themes of postmodern thought, and with it of architecture. Traditional urban contexts, for so long neglected by mainstream Modern architecture, were the inspiration for some of the most persuasive buildings of the late twentieth century – from major complexes such as Stirling and Wilford's Staatsgalerie in Stuttgart to countless small interventions. For many architects, a preoccupation with the creation of 'place' has also been the catalyst for conceiving buildings as miniature cities, an approach perhaps still best exemplified by Hans Hollein's Abteiberg municipal museum in Mönchengladbach, Germany, completed in 1983 – a 'compacted composition' of distinctive forms and materials of the kind advocated by Colin Rowe and Fred Koetter in their influential book, *Collage City*.[43]

This brief review of the interaction of materials and place confirms that any attempt to understand the 'nature', as opposed to quantifiable properties, of materials independently of their use in a specific location is misleading. Ignoring this relationship may suit the aspirations of those in search of an international style, but their reasoning is grounded in ideology, not the science of materials – whose qualities and meanings in architecture are inescapably place-specific and time-bound. And it is to the actions of time we now turn.

The commercial landscape of the Las Vegas strip (above and right) was the subject of investigation by Robert Venturi and colleagues in the 1970s.

Above and above left: Frank Gehry distilled the materials of the group of three studio-houses on Indiana Avenue in Venice, California, from the surrounding 'ugly and ordinary' context.

Top right: Building as place: Abteiberg municipal museum in Mönchengladbach by Hans Hollein.

PIVVENT

SETANN N

SENA

Eroded inscription,
Roman Forum.

Then Marco Polo spoke. 'Your chessboard, sire, is inlaid with two woods: ebony and maple. The square on which your enlightened gaze is fixed was cut from the ring of a trunk that grew in a year of drought: you see how its fibres are arranged? Here a barely hinted knot can be made out: a bud tried to burgeon on a premature day, but the night's frost forced it to desist.
Italo Calvino[1]

Reviewing a travelling exhibition of Le Corbusier's early villas in 1959, a mere 30 years after their completion, Nikolaus Pevsner became deeply depressed. Not only had several of these seminal works been neglected or insensitively altered, but also almost all appeared to be in a state of serious decay. 'Le Corbusier's houses can't please in decay', Pevsner observed. 'Concrete structures with walls designed to be rendered white make bad ruins. What we are used to enjoy in decay, according to our upbringing, but perhaps also according to just laws of aesthetics, is weathered stone and lichens. … These white surfaces must be white, these metal window frames free from rust. The Villa Savoye at Poissy should greet us on its hill-crest as an eternal vision.'[2]

The white architecture of the International Style was a challenge to those two great natural modifiers of buildings, climate and time. The speed with which, in the absence of regular maintenance, it deteriorated in all but the most forgiving of environments was a significant reason why Le Corbusier, for one, turned to more traditional materials and rougher finishes.[3] His more recent works, especially the Maisons Jaoul, noted Pevsner, 'possess this same quality of the *non-finito*, the roughness, the sympathy with the accident, the licence for things to grow where they choose, with which nature is now trying to endow the early villas'.

Painted white and stripped of almost all the features, originally known as *weatherings*, which were designed to cope with rain and wind –

projecting cornices, copings and cills – the new architecture was almost everywhere a hostage to fortune. Its owners, not surprisingly, frequently declined to meet the high costs of keeping it pristine. And in the case of the workers' housing at Pessac, they had neither the means nor the inclination, preferring to add more traditional features and materials to render the strange new buildings more resilient and house-like: 'Life is always right', observed Le Corbusier, 'it is the architect who is wrong.'[4]

Time's critique of the Modernist aesthetic was not simply a matter of maintenance. Recalling an early project built in brick, Richard Meier noted that a wall running from inside to out quickly became covered in a thin film of moss, and in the process destroyed this would-be expression of 'spatial continuity'.[5] Meier's subsequent reinterpretation of the early Corbusian style using durable coated-aluminium and other panels solved the technical problem, at least for a reasonable building life, but the issue of attitude remained. The dream of a pure 'white' architecture capable of resisting the actions of time revealed both a preoccupation with appearance rather than constructional substance, and the conviction that the Machine Age had somehow 'conquered' time. For the young Le Corbusier and his fellow Moderns, the stained surfaces and softened edges, which accompany weathering, were 'moral' as well as practical defects, and had to be vigilantly suppressed through constant maintenance.

Obsession with image is a dominant feature of our media culture of instant effects, and just as genetic scientists now devote their attention to deferring or even, according to some, defying natural ageing, materials scientists are increasingly directing their efforts towards the development of materials that resist deterioration. 'Never before', writes Sophie Trelcat, 'has the struggle against the ageing of materials mobilized so much talent, energy and finance.'[6] Archaeological studies of long-term weathering, mathematical models of the

As seen here at Pessac, early Modernist buildings weathered badly in the absence of regular maintenance.

At Pessac, the residents made good the buildings' technical deficiencies by adding pitched roofs.

evolution of chemicals in time, and accelerated ageing in building research-facilities are all being marshalled to test and improve materials. Composite forms, such as carbon-epoxy-reinforced wood, resin mortars and super-high-performance concretes, are developing, whilst nano-technologies, working at the molecular scale, promise materials tailor-made to specific needs – reversing the traditional sequence of decisions in choosing a material. Even the most ancient, such as stone, can be 'improved' by the application of non-pathogenic bacteria, which synthesize calcium carbonate to form a hard, naturally protective coat.

The desire for instant effect, and accompanying dislike of ageing, is symptomatic of deeper issues in contemporary construction. Built as skins of precisely sized and increasingly thin materials – as often as not of stone cladding on metal hangers – the buildings that dominate the centres of modern cities may weather better than Le Corbusier's Purist villas, at least in the medium term, but are almost equally incapable of tolerating wear, or the patching and changes over time through which cities have traditionally evolved. Modern buildings ask to be disassembled or re-clad rather than gradually remodelled, with obvious implications both for the use of resources and for the continuity that cities have traditionally provided.

Recently restored, the Villa Savoye epitomizes the time-defying aspirations of early visions of modernity.

The determination to defy the effects of time is hardly new: all worthwhile architecture is an act of faith in the future and, to a greater or less extent, a defiance of the corrosive action of weather. The Classical treatises on architecture, beginning with Vitruvius, contain far more information about the selection and use of materials than they do about 'design', and a major concern, then as now, is with their durability. Palladio, quoting Vitruvius, explains that timber 'ought to be felled in autumn, or during the winter season, in the wane of the moon', and then seasoned for at least three years before it is 'dry enough to be made use of in planks for the floors, windows, and doors'.[7] Similarly, soft stones – such as freshly cut travertine, which can sometimes be cut with a spade – should be placed under cover for two years to harden so that they are 'much fitter to resist the inclemencies of the weather'.[8]

In Victorian England, constructional polychromy made use of new 'weatherproof' glazed and hard engineering bricks, and as such was a deliberate challenge, not only to time and weather, but also to the greatest advocate of their beneficial effects, John Ruskin. For Ruskin, 'a building cannot be considered in its prime until four or five centuries have passed over it',[9] because 'the greatest glory of a building is not in its stones, nor in its gold. Its glory is in its Age … in walls that have long been washed by the passing waves of humanity. … It is in that golden stain of time, that we are to look for the real light and colour, and preciousness of architecture.'[10] The sentences omitted from this passage are replete with those high moral sentiments that render Ruskin's writing unpalatable to many modern tastes, but his love of the effects of a nobly weathered building was as much visual as sentimental. Writing home to his father from Venice in 1845, Ruskin expressed his delight in the recently invented daguerreotypes,[11] which were almost like 'carrying off the palace itself – every chip of stone and stain is there'.[12] And pondering the

beauties of humble Lakeland cottages, he noted that 'both the coverings and sides of the houses have furnished places of rest for the seeds of lichens, mosses, ferns and flowers'.[13]

Ruskin's pleasure in the visual effects of weathering had its roots in English aesthetic theories of the eighteenth century. A precociously early example of this sensibility was expressed in 1724 in a letter written from Rome by the painter, poet and farmer, John Dyer. Attempting to describe the impression made by the ruins, he explained that 'a certain disjointedness and moulder among the stones, something so pleasing in their weeds and tufts of myrtle' blotted out 'the traces of disagreeable squares and angles' and thereby added 'certain beauties that could not be before imagined, which is the cause of surprise no modern building can give'.[14] Half a century later, in his Discourses given at the Royal Academy in London in 1786, Sir Joshua Reynolds advised young architects to trust to happy accidents rather than always rely on regular plans. The resulting 'variety and intricacy', he explained, would be of as much advantage to architecture as they were to the other arts.[15]

In 1794, William Gilpin gave coherent expression to the emerging passion for the seemingly accidental with the publication of his celebrated *Essay on the Picturesque*. 'The two opposite qualities of roughness and sudden variation, joined to that of irregularity,' he explained, 'are the most efficient causes of the picturesque.' In architecture, time itself can be the means of achieving such qualities, because it replaces the 'embellishments that belong to architecture, the polish of its columns, the highly furnished execution of its capitals and mouldings, its urns and statues' with 'what may be called the embellishments of ruins … incrustations and weather stains … the various plants that spring from or climb over the walls'. Time and the 'progress of vegetation' were also, he suggested, effective means of healing 'deformities' and 'gashes in the ground', such as quarries and gravel pits.

Courtyard of Palazzo dei Conservatori, Rome: the 'golden stain of time'.

Made of local stone and worn by time, the walls of this Cotswold village seem part of the earth.

Traditionally, English cemeteries were designed to weather (above), whereas those of Italy (opposite) aspire to defy time.

The fascination of ruins: illustrations from *Churton's Monastic Ruins of Yorkshire*, 1943 (top) and *The Ruins of Balbec, otherwise Heliopolis in Cœlosyria*, by Robert Wood, 1757 (above).

It would be an exaggeration to suggest that the theory of the Picturesque marked the emergence of a wholly new sensibility in Europe – Leonardo da Vinci, after all, had commended the random stains found on walls to the attention of painters[16] – but it gave new coherence to previously unstructured ideas, and acted as invaluable preparation for the assimilation of Japanese aesthetic values in the late nineteenth century. In the process, it challenged the hegemony of the Classical theory of beauty – which preferred smoothness to roughness, precision to vagueness – and acted as a stimulus to new attitudes to the past. Once again Ruskin, and later William Morris, were the key thinkers.

Detesting buildings that had been 'scraped and patched up into smugness and smoothness more tragic than uttermost ruin',[17] Ruskin argued that the traces of time should be preserved as a record of the building's life, not erased under the guise of returning it to its original state. 'It is impossible', Ruskin declared, 'as impossible as to raise the dead, to restore anything that has ever been great or beautiful in architecture.'[18] The reaction against the Victorians' overly zealous determination to restore medieval buildings became known as the 'anti-scrape' movement, and stimulated William Morris to establish the Society for the Protection of Ancient Buildings in 1877. Arguing for the *conservation*, rather than *restoration* of old buildings, Morris explained that it was impossible to do 'the same sort of work in the same spirit as our forefathers' because 'we are completely changed and we cannot do the work they did. All continuity of history means is after all perpetual change.'[19] When working on an historic building, as much of the old as possible should be retained, Morris argued, and in any changes it should be made overt what is new and what is old. Properly conceived conservation could involve, as James Stevens Curl observes, 'considerable intervention, even much new building',[20] always providing that it respected, and ideally enhanced, the existing fabric.

Cemetery, San Miniato, Florence.

Built ruin: the Magdalenenkapelle in the Nymphenburg, Munich, 1725-8.

The work of Carlo Scarpa on the Castelvecchio in Verona is, perhaps, the most celebrated and poetic twentieth-century example of such an approach,[21] and a similar determination to juxtapose old and new motivated Sverre Fehn's deeply moving Bispegard Museum in Hamar, Norway, developed over the remains of a medieval bishop's palace (see also page 17).[22]

Contemplation of the ruins of Rome during the Grand Tour of Italy undertaken by many young gentlemen and budding artists was a vital stimulus to the revaluation of the past, but when Adolf Hitler visited Rome in 1938 the Eternal City provoked rather more ambitious thoughts. Returning to Germany, he realized that he had a duty to ensure a legacy as inspiring as that of the Eternal City. Advised that steel and reinforced concrete might well prove too perishable to last the planned 1000 years of the Third Reich, he made it official policy – known as the *Teorie von Ruinwert* – that only stone and brick should be used in official Nazi buildings.[23]

Building a legacy for the future has, needless to say, long been a stimulus to great architecture: 'I shall be expelled,' said Cosimo de' Medici, 'but my buildings will remain.'[24] What makes Hitler's aspirations peculiarly modern, however, is the idea of building with the nobility of the ruinous end condition in mind. What excited him about this propsect,

of course, was not so much the picturesque delights of accident and decay, as the feeling, widely shared amongst Romantic Classicists of the eighteenth century, such as Piranesi, that the full grandeur of architecture was revealed, rather than 'softened', by partial ruination. Hence, in part, Sir John Soane's predilection for making presentation drawings of his designs as ruins, and hence, certainly, Louis Kahn's passion for the remains of Egypt, Greece and Rome, which he visited for the first time in middle age, as a Resident Architect at the American School in Rome.[25]

Kahn was no lover of the paraphernalia of modern building – 'it was easy for Ledoux,' he famously observed, 'no pipes' – and after his encounter with the ruins of the ancient world he dreamt of constructing 'openings without frames' and 'wrapping ruins around buildings'.[26] The latter, first proposed for the American Embassy in Angola, were given functional justification as means of shielding the interior from the sun. Much the same motivation lay behind Lewerentz's idea of placing frames over, rather than in, the wall-openings, so that from inside the contact between brick wall and nature was seemingly unmediated, even by glass.

The contemplation of ruins has inspired thoughts about the beauties of the most ephemeral of architectural effects – Ruskin's

Juxtaposition of old and new: Castelvecchio, Verona, converted by Carlo Scarpa in the 1960s (above) and Hamar

Bispegard Museum, Norway, by Sverre Fehn (right).

Staircase in Le Thoronet: worn and polished by the feet of generations of monks.

'golden stain of time' – and it has focused attention on what, in the West at least, have widely been seen as architecture's most enduring qualities of geometry, structure and form. Both the ephemeral and permanent aspects came together in Aldo Rossi's youthful reminiscence of seeing fog enter the church of Sant'Andrea in Mantua: 'It is the unseen element that modifies and alters, like light and shadow, like stones worn smooth by the feet and hands of generations of men.'[27]

From something as ephemeral as the appearance of fog, to changes in light and humidity, the materials of building are inescapably caught up in the play of time. As Marco Polo pointed out to Kublai Kahn, natural materials have time inscribed in their very structure – from the decades or centuries it takes to produce timber, to the untold millennia of sedimentation, geological transformations and weathering locked in stone. Those, such as gold, granite or marble, most able to defy physical deterioration by atmospheric pollution or wear have frequently been amongst the most valued. Gold leaf still finds occasional uses as a protective finish on buildings, and its physical permanence is matched by stainless steel (which really does live up to its name) and other metals, including that recent arrival in building, titanium, made famous by Frank Gehry's

Guggenheim Museum in Bilbao (see page 215). Used at suitably expensive levels of purity, titanium, it is claimed, offers an essentially unchanging finish – although in Bilbao, as we noted on page 28, it is already showing signs of weathering.[28]

The most widely used metals in building are, like most materials, subject to a range of chemical effects. Freshly cut lead has a shiny metallic surface, which dulls rapidly by oxidation on exposure to the atmosphere. Similarly, copper oxidizes to a brown colour, and in polluted areas the colour can verge on black. After several years – typically between five and ten – a green patina begins to form, and the surface becomes mottled green all over. This process is electrochemical and depends on the

Eternal youth: gilded, open-work dome crowning Josef Olbrich's Secession Building in Vienna.

Forty years old, the copper on St Catherine's College, Oxford, is now at an advanced stage of patination.

presence of a film of moisture and of atmospheric pollution – in remote mountainous regions copper does not need regular cleaning to remain as copper-coloured as a favourite cooking pan.

Under normal conditions, it takes about 70 years for the surface of copper to become completely mineralized and acquire its distinctive, verdigris-coloured patina – which for Frank Lloyd Wright made it 'the only sheet metal that has yet entered into architecture as beautiful permanent material'. The patination of copper can be accelerated chemically, or inhibited by applied coatings. Many architects favour pre-patinated sheets, although the chemically induced colour can seem 'unnaturally' uniform – Ruskin would surely have condemned it as a perverse abuse of nature.

The patina that results from weathering or use – as for example the polishing of surfaces through repeated contact with hands or feet – is generally regarded as a desirable sign of age. Rust, on the other hand, is not, largely because we know that, left to its own devices, it will eventually destroy the iron or steel on which it has taken hold. The invention of Cor-ten, or 'weathering' steel as it is now more commonly known, required us to radically re-think the familiar association of rust with decay. Scratch Cor-ten steel and it happily re-oxidizes, and, like

old furniture, it should not be cleaned, because cleaning only promotes further corrosion. Far from being a sign of neglect and decay, the rust of Cor-ten steel is a protective layer more effective, because it needs minimal maintenance, than paint or other coatings. Rust has now to be appreciated as an aesthetically desirable 'finish' – always providing the need to avoid potentially unsightly drips on porous materials is considered. For a sculptor such as Richard Serra, placing large sheets of apparently rusting steel in public spaces added to the 'challenge' of his work's abstraction,[29] whilst for Anthony Gormley, the weathering steel of his millennial 'Angel of the North', in the north of England, carried evocative associations with the ships' hulls that used to be built nearby.

Changes to stone, brick and concrete due to weathering are generally slower than with metals, but can be no less far-reaching. Most dramatic, especially in urban areas, are those that result not from changes to the stone itself, but from the accumulation of atmospheric deposits on areas protected from cleaning by rainwater. This process can have surprising consequences, and few are more striking than the transformation of the uniform cladding of Marcel Breuer's De Bijenkorf Department Store in Rotterdam into what might, at a glance, be taken as a display of artfully matched veneers.

Weathering steel: 'Angel of the North' by Anthony Gormley.

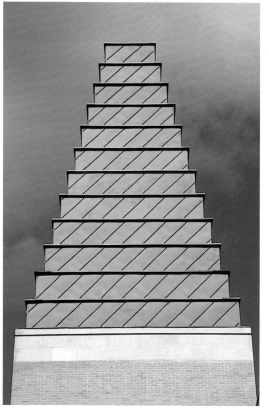

Prepatinated copper: Said Business School, Oxford, by Dixon and Jones.

Naturally patinated copper: Helsinki Technical University, Otaniemi, by Alvar Aalto.

The stone-clad De Bijenkorf
Department Store in Rotterdam
by Marcel Breuer has been
totally transformed by these
unexpected weathering patterns.

The layered composition of Palladio's San Giorgio Maggiore, Venice, is clarified by weathering.

In Venice, the white Istrian stone turns almost black due to soot where it is protected from the washing of rain, an effect that lends to the Doge's Palace a permanent feeling of light and shadow, and that Palladio appears to have deliberately exploited to clarify the layered compositions of the façades of the churches of San Giorgio Maggiore and Il Redentore.[30] The equally striking 'whitewash and soot' effects on the white Portland Stone of Nicholas Hawksmoor's churches in London's East End are, perhaps, less calculated – but nonetheless often serve to emphasize aspects of the design.

Reflecting on the spectacle of fog entering Sant' Andrea to which we have already referred, Aldo Rossi relates in his *Scientific Autobiography* that it made him realize that 'architecture was made possible by the confrontation of a precise form with time and the elements, a confrontation which lasted until the form was destroyed in the process of this combat.'[31] In pre-industrial Japan, this confrontation assumed a radically different character to that in the West. In a country subject to frequent earthquakes, and the devastating fires that often came in their wake, architecture achieved permanence not through resistant materials but through persistent forms. The paradigm of this attitude is the Shinto shrine at Ise (see page 14). Ritually built and re-built every 20 years over some 14 centuries, with only occasional gaps because of war, the structures at Ise have achieved immortality through cloning. Writing in the 1930s, following his first, life-changing visit to Japan, Bruno Taut observed that seen in pictures, 'they seemed to be merely huts … and rather affected at that'. But after encountering them at first hand he realized that they 'are not human ideas and conceptions deliberately solidified in order to secure an eternal existence for human production', but rather 'stress the refinement of the transitory, the projection of the moment into the universe'.[32]

Although the central buildings at Ise, archetypes of native Japanese architecture,

The 'whitewash and soot' effects on Hawksmoor's St George in the East, London, result from differential exposure to washing by rain.

were perpetually renewed, this fascination with the transitory by no means implied insensitivity to the long *durée* of time. Just as old people were revered, so too were the effects of ageing on buildings. The most celebrated example is the low wall that frames the *kare-sansui*, or dry garden, of the Ryoan-ji temple: although well protected from weather, thanks to its deeply overhanging thatched coping, it is richly stained by resins and oils slowly seeping out from within the construction. This wall is certainly exceptional, but the sensibility that valued it informs every aspect of Japanese aesthetics. The impermanence of the raked lines in the gravel at Ryoan-ji – freshly raked every day by novices at the temple – heightens the sense of time made material in the infinitesimally slowly changing wall that encloses them. In a similar way, the flawless surfaces of the regularly renewed paper in the sliding *fusuma* screens serve to heighten our awareness of the gradual mellowing of the timber that frames them.

Above and top: The wall around the dry garden at Ryoan-ji in Kyoto is stained by resins oozing out from within its fabric – a mark of age which is highly esteemed in Japan.

Tea-house in the Shugakuin Imperial garden, Tokyo.

Aalto's summerhouse on Muuratsalo evokes the time-worn surfaces of an Italian piazzetta.

Blue-tiled panel at Muuratsalo: metaphoric window onto a southern sky?

In building this courtyard at Yale, James Gamble Rogers buried the slates, laid the paving to create puddles, and re-leaded windows after having them broken at random – all to make a 1930s building seem as ancient as its Oxbridge models.

It is surely no coincidence that the two major twentieth-century architects who were acutely conscious of the potentially beneficial effects of time on buildings and materials, Wright and Aalto, were both deeply marked by contact with Japan, as also was Scarpa, whose beloved *stucco alla veneziana* grows more beautiful with age. Wright expressed the hope that 'nature, by invitation, would become the ornament of the building',[33] illustrating the idea with a picture of an icicle depending from the eaves of his Wisconsin home, Taliesin East, whilst Aalto's summerhouse on Muuratsalo is a hymn to the pleasures of ageing. Although as a good Modern architect and quasi-functionalist, Aalto explained their rich textures as technical 'experiments', designed to test the durability of different bricks, tiles, mortars and types of pointing – and to make the house tax-deductible![34] – the underlying motivation was far from prosaic. 'I always have a journey to Italy in mind',[35] Aalto often professed, and on Muuratsalo he saved himself the trouble by building his own fragment of the beloved land, a homage to the patched walls and bricked-up openings of Italian streets and piazzas – a rectangle of deep blue tiles, complete with structurally redundant timber lintel, neatly reverses inside and out by doubling as an 'open window' onto the southern sky.

In Aalto's work, a quasi-Japanese sensitivity to the patination of materials by time is allied to a Picturesque fascination with its effects. He delights in placing untreated wood next to relatively unchanging marble, glazed tiles against rough brick or stucco, or in showing polished copper inside as a foil to its patinating counterpart outside. Nature is not so much invited to become the 'ornament' of the building, as to transform it. At the Villa Mairea, for example, poles for climbing plants frame window openings and wrap around a corner, inviting vegetation to undermine the clarity of the forms. As at Muuratsalo, the effects of weathering seem almost to be built in.

At the Villa Mairea, Noormarkku,
Finland, Aalto delighted in
juxtaposing 'new' and 'old'
materials.

Plants trailing over the Villa
Mairea's walls moderate
'the shock of the new'.

Similarly, Aalto's partial revetments of stone or tile, employed to articulate the overall composition or to mark or ease transitions, can almost equally well be read as remnants of all-over claddings. And on a larger scale still, whole buildings are conceived as Picturesque compositions, for which Uvedale Price's words – 'roughness and sudden variation, joined to … irregularity' – seem an apt description. Aalto's buildings were clearly not in any literal sense 'built ruins', but by adopting compositional tactics strikingly similar to those for which ruins came to be admired, they certainly invite us to see them less as static forms than as places evolving in time.[36]

The Japanese influence on twentieth-century art and architecture has been pervasive, and even without the overtly Japanese steps leading up to his own house in Los Angeles, it would not be difficult to detect oriental influences in the work that brought Frank Gehry to international attention. The idea of peeling away the layers of construction so as to reveal the process of its making echoes precisely the Japanese love of exposing the framework below the mud plaster in the tea-houses at Katsura. Just as Gehry made poetry out of that by now most prosaic of constructional forms, the ubiquitous timber frame, so too the Japanese masters of tea based their work on peasant, rural building types, to demonstrate the superiority and refinement of Imperial taste over the vulgar, *arriviste* Shogun rulers. And in both, a significant measure of our enjoyment comes from seeing a time-bound process revealed, the ephemeral made permanent. In the West, deliberately inscribing process in form, time in material, is a pervasively modern idea – and one to which we will return.

The partially finished surfaces of the Shoka-tei tea-house at Katsura reveal the underlying construction.

Helsinki Technical University, like many of Aalto's late works, hints at the Picturesque effect of ruins.

Inspired by half-built timber houses and traditional Japanese architecture, Frank Gehry exposed the layers of construction in extending his house in Santa Monica, California.

Chapter 6
Use

Paving in Prague.

A glass jug, a wicker basket, a coarse muslin huipil, a wooden serving dish: beautiful objects, not despite their usefulness but because of it...
Octavio Paz[1]

Two lines of stone paviors, diagonally incised to give added grip and spaced to fit the wheels of a horse-drawn carriage, thread their way up a narrow driveway, whilst for passing pedestrians, broader slabs offer a similarly inviting passage across a choppy sea of cobbles. Modern vehicles no longer demand such exquisitely wrought paving as this two-centuries-old survival in a driveway in the Beacon Hill district of Boston, but the obvious rightness with which it is attuned to the pattern of use makes its appeal perennial. In the quads and courts of Oxford and Cambridge colleges, the juxtaposition of smooth and rough is similarly satisfying, and has the added twist that the bands of cobbles or setts that line the paths are also a warning, as much tactile as visual, not to stray onto the grass – a surface reserved, in those ancient institutions, for Fellows or other senior members of the College.

Comparable, if generally less striking, changes of materials to these are also ubiquitous in buildings. The floor surface may run from outside to inside to stress 'spatial continuity', but such transitions are more typically marked by moving from rough to smooth, hard to (relatively) soft. The choice of materials to suit different uses is often prosaic and taken for granted – waterproof tiles in kitchens and bathrooms; hard-wearing surfaces for corridors or stairs, 'finer' ones in occupied rooms – but their mutual adjustment and co-ordination, psychological as well as physical, offer manifold tactile, as well as visual, pleasures. In a world increasingly dominated by the sense of sight and the pervasive demands of visual media, many modern buildings are strikingly lacking in these qualities, all the more surprising given that touch, as Lucretius pointed in *De Rerum Natura*, is 'the sense of our whole body'.[2] Noting this deficiency, the engineer Peter Rice has suggested that members of his profession now have a duty to 'use their understanding of materials and structures to make real the presence of the materials in use in the building, so that people warm to them, want to touch them, feel a sense of the material itself and of the people who made and designed it'.[3]

In the buildings of Alvar Aalto, invitations to touch, and a responsiveness to the occupant as an embodied subject, not simply a mobile pair of eyes, abound. Consider Säynätsalo Town Hall, for example. The design was inspired, in part, by arcaded Italian courts, around which the

Private driveway, Beacon Hill, Boston, Massachusetts.

In Cambridge colleges, the rough cobbles remind you that the grass is reserved for Fellows.

In Asplund's extension to Gothenburg Town Hall, the slender balusters seem to flex in response to use.

movement of officials was democratically open to the citizens. The climate of Finland necessitated glazing what became a single-banked corridor, and so, to emphasize the building's public nature, Aalto brought the brick paving into the foyer (the courtyard was originally almost as much brick as grass, not the suburban lawn it has been allowed to become) and wrapped it around the glazed corridor as a ribbon below a brick bench/radiator. From the entrance, the paving doubles back and runs all the way up, between fair-faced brick walls, to the threshold of the council chamber, where the surface changes abruptly to highly polished timber. Its dignity reinforced by the dim, almost medieval lighting, the space demands silence and focuses attention on the spoken word.

In Säynätsalo, every detail is thought through, with a similar commitment to enriching the user's experience. The door handles, for example, are woven from leather thongs: a pleasure to handle, they impress themselves on the memory as much through touch as sight. Aalto's concern with the way that the qualities of materials could both respond to activities and evoke an atmosphere conducive to them, is reflected in his critique of the shallow 'rationality' of much so-called functional design. Soon after the appearance of bent-metal furniture, his friend, the Danish critic Poul Henningsen,

pointed out that such chairs were 'so cold they give the modernly dressed woman a cramp in the thigh', and Aalto himself went on to suggest that criticizing objects as 'too noisy, too light-reflective, and too good a heat conductor' was, in fact, a way of giving 'scientific terms for things that when put together form the mystical concept of "cosy"'.[4]

'Cosiness' is not a declared objective of most modern architecture, and whilst Aalto did not mean by it anything cloying or sentimental, his work abounds in materials and details intended to humanize the physical environment. In the Villa Mairea (1937-9) in Noormarkku, Finland, for example, the floor surfaces suggest a sequence of increasing intimacy, from stone, to tile, to rugs on tiles, to polished timber boarding. The handle you grasp on entering or leaving the house – 'the handshake of the building', as Juhani Pallasmaa aptly describes it[5] – is cast in bronze, and shaped to the hand. It might strike the non-Finnish observer as bone-like, but is readily recognizable as a 'monumental'

Brick floor and timber handrail leading to the council chamber of Säynätsalo Town Hall.

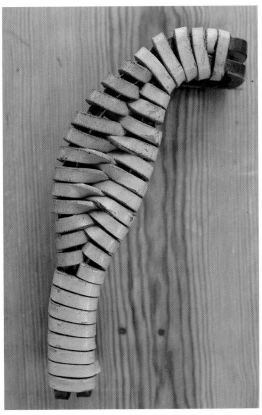

In Säynätsalo, the bronze, leather-wrapped door handles are delightfully receptive to the hand.

Transitions from stone to tile and then timber-boarding suggest increasing intimacy in the Villa Mairea.

Wrapped with rattan, the steel columns of the Villa Mairea (left) are warm to the touch – and recall the protective bamboo claddings of the cryptomeria trees at Ise (below).

Living room, Villa Mairea: Aalto happily sought to evoke a feeling of domesticity.

Grasping the door-handle of the Villa, you are reminded of the pieces of tree-branch used on saunas.

form of the wooden handles, straight from the tree, traditionally found on that most Finnish of buildings, the sauna. Throughout the house, the other handles and latches are similarly individual and inventive, varying in size and gravitas according to their place and role.

The black-painted steel columns are domesticated by being wrapped with rattan, which, like a cat's fur, positively asks to be stroked. During 1940, with Finland at war with Russia, the material was hard to find and, once obtained, proved tricky to bend tightly to the radius required. Aalto would not, however, entertain its omission. Partly this was because the columns were metaphoric pine trees in the 'forest space' of the interior[6] – the rattan evoking the golden core exposed when the black bark peels away – and partly because this conspicuously handmade addition mediated the steel's 'industrial' associations and cold surface. The result is reminiscent of the bamboo wrapped around the cryptomeria trees on the approach to the shrines at Ise: the purpose is prosaic – to protect the bark from the attentions of deer – but the effect is to emphasize that you are walking along a man-made route through nature.

Most of Aalto's public buildings are characterized by what George Baird has aptly called 'a network of touch',[7] which serves both as guide and welcome. In keeping with his criticism of metal furniture, almost all his handrails – after a brief and brilliant exploration of the machine aesthetic at Paimio Sanatorium – are warm to the hand. Made of wood or tubular metal wrapped with leather, they also frequently, as in the brick corridor/stair at Säynätsalo, run across level areas to lead you to your destination. In the Viipuri library, the railings provide both an ingenious means of separating the routes in and out, and an evocative image of the comings and goings of readers: elements so conspicuously designed for use suggest human presence even when the space is empty.

For Aalto, this passion for what may seem merely the minutiae of architectural design was fundamental, not incidental, and his sensitivity to the factors involved is perfectly demonstrated by the wooden railings that run along the balustrades of the access galleries in the Festival Hall at Jyväskylä University. When they meet the circular columns, the rails bend both inwards and upwards. Visually, the reason is not obvious,

Finlandia Hall: the mature Aalto regarded bare metal as unwelcomingly cold to the touch.

Paimio Sanatorium: the rail is authentically Modern, whilst the painting anticipates discoloration by use.

Combining wood and metal was one of Aalto's ways of making user-friendly handrails.

but when you run your hand along a rail you quickly discover that this double movement responds more comfortably to that of hand and arm: had it merely deflected sideways it would have felt – although not looked – awkward. Aalto was convinced that it was by attending to such 'small details of life' that significant architectural ideas could be discovered, and his concerns find a telling echo in Theodor Adorno's reflections on the growing brutalization of life by crudely conceived technology: 'What does it mean', Adorno asked in *Minima Moralia*, 'that there are no more casement windows to open, but only sliding frames to shove, no gentle latches but turnable handles, no forecourt, no doorstep before the street, no wall around the garden?'[8]

The overt invitations to occupation and appeals to senses other than sight that we find in Aalto's work are far less frequent in much avowedly Modern architecture, at least until recently, but they find frequent echoes in older buildings. Many Renaissance palazzi provide benches for the citizens around their perimeters, and in Florence it was a legal requirement to do so. This example was echoed by McKim, Mead and White on Boston Public Library, completed in 1878, where the bench provides a vivid reminder of the kinship between human limbs and Classical forms. The fact that it can also be read as a moulding that mediates the junction

with the ground happily prevents it being seen as uninvitingly empty when not in use.

The plinths, columns and mouldings of Classical bases frequently invite informal inhabitation, something Aldo van Eyck saw as a mark of the style's inherent 'generosity'.[9] Building on this idea, Herman Hertzberger argues that such seemingly casual opportunities to sit, lean and in other ways use buildings in ways that transcend any narrowly 'functional' reading are a valuable means of enabling us to feel at home with them.[10] Determined to offer forms that invite but never dictate such appropriation, Hertzberger frequently favoured the 'neutrality' of low walls that could double as benches, although in the Vredenburg Music Centre in Utrecht he provided more purpose-designed places to sit and perch. The children in his schools in Delft and on the Apollolaan in Amsterdam happily make inventive and playful use of such invitations to inhabitation, and the square holes in the floors, filled with wooden cubes, which double as tiny seats, are amongst his most felicitous inventions.

Handrail, Jyväskylä University.

Continuous benches along
many Italian buildings create
a habitable edge to public spaces.

Top: Classical mouldings invite
informal use – a sign of their
'generosity', said Aldo van Eyck.

Above: Boston Public Library
by McKim, Mead and White.

Montessori School, Delft,
by Herman Hertzberger: 'play
hole' filled with wooden cubes.

Throughout the Vredenburg
Centre (Utrecht), Hertzberger
created opportunities to sit
and perch.

When making the plywood linings of the waiting rooms for the chapels at the Woodland Crematorium in Stockholm swell into a bench, Gunnar Asplund surely had Classical precedents in mind, perhaps with the added stimulus of the acoustic panelling in the lecture theatre of Aalto's Viipuri Library. There, the timber slats make the opposite journey, billowing across the ceiling like a wooden weather-front and then descending down the end wall. The invitation to sit on Asplund's bench is direct and sensuous, and made all the more appealing by the ease with which plywood appears able to assume such a shape. The *actual* effort of forming it in this way is considerable, but the result seems entirely 'natural', both to the intended use and to a material made of thin laminations.

Plywood was new to architecture in the 1930s, and seen as full of promise. Frank Lloyd Wright considered it offered 'a new lead into a fascinating realm of form',[11] whilst for Richard Neutra it was 'the most significant of the more recently perfected structural items which ushers in a renaissance of wood construction and brings it up to date'.[12] Asplund was, on the whole, less interested in its structural capabilities. For him, plywood offered a recognizably *modern* way of giving new life to traditional forms and uses. For example, throughout the public spaces of the Law Courts extension he added to Gothenburg Town Hall, plywood is used to line walls in a manner that echoes traditional wainscoting. The result, so apt to its use, combines the gravitas of an older, more formal interior, with an unmistakably welcoming and contemporary air.

Asplund's use of timber recalls the way in which many masonry structures – the 'ruins' of Kahn's ideal architecture – are made habitable by 'furnishing' with wood. Viewed in this comprehensive light, such furnishings can be considered to embrace the control of climate through timber-framed roofs, windows and doors; the provision of built-in or 'structural' furniture, such as benches and church pews; and, of course, the lining of walls with timber panelling. In the Mellon Center for British Art at Yale University, Kahn used oak panelling to create an ambience appropriate for pictures, many of which had first been displayed in English country houses, whilst few buildings of any period can offer more compelling or inventive examples of such timber 'furnishings' than those of Charles Rennie Mackintosh's Glasgow School of Art, from the cubic cage of the main staircase to the carpentry 'forest' of the library.

The appeal of materials may be thermal as well as visual or tactile. In climates of hot days and cool nights, thick stone walls are welcome

Timber panelling turns into bench (Gunnar Asplund: waiting room, Woodland Crematorium).

Stone made habitable by carpentry: library in Glasgow School of Art by Charles Rennie Mackintosh.

The hard-surfaced, reverberant main gallery of the Thorvaldsen Museum sounds vast.

Modern, yet familiar: plywood
lining of public spaces
at Gothenburg Town Hall
extension.

Like old stone churches, Reima
Pietilä's Kaleva Church in
Tampere, Finland, is furnished
with timber.

reservoirs of 'coolth', whereas in the north
their coldness was traditionally ameliorated
by hanging the walls with fabrics or lining
them with an insulating material such as wood.
Further south, on the other hand, the display
of fabrics and carpets might be reserved for
special occasions: hence we learn that Piero de'
Medici received visitors by hanging the walls
of his palazzo with 'tapestries . . . rich cloths
of gold, of silver and silk' and by covering floors
and balconies with decorative carpets.[13]

Materials also dramatically affect the sound
of rooms. Except in performance spaces such
as concert halls and theatres, where acoustic
considerations are of paramount importance,
this is probably the least consciously considered
aspect of architecture. Yet the impact on
our perceptions of space and 'atmosphere'
is immediate. Vaulted, hard-surfaced and
populated with marble figures, the reverberant
interior of Bindesbøll's Thorvaldsen Museum
sounds vaster than any comparably scaled
space in Copenhagen: the suggestion of Roman
grandeur is entirely appropriate in this home
for Neoclassical sculptures, but it would be
unnerving as a place for mere mortals to live.

By playing on our expectations, the
Thorvaldsen Museum sounds bigger than
it appears, whereas in Norman Foster's far larger
Sainsbury Centre for the Visual Arts in Norwich,

Kahn specified oak panelling
for the Mellon Center at Yale
University to evoke memories
of English country houses.

Jørn Utzon's unrealized
acoustic ceilings for Sydney
Opera House were shaped
to distribute sound and
intended to be made of
structural plywood box-beams.

Sainsbury Centre for the Visual
Arts, University of East Anglia,
by Norman Foster.

England, you experience the opposite. The vast, metallic space sounds almost claustrophobic, as your voice seems to die in the air in front of you. The explanation is technical not material: electronically generated 'white noise', designed to suppress the sound of chatter and feet, is used to promote an atmosphere conducive to contemplation and study. Practically, the result is clearly a success, but the discrepancy between what our eyes expect and what our ears hear is slightly disconcerting.

Although electronic means of manipulating reverberation times are increasingly common, especially to cope with the varied needs of different types of music, the basic acoustics of performance spaces are still initially established by specifying more or less reflective or absorbent materials. The deep, marble-clad fronts of the 'cubic clouds' that form the balconies in Aalto's Finlandia Hall, for example, are calculated to reflect sound, which their occupants would otherwise absorb. In designing the tragically unrealized interiors of Sydney Opera House, Utzon faced a double problem: the ceilings had both to reflect sound throughout the interior and exclude noise from the surrounding harbour.

The solution was found nearby, in a factory that had developed unique ways of bonding plywood and metal to give added strength or acoustic performance. Layered with lead, plywood could provide the requisite sound exclusion, whilst its structural properties could be exploited to create rippling 'acoustic beams' with similar reflective properties to the richly ornamented bowed fronts of Baroque and Edwardian theatres.[14] For the interior of the Melli Bank he designed in Teheran, Utzon needed to absorb rather than reflect sound, and instructed his assistant to find something rough – 'like the sweater you are wearing' – to soften the sound of the space. A suitably porous, rough brown brick was found, but proved too peasant-like for the client, who ordered it to be replaced with more luxurious-looking acoustic panels.[15]

Several of the topics we have touched on in this brief survey occupy the problematic ground between (more or less) permanent architecture and the generally more ephemeral realm of furnishing and decoration. Despite occasional attempts to regard these two domains as inseparable – as, for example, by exponents of Art Nouveau – they remain practically and, many would argue, properly distinct. For Aldo Rossi, the architect should be 'totally indifferent' to industrial design, decoration and all that belongs to the 'life of the building',[16] and in much contemporary practice the separation is institutionalized in the distinction between the 'shell and core' of envelope, structure and services, and the subsequent 'fit-out' to suit the needs of a particular occupant.

Adolf Loos had a radically different view of these issues, grounded in Semper's ideas on 'dressing'. By correlating architecture and clothing, and declaring 'colourful, woven carpets' the 'true and legitimate representative of the wall', Semper invites us to see the materials that might traditionally be considered merely added decoration as in fact the legitimate makers of architectural space. For Loos, this insight was central, and a catalyst for his most radical innovation, the mode of spatial composition he called the *Raumplan*. Writing about 'The Principle of Cladding' in 1898, Loos

The timber wall panelling and
marble 'cubist cloud' balconies
of Aalto's Finlandia Hall were
designed, respectively, to
absorb and to reflect sound.

used words that might almost have been Semper's: 'The architect's task is to provide a warm and liveable space. Carpets are warm and liveable. He decides for this reason to spread one carpet on the floor and to hang up four to form the four walls.'[17]

Just how literally Loos meant this became clear five years later, when he published the re-modelling of his own apartment in the Viennese magazine *Kunst*. The article included a now famous (to some, notorious) photograph entitled 'My wife's bedroom'. It shows a room almost filled by a thick-pile carpet, which turns up to engulf the bed and is in turn framed by heavily pleated curtains, so substantial that the niche for the bed and bedside tables appears almost literally to have been 'carved' out of them. This was not, in Loos's view, mere decoration, but an *architecture* ideally attuned to the (feminine) use of the space. He happily referred to his thin-slice marble claddings as 'permanent wall-paper',[18] but was trenchant in opposing mere decoration and ornament. Indeed, his love of fine materials was in part motivated by his belief that they eliminated the need for decoration – even the 'most depraved', he argued in his most famous essay, 'Ornament and Crime', would hesitate to decorate materials of intrinsic interest.[19]

With the development of the *Raumplan*,[20] in which the spatial composition evolved around a series of discrete but interlinked volumes on many levels, Loos found a way to allow each room to assume the proportions and materials he considered appropriate to its particular use. This idea matured through a sequence of houses designed in the 1920s and is seen at its most complex and refined in the Müller House of 1930 in Prague. A large, central staircase is usually the pivot of the *Raumplan* composition, and in the main living room of the Müller House, Loos transforms it into a giant block of stone by arranging slabs of his favourite green Cipolin marble – the same as that he used on the exterior of the Looshaus in Vienna – so that their pronounced veining creates a continuous design running right across its length.

Around the stair, the spaces are differentiated by materials that evoke and signify an atmosphere appropriate to their designated use. The lady's reading room, for example, is characterized by light, glazed wood with its grain clearly visible, in striking contrast to the 'seriousness' of the adjacent library, where Loos set dark mahogany against white walls – a more 'public' expression appropriate to this male-dominated world. Walk to the top of the house, and you discover children's bedrooms as cheery in brilliant blue and yellow as anything made around the same time by those Swedish pioneers of liberated, child-centred living, Carl and Karin Larsson.[21]

Although later critics were to interpret the *Raumplan* as a precursor of the 'flowing space' of the modern open plan, nothing could have been further from Loos's mind. In his houses, the links established between rooms by connecting them volumetrically, and by running materials from one into another, cleverly unify what would otherwise be a disconcertingly disparate series of spaces. But they never suggest spatial continuity of the modern kind, nor threaten what to Loos are vital distinctions between rooms designed as monumentally permanent and emphatically material expressions of use.

For Adolf Loos, architecture began with the shaping of rooms in response to different uses, and in the Müller House in Prague the children's bedrooms are finished with brilliant, cheerful colours.

The Müller House's living room
is dominated by the open central
stair – finished in green Cipolin
marble it becomes like a giant,
sculptured block of stone.

Chapter 7
Junctions

Skylight, Gary Group offices,
Culver City, Los Angeles,
by Eric Owen Moss.

Often it is the expressiveness of the jointing which humanizes structures and gives them their friendly feel.
Peter Rice[1]

Detailing the junctions between different materials and surfaces occupies a surprising amount of time on most architectural projects. The task is both practical and formal, as Mies van der Rohe made clear by adopting the truism, 'God is in the details.'[2] The technical use of the word 'detail' entered architectural vocabulary in the eighteenth century, courtesy of the Ecole des Beaux Arts in Paris, where 'details' were likened to words in a language. Just as a piece of literature acquired 'character' through the choice and ordering of words, so, argued French architectural theorists, the character of a building depended greatly on the definition and mutual adjustment of its 'details'. In recognition of their crucial role, Beaux Arts teachers and practitioners developed a special kind of drawing – known as the *analytique* – on which the interrelationships between the different parts of a building were shown at a variety of scales.

When the methods of building were grounded in longstanding craft traditions, it was not unusual for architects to provide only small-scale plans and full-size details of key points in a design, such as the profiles of mouldings, and door- and window-frames, to enable the builder to complete the work.[3] The technical construction details, for which architects are now responsible, could mostly be taken for granted by being executed in accordance with accepted practice. With the advent of industrialization, everything began to change. 'Details' ceased to be matters for craftsmen on site and became the domain of the 'production', or 'working', drawing produced by architects or their draughtsmen – and, increasingly, by engineers. Reacting against the withering of centuries-old traditions of workmanship that this entailed, proponents of the Arts and Crafts sought to return the detail to the domain of the craftsman, who could thereby retain a margin of autonomy within the system of production. William Morris's rejection of the machine had more to do with his absolute opposition to the division of labour, and consequent de-skilling of craftsmen, which came in its wake, than with any narrowly 'aesthetic' consequences of machine work.[4]

Although they originated in response to practical, external stimuli, these contrasting attitudes are reflected in the two basic ways in which architects approach the task of 'detailing'. Either the overall architectural concept is intended to determine every aspect of the design, from spatial and structural configuration down to the smallest details – which are seen as 'reinforcing' or 'reflecting' the overall intention. Or the design is allowed to 'grow' as the guiding idea and appropriate details develop alongside, and mutually modify, each other. The latter approach might seem to be more suited to the use of traditional materials, and is certainly more difficult to sustain on complex, technologically sophisticated buildings, but the difference is essentially a matter of attitude. Mies van der Rohe's work exemplifies the first approach, but the predominantly steel-and-glass buildings of Günter Behnisch frequently demonstrate the kinds of adjustment to local

Construction exposed:
Cartier Foundation, Paris,
by Jean Nouvel.

Constructional form: end-fixings
for post-tensioning cables, shell
plinth, Sydney Opera House.

opportunities of site and programme that are characteristic of the second.[5]

Just as attitudes to matters of detail have been radically changed by the advent of industrialization, so too have the practical demands placed on details. Traditionally, buildings were *built*, now they are increasingly *assembled*: whereas materials were once worked, or at least could be adjusted and finished on site, now they increasingly come as pre-formed components or assemblies, which admit of little or no modification – and certainly not of the kinds that can be effected outside a specialist fabricator's workshop. Sensing the growing difficulty of quality control, Viollet-le-Duc looked forward to the large-scale, off-site prefabrication of building assemblies and components,[6] and whilst it could be argued that nothing built in the twentieth century was as compelling a demonstration of the potential of industrialized building as the Crystal Palace, industrial methods have now penetrated most aspects of construction. Compared with more sophisticated industries, contemporary building sites may appear (and often be) messy and inefficient, but they have far more in common with the factory than with the world of medieval guilds.

For all that has changed, however, the basic issues to be considered in detailing the junctions between materials and components have not:

'at the level of detail', as James Gowan has remarked, 'the language is common'.[7] Materials still change shape and size in response to changes in temperature and humidity, and fixings and junctions must allow for this movement. In the case of a non-porous stone such as granite this may be so minimal as to be insignificant; in the case of timber, especially increasingly poorly-weathered timber, it is almost always critical. The consequences of the failure to account for such movements can be dramatic and unexpected. For reasons that (so far as I am aware) still elude satisfactory explanation, the thin sheets of white Italian marble that Alvar Aalto specified for the cladding of Finlandia Hall in Helsinki began to bow and then spring their fixings, necessitating their replacement less than 30 years after completion.[8]

The Italian marble on Aalto's Finlandia Hall in Helsinki gradually bowed and had to be replaced.

Lutheran Seminary, Stuttgart, by Günther Behnisch.

Frame and cladding: building under construction, Philadelphia, 1992.

Apartments, 860 Lake Shore Drive, Chicago, by Mies van der Rohe.

Achieving the perfectly spherical
surfaces of Sydney Opera House
required extreme precision
in the hidden fixings for the
precast concrete 'tile lids'.

Cast steel gerberette,
Pompidou Centre, Paris,
by Piano and Rogers.

Junctions not only have to account for thermal and other types of movement, they must also allow for tolerances in the manufacture and working of materials and components. Steel may be cut to within a fraction of a millimetre of a specified size, whereas in situ concrete walls are typically cast to tolerances of plus or minus ten millimetres (three-eighths of an inch), and even pre-cast concrete components are rarely produced to tolerances better than double this. The 'abstract' planes demanded by much modern design are especially unforgiving, because any deviation is immediately perceived as a defect, and there are no mouldings to cover discrepancies. To achieve the perfectly smooth spherical surfaces Utzon called for on Sydney Opera House, the pre-cast 'tile lids' were packed on shims at each corner. And to determine the depth of shims required, the following day's fixing points were surveyed at the end of each day's work, and the dimensions sent to be calculated overnight on one of Sydney's only two suitable computers (it *was* the mid 1960s!).[9]

With massive members, it may still be sufficient simply to place 'stone on stone' – the basis of ancient 'trilithons' such as Stonehenge. More typically, such structural junctions lead to the practical and aesthetic refinements exemplified by, say, the Greek Doric order –

with its 'swelling' capitals to receive the load – or by the intricate carpentry of traditional Japanese architecture, designed to allow for movement during earthquakes. Nowadays, with craft skills at a premium, the traditional role of joinery is frequently replaced by purpose-made connectors, such as the steel plates, shoes and bolts commonly associated with structural timberwork. Such secondary connecting elements can play a major role in the architecture, none more so than the massive cast-steel 'gerberettes', which join columns to beams and an array of counteracting tie-rods on the Pompidou Centre in Paris.

Architecturally considered, most junctions in buildings embrace formal as well as technical issues, and design responses can be said to fall somewhere on a scale between 'celebration' and 'suppression': in doing so they define much of the character of the resulting architecture.

Column meets beam:
stone capital, Karnak, Egypt.

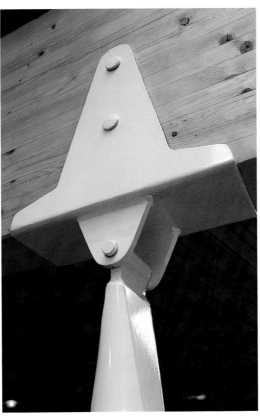

Metal connector, refectory,
Stockholm University,
by Ralph Erskine.

Paired timbers ensure loads
remain axial: chapel, Helsinki
Technical University, by Kaija
and Heikki Sirén.

The eye is acutely sensitive to joints in or between materials, and the effects of even the slightest systematic marks in a surface can be considerable. Take the case of external rendering, for example. Traditional materials allowed entire walls to be covered without visible lines between different work sessions, whereas many modern renders require 'daywork' joints, radically changing the possible aesthetic effect.[10] In a stone building such as the Cistercian abbey of Le Thoronet in southern France, the stone joints are so fine that the walls appear almost as homogeneous as the solid walls cut directly in the earth by early Ethiopian Christians. Many architects are now experimenting with structural members assembled off-site and held together by post-tensioning wires. On Portcullis House, designed by Michael Hopkins to provide additional space for British Members of Parliament, the joints might almost be taken for cladding, whereas on a new building in the City of London by Eric Parry the erratically placed columns appear almost monolithic.

Before they became part of a language of ornament, architraves and skirting-boards were means of masking potentially unsightly junctions between different materials. Orthodox modern architecture, by contrast, generally favoured keeping materials apart rather than

Top: The fine stone joints of Le Thoronet create homogeneous walls as a canvas for light.

Above: Wall without joints: rock-cut Church of St George in the pit, Lālibalā, Ethiopia.

Prefabricated columns made of post-tensioned stone blocks at Portcullis House, London, by Michael Hopkins.

Post-tensioned stone columns with suppressed joints at 30 Finsbury Square, London, by Eric Parry.

letting them meet, as, for example, in the once ubiquitous 'shadow gap' joints between door linings, skirtings and walls. The motivation was partly the 'honest' refusal to cover construction, but mostly the desire to present surfaces as abstract, flat planes. The formal objectives were at odds with an easily damaged material such as plaster, necessitating the introduction of metal 'stop beads' to give the tradesmen a line to work to, and to prevent mechanical damage to the vulnerable exposed edge.

Although consistency in detailing is generally considered a defining feature of buildings of architectural merit, the attitude to consistency may allow for variations in the handling of different junctions. Some may be emphasized, whilst others are underplayed, in the same 'consistently' detailed building: to demand otherwise is to risk the entire ensemble degenerating into a cacophony of overstated details. Mies van der Rohe, for example, made much of the way steel sections turn corners, but happily allowed them to disappear without elaboration into the ground – much as the cruciform columns of the Barcelona Pavilion pass neatly and unceremoniously through the floor with no suggestion of support. In Can Lis, as we noted earlier, whilst Utzon was generally keen to reveal the nature of the construction and used exposed lintels as an element of the

architectural order, on the openings that frame the primary views, the structural means are suppressed (see page 112).

For Louis Kahn, 'adoration of the joint' was the beginning of properly architectural ornament and a means of recognizing in the finished building the process by which it had been built – exemplified by his detailing of concrete at the Salk Institute, which we discussed in Chapter 3. Kahn's prescription applies equally well to traditional buildings. Many of the mouldings and other elements of the Classical style developed from refinements of the practical necessities of building, such as mastering joints, shedding water and providing support, and only in the hands of the most sophisticated Mannerist

Top: Articulate corner: 860 Lake Shore Drive by Mies van der Rohe.

Above: Column/floor junction, Barcelona Pavilion.

Junctions revealed: frameless door laid over concrete structure in Jørn Utzon's Bagsværd Church.

Junctions mastered: timber mouldings, ESTEC centre, Nordwijk, The Netherlands, by Aldo van Eyck.

can they happily lose all contact with some feeling for these origins. Gothic roof bosses were likewise means of disguising the potentially awkward junctions between several ribs before they were taken as opportunities for ornamentation. Their elimination by late Gothic masons in favour of ribs that deftly fly past or through each other was certainly an expression of the impetus towards 'dematerialization' we noted in Chapter 2 – but it was also a bravura demonstration of that virtuosity in cutting stone which enabled them to dispense with the necessity of 'adoring' the joints through ornamental elaboration.

As architects came to terms with appropriate ways of expressing the cladding of surfaces with thin stone, decisions about the expression of the junctions between panels, and of the means of fixing them, were vital to the architectural effect. By opting to express the bolts that acted as temporary fixings, and by giving each piece of stone a shallow profile like a flattened baluster, Otto Wagner's Post Office Savings Bank in Vienna made its mode of construction abundantly clear. In the Stoclet House in Brussels, Josef Hoffmann, like Adolf Loos, took the opposite route, suppressing all joints and fixings, but using a figured stone and 'binding' the edges with a rope-like moulding. Anyone with the least familiarity with stone would immediately recognize that these could not possibly be other than thin sheets, and hence unashamedly 'modern'.

On the Zacherl House – the first building in Vienna to be clad entirely in granite – Jože Plečnik adopted a middle course, dispensing with the mortar that, once set, actually held Wagner's cladding in place. He opted instead for concealed iron fixings backed up by small, T-shaped granite strips, which both covered the joints between panels and helped to restrain them. This detail was almost certainly motivated, at least in part, by Semper's descriptions of the Egyptians' decoration of smooth granite pylons with rod-like profiles – which, characteristically, he explained as a derivation from carpentry (the result is reminiscent of 'board and batten' construction).

As Otto Wagner's bank demonstrates, even small fixings, rhythmically repeated, can play a major role in the visual expression of a building. The effect of the insistent repetition of the bolt-head covers is highly decorative – and, as Ákos Moravánszky points out, so felicitous that it prompted purely ornamental imitations, such as the ceramic knobs on a corner shop in Budapest, completed by József and László Vágó in 1909.[11] The massed rivets of plated-steel structures greatly add to the impression of strength, and also offer

Top: Adoration of the joint: roof bosses, Exeter Cathedral, England.

Above: Intersecting ribs, Vladislav Hall, Prague Castle, by Benedikt Ried.

Top: Granite cladding and fixings/cover strips, Zacherl House, Prague, by Jože Plečnik.

Above: Thin stone cladding 'bound' by edge mouldings: Palais Stoclet, Brussels, by Josef Hoffmann.

Riveted steel-plate construction, Tyne Bridge, Newcastle-upon-Tyne.

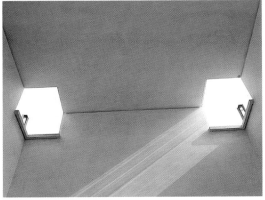

the satisfying feeling of being able to grasp how, and with what effort, the structure was assembled. This satisfaction is not so readily afforded by many modern structures, where welding frequently eliminates more expressive joints. By comparison with older designs such as the Tyne (England) and Sydney Harbour Bridges – both made by the Yorkshire firm of Dorman Long – the suave forms of Santiago Calatrava's structures appear plastic, like large-scale pieces of industrial design, and it comes as no surprise to learn that some of their members are more decorative than rigorously structural.[12]

Modern architecture affords no more sustained exploration of the expressive possibilities of junctions and joints than the work of Carlo Scarpa. At the Gipsoteca Canoviana in Possagno, Italy, two corner-junctions of wall and roof planes were dissolved and expressed as a glass cube. Wright – Scarpa's acknowledged master – would doubtless have approved this miniature example of 'the destruction of the box', but it was no mere show of virtuosity. By washing the walls with light, it enabled Scarpa to reverse the normal tonality of plaster casts, allowing them to appear as solid figures against a bright background, rather than as the more familiar deathly white against a coloured ground.

In the Castelvecchio in Verona, the junctions between materials – or, more accurately, the consistent refusal to allow different materials to meet directly – become the means of giving expressive life to the building's history.[13] Different phases of the site's construction are exposed by cuts – as, for example, in the glazed slot between the tower and wall in the northeast corner, next to the river. Where a new section of roof is required, it is made of copper, not tile, and seems to have been slid out from below the existing roof. New staircases are made to appear to float above or between floors, whilst existing ones are renewed by laying new, crisply delineated stones over the old, which – like the new floors throughout the Museum – follow a strictly orthogonal geometry and stop short at their ends to reveal the previous layer of history.

Top: New copper roof sliding out from below old tiled roof, Castelvecchio, Verona, by Carlo Scarpa.

Above: Corners dissolved: Canova plaster-cast gallery, Possagno, Italy, by Carlo Scarpa.

In the Canova plaster-cast gallery, Scarpa uses corner windows to wash the walls with light.

Even with wholly new elements of construction, Scarpa generally introduced a third, in-between, element to effect junctions. The rails that protect a glazed opening above an excavation in the ground floor, for example, are loosely hung from sturdy steel uprights, their frailty reinforcing psychologically the warning of the minimal physical barrier. Elsewhere, metal fixings are made to step sideways, or paired to receive other members. On the bridge into the Querini Stampalia Library in Venice the same principle dictates that the timber handrail is made in straight sections and joined by bronze castings, rather than 'scrolling' the wood itself to effect a change of direction in the traditional manner. Scarpa's work required a level of craft skill that is now almost unobtainable in the developed world, save for major restoration projects, but the union of constructional means and expressive ends remains a potent example of the way in which a compelling and richly varied whole may emerge from paying exhaustive attention to its parts. Operating within the framework of an existing building clearly facilitated this way of working, and it has to be said that none of Scarpa's new-build projects comes close to the quality he achieved in his transformations of existing fabrics.

The earth is the inescapable context for buildings, and mediating the junction between ground and building offers manifold expressive possibilities. All buildings require some kind of foundation, but it is not generally thought necessary to express this fact – indeed in his work in Dacca especially, Louis Kahn often seemed to enjoy dumping his buildings rather unceremoniously on the ground in the Roman manner.[14] Ruskin considered a clear expression of the foundation essential: it is 'most necessary', he wrote in *The Stones of Venice*, 'that this great element of security should be visible to the eye.'[15] He likened the effect to that of an animal's paw,[16] and this principle was studiously observed by Frank Lloyd Wright in his Prairie Houses. Wright's walls almost invariably rested on a visible stone base, and he saw the resulting 'earth line' as an expression of the building's attachment to the ground[17] – its horizontality was reinforced by similarly emphatic timber or stone copings.

Mies van der Rohe's Farnsworth House, in total contrast, expresses a sublime detachment from the earth, and its columns therefore disappear unceremoniously into the grass. Much the same, of course, is true of the Villa Savoye, where Le Corbusier despatched the pilotis straight through gravel. Like many traditional Japanese houses, the Katsura Detached Villa in Kyoto also has suspended floors raised significantly above the ground. But there the

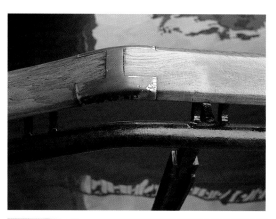

Top: Brass connector on the handrail of the bridge into Scarpa's Querini Stampaglia Foundation, Venice.

Above: New meets old: floor junction, Castelvecchio, Verona.

In the Castelvecchio, Scarpa protects this opening in the floor with conspicuously fragile railings.

Articulation of the in-between: railing/wall junction in the Castelvecchio.

Above: Interaction
of architecture and nature:
Katsura Detached Villa, Kyoto.

junction between column and ground is turned to totally different expressive ends. By shaping their ends to lock tightly onto an un-worked stone, the columns become an expression of the reconciliation of architecture and nature – at one with the diffusion of the building's geometry into the surroundings, and with the countervailing and seemingly random encroachment of stones, which interrupt the lines of steps and walls.

Practically, of course, the timber columns at Katsura demanded the protection from damp that the stone bases afforded, whereas steel and concrete can more easily be made to perform a constructional disappearing act. But the differences in making convey radical differences in meaning: the Villa Savoye and Farnsworth House remain avatars of universality in architecture, whereas Katsura declares a Shinto-inspired devotion to the spirits of place and matter. The economies of modern construction may have eliminated many of the possibilities open to earlier builders, but carefully considered junctions and detailing remain a basic discipline of the architect's craft, and retain their expressive potential.

Top: Articulation of materials
by function: bridge into Querini
Stampaglia Foundation.

Above: Detachment from
the earth: Farnsworth House
by Mies van der Rohe.

The walls of Wright's Robie
House in Chicago rest on visible
stone foundations.

Chapter 8
Surfaces

Inspired by Islamic architecture, the shells of Sydney Opera House are clad with more than a million tiles.

*Oh, those Greeks! They knew how to live.
What is required for that is to stop courageously
at the surface, the fold, the skin, to adore
appearance, to believe in forms, tones, words,
the whole Olympus of appearance. Those
Greeks were superficial – out of profundity.*
Friedrich Nietzsche[1]

Above the entrance of the Schullin
Jewellery shop, which Hans Hollein completed
in 1974 in Graben, one of Vienna's most
fashionable shopping streets, the brownish
black granite cladding is fissured to reveal
receding layers of differently coloured brass
penetrated by stainless-steel tubes that act
as intakes for the air conditioning. The image
is evocative, at once erotic and geological: the
voluptuous brass layers suggest liquidity, an
image of those primordial magma flows, from
which granites condensed.

Flat and polished to perfect smoothness,
the granite's shiny surface is also 'geological',
concealing a mountainous, if unusually rounded,
landscape in miniature. The eye can focus on
surface or inner landscape, but not both at the
same time – a slightly disconcerting effect, like
the double exposure of a photograph that has
been moved slightly during development.[2] The
illusory space created by the granite's polished
surface is ideally suited to enhancing the allure

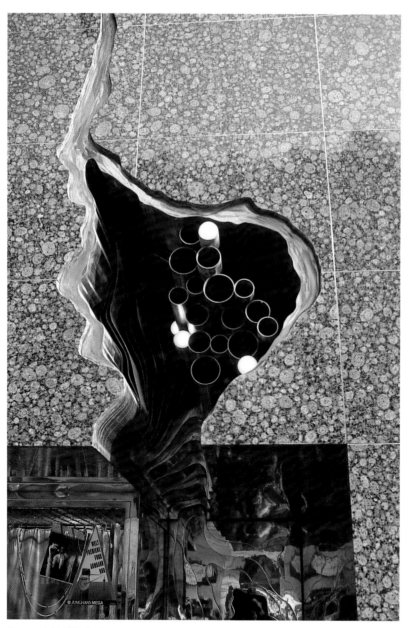

Above and right: The frontage
of Hans Hollein's Schullin
Jewellery shop in Vienna
is an alluring invitation to enter.

of this tiny temple to luxury consumption. But on many buildings where polished granite is used as a hard-wearing and easily cleaned cladding, often at ground level, such a disjunction between the actual and apparent surface is damaging to the intended impression of solidity.

Hollein's shop-front plays with several aspects of building surfaces. The cladding is intrinsically appealing, made as it is of the kind of fine material that Adolf Loos believed would replace ornament in an industrial civilization, and the chosen finish – polishing – is crucial to the intended effect. At the same time the surface has been opened to suggest 'hidden' depths, persuading us that it is also an intimation of the interior that lies in wait: Hollein certainly does not disappoint, the shop being every bit as luxurious as its entrance.

In a commercial setting such as a jewellery shop we have come to expect polished surfaces and rich materials, but in general our culture and language teach us to be suspicious of judging by appearance, of coming to 'superficial' assessments based on the surfaces of things. Rather than dwell on the direct, sensuous appeal of colour, texture and material, the 'discerning eye' is educated to value the forms and spaces that surfaces define, and to scrutinize them for revelations of internal structure. As with natural organisms, the skin is 'read' as a sign of inner organization: Berlage used precisely this biological analogy in arguing that the cladding of a building should not be, as he put it, a 'loose cover that would fully deny the natural construction', but be 'grown together with the interior structure'.[3]

In Modern architecture, the 'interior structure' was the spatial composition, not just the physical means of support, and its expression should be, as Hitchcock and Johnson specified in defining the formal characteristics of 'The International Style', 'an effect of volume, or more accurately, of plane surfaces bounding a volume'.[4] Black and white photography of early Modern architecture promoted the belief that their surfaces were a uniform white veil, whereas several leading Modern architects used colour extensively as a means of breaking cubic forms down into different planes. At Pessac, Le Corbusier not only broke down the boxiness of the individual houses with colour, but also deployed it to make them advance or recede as part of an overall urban composition of volumes in space.

Bruno Taut's houses at the Weissenhof in Stuttgart (above) and Le Corbusier's at Pessac (right) illustrate the use of colour to create the impression of a volume bounded by plane surfaces.

The Villa Savoye epitomizes
the Modernist ideal of spatial
richness contained by taut
surfaces.

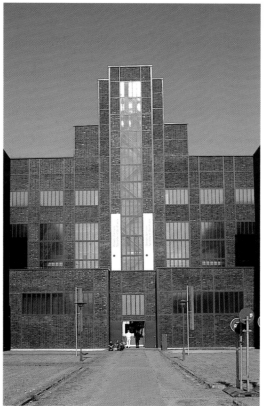

Zeche Zollverein mineworks
near Essen: massive,
but treated as a composition
of flat surfaces.

Asplund set the window-frames
of the Karl Johan School
in Gothenburg flush with
the wall-plane.

To present the bounding surfaces as 'stretched planes' and not gravity-bound supporting walls, they were made as thin as possible and designed to create an unbroken effect. Hence the preference for bands of ribbon windows – Le Corbusier's *fenêtres en longueurs* – and for placing the window frames at the outer rather than inner edge of the walls, so that the glass becomes part of the surface. The aim was precisely the opposite of traditional windows, where the frames were deeply set to reveal the wall's thickness and produce a strong shadow, and generally sufficiently widely spaced so as not to threaten either the structural or visual integrity of the wall plane.

The planar character of the new architecture was also stressed by suppressing any suggestion of material weight. For the most part this meant using smooth stucco – with the consequences for weathering that so troubled Pevsner – but it could equally effectively be conveyed by the smooth, jointless, thin-stone cladding favoured by Adolf Loos. Indeed, the texture and scale of large sheets of polished stone was found to combine very effectively with sheets of glass to form a slick, continuous skin – as seen, for example, on the base of Howe and Lescaze's PSFS Building in Philadelphia (best known, thanks to Robert Venturi, for its huge roof-top sign[5]). Such usages were a perfect fulfilment of Otto Wagner's prediction that Modern architecture would be characterized by 'panel-like treatment of surfaces' and 'the greatest simplicity'.[6] Influenced by the Bauhaus, some of the finest German industrial buildings of the 1930s – such as those at the Zeche Zollverein mineworks near Essen – achieved a similar lightness and volumetric quality using flat planes of brickwork.

The Modernist emphasis on surface-as-plane, and its realization through light construction and continuous bands of glazing, were, of course, made easier by frame construction. But the aesthetic goal was not bound to these technological means, and

in Scandinavia during the 1920s – before the widespread penetration of the new ideas from further south in 1927 – precisely analogous goals were pursued as part of that 'light' style that made its international debut at the 'Paris Exhibition of Decorative Arts' in 1925. Dubbed 'Swedish Grace' by the editors of the English *Architectural Review*, and, following a 1982 travelling exhibition,[7] now generally referred to as Nordic Classicism, it took some of its inspiration from the almost equally 'light' Classicism of many of the buildings documented in Paul Mebes's influential book *Um 1800*, published in 1920.[8] The emphasis on clarity of volume and proportion as 'eternal' architectural disciplines was much the same as that of the Modernists, echoing the call for a return to Classical values following the Great War, and also reflecting a local reaction against the massive, granite walls adopted as expressions of national identity around the turn of the century (of which more in the next chapter).

Stucco was again generally the preferred finish, and the windows – albeit as holes in the wall rather than ribbons of glazing – were frequently set flush with the surface. On the Karl Johan's School in Gothenburg, completed in 1924, Asplund achieved something almost equally immaterial with walls of thin, buff-coloured Roman bricks, but generally the Nordic Classicists suppressed any expression of the material. Explaining his choice of colour for the

The seamless plastered drum of Asplund's Stockholm Public Library appears weightless.

Ivar Tengbom aimed to dematerialize Stockholm Concert Hall by painting it 'the colour of condensed air'.

Polished granite and flush glazing form a slick skin on Howe and Lescaze's PSFS Building.

new Concert Hall in Stockholm, Ivar Tengbom said that he wanted a blue 'like condensed air',[9] and in the interior of the city's new Public Library, Asplund achieved an even greater feeling of weightlessness: the drum, legible and all-enveloping around its lower, book-lined stages, dissolves into an atmosphere of white light above.

These and similar expressions of dematerialization have, as we discussed in Chapter 2, been a recurring theme throughout architectural history. The sense of dissolution of mass and feeling of weightlessness is frequently induced by the use of all-over colour and pattern, as for example in Islamic tilework – of which the Moorish Alhambra Palace in Granada, Spain, provides a wide range of superlative examples – and in the Chinese fondness for painting structural timbers – a practice that transforms the interior of the circular Temple of Heaven in Beijing into a delirium of colour. Visits to the mosques of Iran were crucial to Jørn Utzon's decision to tile the spherical surfaces of Sydney Opera House's 'shells'. For the individual tiles, Utzon likened the result he was after to the contrast between smooth, freshly fallen snow and the glistening, lumpier surface of frozen snow exposed by the wind. He found a precedent for such an effect in half-glazed Japanese ceramics,

but it took three years' of development work by the Swedish tile-makers Höganäs to achieve the precise quality he wanted. Incorporating a crushed chamotte (a fine aggregate produced by crushing previously fired clay) produced a 'live' surface, which showed through the subsequent glazing – rather like the 'mountains' below the polished surface of granite. The desired contrast between glazed and matt areas is produced by using unglazed ones along the edges of the fan-shaped 'tile-lids' – unlike the glazed tiles, their edges do not chip and crumble when cut.

The result is stunning, one of the most radiant and alive surfaces in architecture, yet – as Berlage would have it – 'completely grown together with the structure', so that the lines of matt tiles describe the underlying geometry of the concrete structural ribs which support the shells. As passing clouds, the sun or viewer move by, the surfaces glow, gleam or flash with light. From closer to, successive waves of tiles scintillate like diamonds or tiny stars. Move closer still and focus on a single tile, and miniature constellations appear and disappear below the gently undulating surface. Devoid of colour, yet uniquely receptive to the colours of light and sky, the shells present an ever-changing spectacle. Walk down the narrow 'street' between the halls and you feel as if you might almost be moving between blue shade

The tiled shells of Sydney Opera House are exceptionally responsive to changes in light.

The key to Sydney Opera House's responsiveness to light lies in the combination of specially developed tiles. The glazed ones, almost colourless but richly textured, are uncut and bordered by plain matt tiles, cut to fit the segmental geometry.

Sgrafitto, made by scratching away an upper layer of wet plaster, transforms building surfaces into giant drawings, as seen here in a 'rusticated' building in Prague (above left) and on the main building of the ETH in Zürich (above).

Mosques are typically rendered as shimmering tiled surfaces: Dome of the Rock, Jerusalem (left).

and mountains of glistening ice, broken by cast shadows, which glow mysteriously with pools of light reflected from a sunny neighbour. Wait for evening, and the fading sunlight seems to linger, caressing and colouring the tiles as cream and ochre give way to salmon pink and the palest of violets.

The vitality of Utzon's shells depends crucially upon the contrast between the matt and glazed tiles, but on Aalto's Town Hall in Seinäjoki, a related effect is achieved using a single, dark blue tile of his own design – which is also encountered frequently, and in various colours, in Aalto's interiors (a fact that surely has nothing to do with the royalties he received by specifying it!). The tile is convex in form and, laid vertically, the organically swelling curves and horizontal joints are vaguely reminiscent of the growth rings of bamboo. Seen head-on, the broad, white joints are clearly visible, but when viewed obliquely the tiles can present a solid wall of intense blue. Add to these basic geometric facts the varied ways in which the glazed surface responds to the light, and the overall effect is like large-scale corduroy, mutating from solid, shiny blue, to striations of blue and white, to a matt grey-brown. And as with Utzon's tiles, the changes occur as you move around the building, animating what might otherwise have been a slightly ponderous mass.

Aalto clad Seinäjoki Town Hall with curved, dark blue ceramic tiles which, reacting to light like corduroy, appear by turns a brownish grey (above) and blue-black (right).

The technique of *sgraffito* – 'scratchwork' – turns entire façades into giant drawings. This involves covering a wall with coloured plaster, and then adding a coat of wet plaster onto which a design is drawn and, whilst still wet, scraped away to reveal the coloured layer below. *Sgraffito* was used to transform the main building of the ETH in Zürich into a didactic display of scientific heroes, whilst, in an amusing inversion of 'proper' usage, the upper floor of a building in Prague Castle was given graphic 'rustication', complete with shadows – echoing similar, essentially decorative, applications of rustication across entire façades.

Rustication is normally used to emphasize the strength of a wall, but stone can equally well be carved to give the opposite effect. Nowhere, arguably, has this been achieved more delicately than on the exquisite Getty family tomb in Chicago by Louis Sullivan, where the upper half of the tiny building is made to appear as a stone veil, light as lace. As with most carved ornament, Sullivan's motifs stand proud of the stone surface, which has been cut away to produce them. Adrian Stokes has drawn attention to a different tradition – seen, for example in the work of Agostino di Duccio at the Tempio Malatestiano in Rimini – in which the carving is more like a process of 'thinning' into shallow, layered planes. Throughout its long

years of development, Ancient Egyptian architecture resolutely took a different approach: unwilling, one presumes, to sacrifice the wall surface to three-dimensional carving, the Egyptian masters opted to incise their motifs, as if in a large-scale engraving – the resulting effect is seen at its most dramatic in grazing sunlight.

The contrast between rectilinear wall planes and the intricate, natural patterns found in many stones has provided some of the most satisfying surfaces in modern architecture. For Adolf Loos, as we have noted already, the decorative qualities of marbles and wood veneers were a replacement for ornament. On the Bank of Denmark, Arne Jacobsen exploited these qualities to suggest a restrained sense of luxury, heightening the smooth, yet highly figured, sheets of Norwegian Porsgrunn marble by contrasting them with strongly textured paving of granite setts. Although it is manifestly heavy, we read the stone as a patterned surface rather than a weighty substance, much as we do in one of the last century's most celebrated buildings, Mies van der Rohe's Barcelona Pavilion. For all the rhetoric of the Heroic Period about the 'truth' of structure, the Pavilion is experienced as a space shaped by reflections and figures, real and virtual, in the elusive surfaces of polished stone, chrome and the almost imperceptibly tinted planes of glass.[10]

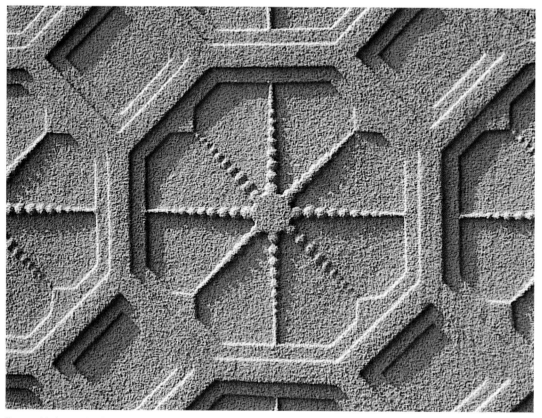

The exquisitely carved surfaces (above) of Louis Sullivan's Getty Tomb in Chicago (right) suggest a delicate, lace-like veil.

Top: The incised motifs on the buildings of Ancient Egypt preserve the integrity of the wall surface.

The Barcelona Pavilion is exceptional in rendering almost every vertical surface reflective, but juxtapositions of shiny/reflective and matt materials have, of course, been widely exploited to give life to surfaces at a variety of scales. On Mackintosh's Glasgow School of Art, the library's west-facing oriel windows catch the sun to appear as scintillating cages of light set against the grey-brown stone, whilst on a commercial development facing Vienna Cathedral, Hans Hollein peels away the matt cladding panels to reveal mirror glass. The result recalls the 'geode' effect of the tiny office tower at his masterpiece, Mönchengladbach Museum, where stone is cracked open to reveal reflective metal and glass.

One of the most frequently recurring treatments of wall surfaces is horizontal banding with contrasting materials or colours. For Ruskin, it was the one 'deeply suggestive' form of decoration, which followed 'naturally' from the wall's construction.[11] It might have originated, he suggested, with the alternation of stronger and weaker materials, such as that of bricks and pebbles in the walls of Verona,[12] and – like the rings of a tree – reflects the wall's 'growth'. The latter idea finds intriguing confirmation in Japanese examples, which Ruskin could not have known: painted bands on walls, which reflect the hidden courses of tiles used to bind the materials at intervals up the wall's height. Whatever its origins or associations, in the West horizontal banding is a recurring feature of building elevations, from the Romanesque of Pisa and Orvieto to the present.

Despite his fervent advocacy of horizontal banding, it could be argued that it breaks what Ruskin called 'the first great principle of architectural colour', namely that it should be 'visibly independent of form. Never paint a column with vertical stripes, but always cross it.'[13] Echoing the principle of colouring-by-coursing, Romanesque Italian *campanili* offer fine examples of such 'crossed' forms, as, on a finer scale, do the remarkable flagpoles that Plečnik designed for Prague Castle.

Top: To clad the Bank of Denmark, Arne Jacobsen chose richly figured Norwegian marble.

Above: On Glasgow School of Art, Mackintosh contrasts the matt grey-brown stone with reflective glass.

The Barcelona Pavilion (top) is a composition of reflective, transparent and translucent surfaces.

On the office tower of Hollein's Mönchengladbach Museum the stone cladding is cracked open to reveal crystalline glass.

The white bands on this wall in Nara, Japan, mark the lines of binding tiles within the construction.

As several of the examples already discussed suggest, the appearance of building surfaces can be dramatically transformed by what might seem relatively minor variations. With brickwork, for example, variations in texture and the choice of mortar and pointing are crucial to the overall effect. Michel de Klerk's Eigen Haard housing in Amsterdam, for example, exploits the contrast between plain, almost white mortar and strongly coloured bricks to emphasize pattern and celebrate the virtuoso bricklaying technique that went into its making. The impact of the repeated 'zippers' up the façades – created by narrow headers, which stand out markedly by comparison with the unusually long stretchers – is also greatly heightened by the contrast between bricks and mortar.

At the opposite end of the spectrum from de Klerk is the Art Museum in Gothenburg, for which Sigfrid Ericson chose roughly textured, buff-coloured bricks, which blend with the flush-pointed joints to produce an homogeneous, stone-like character. The bricks of Jensen-Klint's Grundtvig Church in Copenhagen have a similar colour, but they are harder and smoother, resulting in surfaces that emphasize the integrity of the individual bricks as the units of construction. At Hilversum Town Hall, Willem Dudok opted to recess the horizontal joints, with results that, even at a distance, clearly inflect the crisp, planar effect of the volumetric composition.

The walls of Sir John Soane's Dulwich Picture Gallery are made with London stock bricks, and its surface seems to vibrate with their unpredictable local colours. 'Contemplating a wall of London stocks', James Gowan has mused, 'I feel as if I can solve the problems of the universe.'[14] The subtlety – one is tempted to say the 'life' – of such a wall would be largely lost if either the individual bricks or their courses were emphasized by recessed pointing: the vitality of building surfaces frequently hangs on just such fine adjustments.

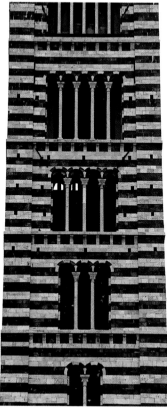

Horizontal banding is a perennial mode of enrichment: campanile, Siena Cathedral.

Kontula Church, Finland, by Käpy and Simo Paavilainen.

Top: House at Ligornetto, Ticino, Switzerland, by Mario Botta.

Above: Extension to the Fogg Museum, Harvard University, by Stirling Wilford.

On Hilversum Town Hall, Dudok treated brickwork as abstract, almost monolithic surfaces.

Made of London stocks, the walls of John Soane's Dulwich Picture Gallery vibrate with colour.

Virtuoso bricklaying: Michel de Klerk's Eigen Haard Housing in Amsterdam.

The brickwork of Gothenburg Art Museum seems calculated to evoke memories of Italy.

Chapter 9
Meaning

Order emerging from Chaos,
or Architecture being reclaimed
by Nature?: Trevi Fountain, Rome.

Each material has its own message and, to the creative artists, its own song.
Frank Lloyd Wright[1]

Contemplating a thick piece of yellow glass, Bruno Taut wrote that it was 'heavy as a building brick', yet 'constantly changing in appearance'. 'It's simply fantastic', he went on, 'what effects the light produces, and yet with a fixed form. The vessel of the new spirit that we are preparing will be like this.' As we noted in chapter 3, Taut's fascination with glass drew on an iconographic tradition stretching back to the Bible, but sitting there at his writing table, the leap from the visual pleasure of the light effects he was witnessing to the 'new spirit' they could symbolize must have seemed direct and unmediated. The fluidity of light in glass offers itself readily as a metaphor for a corresponding freedom of the spirit, just as the strength of iron or hardness of stone may become metaphors for similar qualities in human character.

The ascription of such meanings to materials is based on convention, as was the Abbé Laugier's advice that 'the colours of marbles must relate as much as possible to the character of the subject. It would be equally as absurd to use marbles in green, red, yellow or any other brilliant colour for a mausoleum as it would be to waste black marble on an altar.'[2] The familiar association of black with death, then as now, did not, however, stop it becoming fashionable for dress amongst the aristocracy in the fifteenth century, and subsequently spreading down to the bourgeoisie – as countless seventeenth-century Dutch portraits confirm.[3]

The popular understanding of a material may also be grounded in its origins: being brought back from a crusade in the Holy Land or, like the columns of St Mark's in Venice, secured by pillage from some remote enemy, were once powerful sources of 'added value'. Today, when materials are routinely shipped around the planet and ecological concerns are coming to the fore, the use of local rather than distant sources might well acquire a more desirable cachet. Similarly, whilst the sight, feel and scent of leather upholstery in a car still exude luxury and elegance to many, it is conceivable that its origin as the skin of a slaughtered beast might one day render leather as dubious an asset as fur coats.

Scarce materials frequently acquire special meanings, although this is not generally independent of other valuable qualities. Gold is both hard to find and mine in quantity and singularly resistant to weather, so its use to protect the exposed end grains of timber on some Japanese Imperial and religious buildings

Coloured glass by Antoni Gaudí, Güell Colony Crypt, Santa Coloma de Cervelló, Spain.

The exposed ends of wood on this tiny shrine in Kyoto (above) are painted yellow to emulate the brass or gold cappings traditionally used on grander buildings (right).

was both practical and a sign of status – and imitated on minor structures, for which copper was also deemed inappropriate, by painting the ends of the wood yellow. Rare and intractable stones such as porphyry were especially prized for their decorative value in both the Renaissance and in Ancient Egypt, and, like gold, many are also remarkably resistant to change. Ultramarine, the exquisite blue pigment derived from lapis lazuli, would probably be deemed beautiful by most people regardless of its expense – but it was the latter that lent it a particular appeal, so much so that painters' contracts in the Renaissance would often specify how much was to be used in a given work. As its expense was widely known, ultramarine could give added meaning to a picture, hence the widespread convention for clothing the Virgin Mary in blue.[4]

For much of the twentieth century, conspicuously expensive stones were routinely used as cladding on prestigious but otherwise banal commercial buildings, forcing many architects of artistic ambition to explore ways of creating aesthetic value by finding unexpected uses for cheap and neglected materials – as, for example, amongst some of the work we consider in the next chapter. For Alvar Aalto, however, the currency of white Italian marble was all but impossible to devalue. To mark the importance of the main library on the Helsinki University of Technology campus at Otaniemi, he gave it a partial revetment of marble around its entrance – the 'ruin' effect suggesting not lack of resources but a work of artistic ambition. And to differentiate the School of Architecture from the other departments, Aalto managed to persuade the authorities that its courtyard should be entirely faced with marble – it would, after all, reflect more light into the studios![5] On the Academic Bookshop in Helsinki the use of his favourite stone is more discreet. The frames of the windows facing onto the Esplanade – one of the city's principal streets – are lined with marble, whereas those on the side street are not. In Aalto's eyes, the marble serves both to signify the shop's cultural status – Finland is an intensely literary nation – and to clarify the building's urban situation, much as the Doge's Palace's two principal façades are clad in marble, and the others left as brick.

At Helsinki Technical University, Aalto marked the school of architecture's status with marble.

The openings on the principal façade of the Academic Bookshop in Helsinki are lined with marble.

The public faces of the Doge's Palace are clad with stone, the side and rear left as plain brickwork.

For Gottfried Semper, the meaning of Egyptian monuments in hard stones such as granite and porphyry owed much to the sheer difficulty that 'the soft hand of man' faced in working them with 'his simple tools': '"So far and no further, in this manner and no other!" This has been the silent message for millennia.'[6] Today, however, when we 'can cut the hardest stone like cheese',[7] the massive, somewhat angular forms lack their earlier sense of necessity. Hence, in part, the insistence of Modernist sculptors such as Brancusi on the aesthetic value of direct, hand carving, and preference for similarly abstracted shapes: forms too easily won, or too facile in elaboration, may now be perceived as lacking aesthetic value and meaning rather than as demonstrations of virtuoso technique.

Materials may also acquire meaning through colour: all such associations are ultimately culturally mediated, but some play on what might be thought familiar associations, whilst others are part of complex symbolic systems. For example, the gold stars on a dark blue field encountered as a decorative motif on buildings in Venice – as, for example, on the Quattrocento Torre dell'y Orologio in Piazza San Marco – appear to need no interpretation, but gain in significance as emblems of the Doge Michele Stano, whose insignia was a star. The porches of many buildings in the Islamic world are made palpably cooler by being 'hung' with 'carpets' of blue and turquoise tiles, whilst the similarly tiled domes and mosques of minarets become visual oases in the desert. The effect is immediate, the colours being associated with the cooling presence of plants and water, but by mingling the iconographies of the Garden of Life and of the sky, such tileworks also become doubly reassuring images of Paradise as a Heavenly Garden.[8] No such symbolism, so far as I am aware, attended the use of cool, pale green marble to temper the heat of Florence, or the contrary preference in Venice for 'warm' red Verona marble to add a welcome touch of warmth amidst the damp marshes.

Although these and similar meanings of materials may appear to be securely grounded in readily perceived qualities, they can be inverted by cultural changes. Gold's status as a sign of wealth has rarely been challenged, but in the Renaissance the use both of gold and of ultramarine was criticized as offering an easy route to conveying meaning. Giorgio Vasari argued that artistic value should come from the excellence of a work's invention and design, not from the expense of its materials, and Alberti similarly disparaged the use of too much gold leaf, considering it more artistic to achieve the illusion of light and luxury it conveyed using only coloured pigments.[9] Similar strictures could be applied to the over-indulgent use of luxurious stones in architecture, and some architects prefer to avoid rich materials altogether – hence Herman Hertzberger's attempt to 'democratize' the Vredenburg Music Centre in Utrecht by building it of concrete blocks. The difficulty with such a strategy is that for most viewers the blocks will not be seen 'abstractly', but may bring with them other, less desirable, associations.

In architecture, the changing reception of concrete offers an unusually volatile example of the contradictory meanings that may be assigned to a material. Throughout the first half of the century it was widely seen as the material of the future. As late as 1964 the Danish engineers Christiani and Nielsen could celebrate the Golden Jubilee of their activities in England with a book entitled *The Golden Age of Concrete*.[10] By then, of course, modern cities were beginning to be denigrated as 'concrete jungles' and the word was becoming, as Thomas Raff has written, 'a popular metaphor for

The slenderness of Plečnik's granite obelisk at Prague Castle is a recognition of the material's strength.

Red Verona marble provides a warm welcome to San Zaccaria in Venice.

The blue 'carpet' of wall tiles enhances the coolness of this porch of the Friday Mosque in Yazd.

The domes of many mosques, such as this in Samarkand, Uzbekistan, are tiled as images of a paradise garden.

Top: The gold stars on the Torre dell'y Orologio in Venice were the insignia of Doge Michele Stano.

Above: Hertzberger intended the Vredensburg Music Centre's blockwork as a form of 'democratization'.

vices such as contempt for humanity, narrow-mindedness, and heartlessness'.[11] Concrete never fell completely out of favour with architects, and four decades later, bare concrete walls and a host of concrete products for the house and garden are being promoted as accompaniments of chic contemporary lifestyles.[12]

The example of concrete illustrates the impossibility of architects controlling the reception, the socially ascribed meanings, of their work. To its creators, the crisply rendered surfaces and metal details of early Modern architecture were declarations of faith in reason and industry as means to a utopian future. The transparency of glass was both a health-giving source of light and a metaphor for demystification: 'Things made of glass', declared Walter Benjamin, 'have no aura. Indeed, glass is the enemy of mystification.'[13] In a sanatorium such as Aalto's at Paimio, where the supposed healing power of the sun was celebrated with enormous windows and a brilliant yellow floor covering, the new architecture was widely accepted as an apt expression of the building's purpose. But in homes, even some of the most progressive minds of the period found it hard to accept. Ernst Bloch declared that Functionalist houses had as much 'charm as a sanitary facility', and Bertolt Brecht famously attributed the desire to live in houses that were like 'tiled bathrooms' to the experience of the filth of the First World War trenches.[14]

A familiar and potentially disconcerting strategy of modern designers is transposing materials from one context to another. When Auguste Perret used glass blocks in the façade of the apartments he completed at 25 bis rue Franklin in Paris in 1903, they were advertized as a material for pavement lights. Eleven years later, in Bruno Taut's Glass Pavilion in Cologne, they became a primary material, as they did, even more famously, in Pierre Chareau's Maison de Verre in Paris. Industry was surprisingly slow to catch on to such a potential expansion for its market: the material's meaning, and hence possible uses, were tied up with the strictly 'functional' purpose for which it had been developed. Le Corbusier's choice of a 'factory style' metal mesh as an entrance gate and screen at the Salvation Army Hostel in Paris was an even more provocative challenge to the material's probable associations – and it was originally flanked by frankly decorative panels of glass block, in anticipation of their light-transmitting counterparts beyond.

In the nineteenth century, and in northern Europe especially, materials began to acquire new significance as expressions of national identity.[15] Inspired by the 'Dream of the North', which maintained that Germany and Scandinavia were the heirs of ancient northern peoples whose common cultural roots went back at least to the fall of Rome, architects sought to develop self-consciously national styles grounded in specific materials. This emphasis on material had the added advantage of echoing the growing conviction that a truly modern style would also emerge from re-discovering how to work 'in the nature of materials'.

In Finland and Norway, the focus of attention was granite. Building with the literal bedrock of the nation would, it was argued, root the new national architectures in the landscape. And in the process it would lead to forms more

Steel mesh entrance screen to the Salvation Army Hostel, Paris, by Le Corbusier.

The yellow floors of Paimio Sanatorium celebrate the supposed health-giving powers of the sun.

Wood and steel, nature and culture, are juxtaposed in Monark's Finnish Pavilion at the 1990 Seville Expo.

suited to the severe national climate and correspondingly resilient character than had been achieved by transplanting 'the luscious flower of Italian architecture', which belonged 'to the southern sun and marble'.[16] Granite also had its advocates as the material of the 'fatherland' in Prussia, but there it was more its 'moral' virtues of strength and steadfastness than its presence in the landscape that appealed. For the most part in Germany, Denmark and Sweden, however, brick was regarded as the authentic national material. Ragnar Östberg's new City Hall for Stockholm, arguably the finest achievement of the short-lived National Romantic episode, was built in brick, as was its similarly imposing counterpart in Copenhagen, designed by Martin Nyrop.

Stylistically more innovative, however, were the Finnish attempts to wring a national style out of granite. Seen in the light of what was to come only a few years after it was completed in 1905, Lars Sonck's headquarters for the Helsinki Telephone Company might appear behind the times. To his contemporaries, however, it not only represented an authentic national statement in granite, but also – despite the lingering medieval overtones – a distinctively modern attempt to transcend style and return to architectural basics. The sturdy columns with their primitive, incised motifs support truly enormous lintels: the ensemble recalls prehistoric trilithons, and the sensation of weight is enhanced by the abnormally large blocks placed over the vertical joints between the lintels, as if to help bolster them for the task. The individual granite blocks are emphasized by shaping them so that they project slightly from the wall face implied by the joints, and by mixing a local reddish stone with pale grey ones from further north: the calculated variations of texture and colour have taken the place of ornament in giving character to the walls.

Top and above: Lars Sonck's Helsinki Telephone Company Building uses national granite and pre-classical forms.

Organic form serving national ends: the loosely layered timber boarding of Dezsö Ekler's Reception Hall for the Téka camp at Harangod, Hungary, evokes bird's feathers.

Aalto's critique of orthodox Functionalism was based, in part, on the search for a national inflection of (international) Modern ideas, and, like the architects of National Romanticism, he made extensive use of the associations evoked by materials. Nowhere is this more extensive or compelling than in the Villa Mairea. Seen at a distance in its wooded setting, the Villa could be mistaken for a normal, white-rendered International Style house set amidst pristine nature. But as you get closer you notice that the white surfaces are, in fact, lime-washed brickwork, more Mediterranean vernacular than Machine-Age Modern, a token of the beloved South. Moving around the house, a surprising variety of other materials come into view: timber boarding, teak panelling, slate cladding, a low stone wall, a patch of blue tiles, rough stone steps, circular columns made of concrete and timber. The result is more like a collage than a conventional architectural composition, and, as in a collage, the various materials are intended to act both formally and semantically, by carrying with them into the artistic universe of the work associations from the world at large.

The associations upon which Aalto draws would have been familiar to most progressively minded Finns at the time the Villa was completed in 1940, and showed how it was possible to be both progressive and internationally minded whilst at the same time promoting a distinctive Finnish identity. Despite its later, carefully cultivated image as a haven of 'naturally functional' modern design, Finnish culture in the 1930s was dominated by a backward-looking 'birch bark culture'.[17] The Villa is manifestly and radically modern, but from its courtyard layout to its detailing, it also deliberately recalls Finnish traditions – as well as an eclectic range of influences from what we might now call 'world culture', in particular that of Japan.[18] The low stone wall that frames the sauna echoes similar walls around churchyards; the grass-roofed sauna beside its free-form pool resembles its lakeside relatives; the pieces of sapling that form the balustrade above the dining wing evoke farm fences, but are 'modernized' by being made to float on steel uprights.

Some of the associations are more personal. The client Maire Gullichsen, after whom the house is named, had studied painting in Paris in the 1920s, and the collage-composition itself may well be indebted to her encouragement,[19] and was certainly much

Aalto's Villa Mairea is a collage of material associations: Mediterranean lime-wash and vernacular wood …

… seemingly casual fragments of Modernist structure and luxurious teak…

… and boarding from the Finnish Pavilion at the 1937 Paris World Fair, supported by tree-like pilotis.

The stripped saplings above
the Villa's dining room combine
memories of farm fences with
the floating lines and planes
of Suprematism and De Stijl.

At the Louvain-la-Neuve Medical Faculty, Lucien Kroll collaged materials to suggest growth over time.

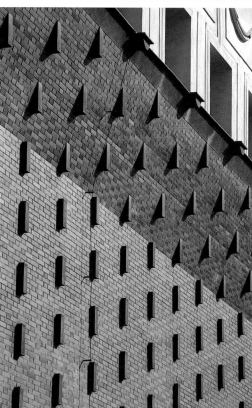

appreciated by her. It was she who insisted that the hard-to-find blue tiles, which erode the corner of the dining room, should not be left off, and that the non-structural section of the birch-like double-column, which supports her studio, should be retained against the structural engineer's wishes. From a distance, the timber weather-boarding of Maire's studio appears 'rustic', but from close-up is discovered to be subtly profiled: it is, in fact, a direct and highly personal 'quotation' of the boarding Aalto used on the Finnish Pavilion at the Paris World Fair of 1937.

Aalto's use of materials and details to suggest both general and specific meanings was unusual, if not unique, in modern architecture, and finds intriguing parallels in the work – simultaneously pre- and post-modern – of Jože Plečnik. Consider, for example, the Church of the Sacred Heart, completed in Prague in 1932. Materially, the church is characterized by the striking contrast between a dark, richly textured and largely blank base of twice-burnt clinker bricks and projecting stone blocks, and the brilliant white plaster of the upper stages and door and window surrounds. Stylistically, the base is singular, whereas the plastered areas are recognizably, if highly individualistically, Classical.

The accepted interpretation of this disjunctive composition, presented by Damjan Prelovšek in his excellent monograph on Plečnik[20] and supported by texts and the recollections of Plečnik's associates, takes its lead from Semper's observation that in antiquity textiles were used on special occasions to enhance the significance of architecture. Here, Prelovšek argues, Plečnik has 'dressed' the church's white walls with an ermine robe – the symbol of royal dignity – represented by the richly textured, and textile-like, brick walls. Whilst willing to accommodate such a reading, Ákos Moravánszky suggests that it should be understood in light of the earlier search for national expression, which was equally prevalent

Jože Plečnik described the richly textured, clinker-brick walls of the Church of the Sacred Heart in Prague (above and right) as an 'ermine robe' cast over the white walls.

in Eastern Europe as further north. The church, in Moravánszky's view, has a similar structure to that which Bartók identified in Hungarian folk music: the brick base echoes the 'ancient layer' of folk music, with its 'archaic colours' and free rhythm, whilst the Classically ordered superstructure, like the second layer of song, has a strict rhythm and architectonic order.[21]

However it is to be interpreted, it is clear that Plečnik's church, like so much of his other work, is motivated by semantic as well as tectonic concerns. This is certainly true of the extraordinary staircase he designed between 1927 and 1931 to link the Third Courtyard of Prague Castle to the Rampart Garden below. Wishing to disturb the historically defined space as little as possible, but keen to provide a canopy over the entrance, Plečnik again turned to Semper for inspiration. The necessarily permanent feature is built as a representation of an ephemeral, mobile structure to be erected on special occasions. Fabric is rendered as riveted copper – and surely no metal canopy was ever 'draped' in such a persuasive manner – and the primary supports, two long timber beams, are borne on four bronze bulls, which appear ready to walk off with their mighty load.

The staircase's arrival below is celebrated with a tall opening, which accommodates two intermediate landings before the stairs finally spill out in a cascade of steps. The construction is based on Semper's speculation about an intermediate metal phase between building in wood and stone. The rounded rustication of the walls suggests stacked logs, whilst the architrave above the opening is clad in copper – the regular pattern of rivets alluding, perhaps, to plated iron structures. Framed by the walls, the single columns that support the landings have the inverted profile and rudimentary capitals that bring to mind such proto-Classical forms as those made famous by the reconstruction of the Palace of King Minos at Knossos.

Having been appropriated, to mostly disastrous effect, by the stylistic Post-Modernism of the 1980s, the issue of meaning has disappeared below the horizon of most architects' active concerns – although Daniel Libeskind's work is a conspicuous exception. The issue is complex and difficult, but the contrasting examples of Aalto and Plečnik suggest that materials can still be turned to semantic ends that transcend simplistic, linguistically motivated attempts to 'build in' meaning, and in ways that are compatible with both abstraction and tectonic expression.

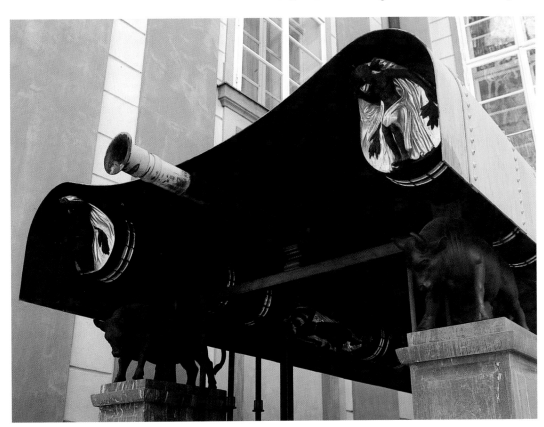

Riveted-copper canopy to the staircase entrance in the Third Courtyard of Prague Castle.

Plečnik's framing of the staircase's arrival in the garden below is a meditation on pre-Classical construction.

Chapter 10
Materiality
and Translucency

The pleasure of 'cheap'
materials: entrance hall,
Kunsthal, Rotterdam
by Rem Koolhaas/OMA.

Wooden floors like light membranes, heavy stone masses, soft textiles, polished granite, pliable leather, raw steel, polished mahogany, crystalline glass, soft asphalt warmed by the sun … the architect's materials, our materials.
Peter Zumthor[1]

In the attitude to materials that they reveal, the library in San Juan Capistrano, California, by Michael Graves, and Arata Isozaki's Tsukuba Civic Centre across the Pacific in Japan, could stand for any number of stylistically Post-Modern projects built between the mid 1970s and mid 1980s. Modelled on the so-called 'Spanish Mission Style', the library simulates an older architecture of mass using a lightweight timber-frame structure covered with plaster. Looking at it, you sense immediately that it is not quite 'the real thing', and have only to tap the hollow walls to confirm your suspicions. Isozaki deploys a variety of claddings – real and simulated stone, mosaic, metals – to more varied but essentially similar ends. Both architects are patently gifted designers, and their buildings are skilfully composed, but they feel more like stage-sets than 'real' places – in Isozaki's case, this is a calculated effect, the Centre being a large-scale exercise in allusive form-making.[2] In both buildings, the feeling of unreality depends, crucially, on the choice and detailing of materials – on the fact that nothing seems content to be itself, but is used to simulate or hint at another reality.

Post-Modern buildings such as these are frequently described as 'scenographic'. To their admirers this suggests, amongst other things, a welcome recognition of the radically altered relationship between architecture and the construction industry, which has rendered any lingering belief in 'truth to materials' anachronistic. Far from being a means by which we construct reality, some argue, architecture should now be embraced as a form of communication based on the manipulation of familiar languages or 'styles'.[3] To Post-

Modernism's detractors, on the other hand, to treat architecture as a form of more or less permanent scene-painting, as a self-referential game of historical allusions and ironic illusions, is to neglect both its central role in the construction of the human world and its grounding in the 'art of building'.

Advocates of stylistic Post-Modernism in the 1980s were undeniably right to emphasize that saturation with the imagery of advertising, television and film is a defining feature of what we have since become accustomed to calling our postmodern culture – even if, as Anthony Giddens and other cultural theorists argue, its salient features suggest that it might be better understood as a continuing form of 'radical modernity'.[4] But they proved to be completely wrong in supposing that, as a consequence, architecture should be made to play the same ephemeral games as other, more evanescent and fleet-footed media. Far from promoting only its like, the world of mediated images generated a compensatory demand for things that were palpably 'real' – tactile, textured, flavoursome, embodied. From fashion to food, furniture to architecture, 'materiality' and 'the body' were destined to loom large as major preoccupations of the *fin de siècle*.[5]

In architecture, the return to reality, to making buildings that want to *be*, not *be about* something, has been a focal theme of theory and practice since the mid 1980s. Kenneth Frampton's advocacy of Critical Regionalism and, more recently, tectonic expression;[6] Michael Benedikt's cryptically elegant manifesto, *For an Architecture of Reality*, with its plea for

Post-Modern simulation:
Tsukuba Civic Centre, Japan,
by Arata Isozaki.

San Juan Capistrano Library,
California, by Michael Graves.

'High Realism': Bregenz Art
Gallery by Peter Zumthor.

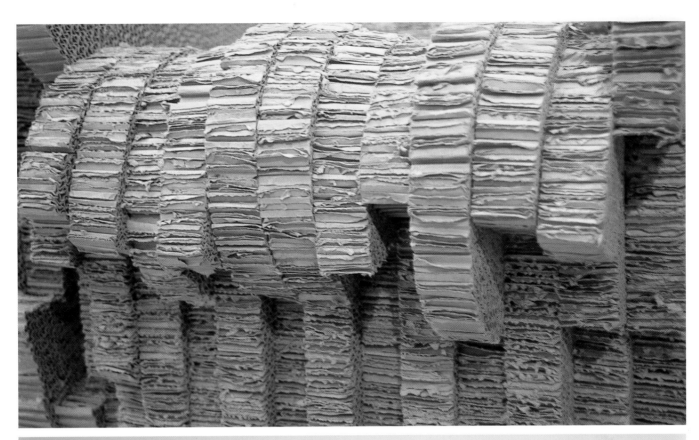

'Tactile, textured, flavoursome, embodied': detail of 'Little Beaver' chair, 1987, by Frank Gehry.

Light-filtering gabions of the Dominus Winery, Yountville, California, by Herzog and de Meuron.

Doors, Chapel of St. Ignatius,
Seattle, Washington,
by Steven Holl Architects.

a 'High Realism' based on 'the direct aesthetic experience of the real';[7] the burgeoning literature about place and the related interest in phenomenology:[8] all in their various ways emphasize architecture as a material practice grounded in the particular conditions of site, construction and materials.

If you had to select one architect whose work most clearly anticipated this new spirit, the choice would surely fall on Tadao Ando, who burst onto the world scene following the completion of the Koshino House at Ashiya near his home town of Osaka in 1982.[9] Built of solid, uninsulated, fair-faced concrete walls twenty centimetres (8 inches) thick, the Koshino House was inconceivable outside its Japanese context – and as a result initially baffled many in the West.[10] The Japanese build widely in reinforced concrete as a means of countering earthquakes, but Ando's insistence on expressing the concrete both inside and out turns the walls into continuous 'cold bridges' with consequent risk of condensation – something he seeks to minimize by using electric heating and efficient air-extraction systems in kitchens and bathrooms. Ando's concrete is worlds apart from Corbusian *béton brut*: fine and delicate like the wood and paper surfaces of traditional Japanese buildings. To get to know and respect the material, the younger members of his office

used to provide free annual maintenance by wire-brushing the external surfaces to eliminate traces of algae and other conspicuous signs of weathering.[11]

Describing his projects as 'bastions of resistance' against the (Western) consumer culture that was sweeping Japan in those years of fevered prosperity, Ando explained that his work reflected his attitude of 'severity' towards living.[12] This is seen at its most extreme in the earlier Row House in the Sumiyoshi district of Osaka (1975-6), which brought him to national attention in Japan. Consisting of two cubic volumes placed either side of a similarly sized open court, the Row House's plan demanded that the residents go outside to cross from living room to dining room or from bedroom to bathroom. Exposure to the elements in crossing the court was considered a stimulus to bodies unhealthily accustomed to artificially controlled conditions, and recalled the journey to the traditional outside toilet – famously eulogized by Jun'ichiro Tanizaki as an ideal opportunity to enjoy such natural delights as 'the chirping of insects or the song of the birds' and 'those poignant moments that mark the change of the seasons'.[13]

Formally, Ando sought to fuse aspects of European Modernism with the feeling for materials, site and episodic composition that typify traditional Japanese architecture and gardens – which in turn, of course, had been a stimulus to European Modernists.[14] His concrete, made with a bluish sand to help 'dematerialize' it slightly, is extraordinary. 'The concrete wood shutterings', explains Ando, 'are done by specialized carpenters, who refer back to the ancient craft tradition of wooden houses.'[15] The detailing of the shuttering to articulate the wall using traces of joints and bolt-holes recalls

Living room, Koshino House,
Ashiya, Japan, by Tadao Ando.

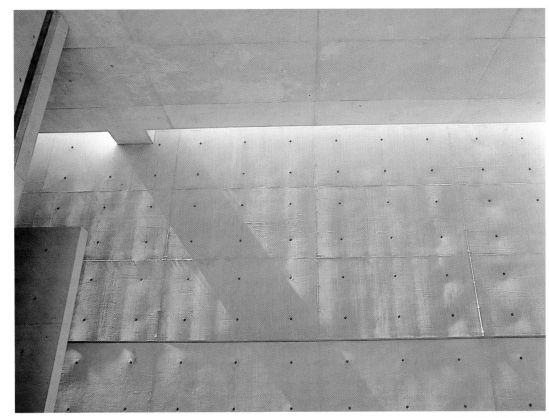

Grazing sunlight transforms
the concrete walls of the
Koshino House's living room
into surfaces that seem
as delicate as rice paper.

'The brickness of the material': the walls of the National Museum of Roman Art in Mérida are made without mortar to distance them from their ancient antecedents.

Ando envisaged the steps of the Koshino House as a 'dry garden'.

Kahn's walls at the Salk Institute. But whereas Kahn makes a point of stressing the wall's thickness, with results that seem weighty and manifestly constructed, in the Koshino house – as in all Ando's work – the interior is experienced primarily as spaces 'created by rays of sunlight'. The walls, as Ando goes on to explain, 'become abstract, are negated and approach the ultimate limit of space. Their actuality is lost and only the space they enclose gives the sense of really existing.'[16]

Although Ando emphasizes the abstraction of the surfaces he creates, the almost unique quality of an interior like that of the Koshino House depends on the fact that the walls appear both abstract and palpable, inseparable from their substance and fabrication. The raking top-light highlights the slight undulations in the wall planes, which occur due to tiny distortions in the shutters, most obviously between the tatami-mat-like 1.8 x 0.9 metre (6 x 3 feet) panels, but also within them. The resulting surface appears as light as a paper screen, and in grazing sunlight can seem almost to ripple. Just as the walls inside are canvases for the play of natural light, the stepped 'dry garden' between the house's two wings was envisaged, like the slate-covered court of the Row House in Sumiyoshi, as a surface on which to enjoy the wetness of rain – Ando sees these as modern counterparts of a traditional *kare sansui* or dry garden. Although the self-conscious enjoyment of 'bad' weather strikes many in the West as strange, it is celebrated in Japanese woodcuts and still practised in everyday life in Japan. I well recall being told, after being prevented by illness from making a trip to Kamakura, that it was a great pity I had been unable to go because 'it would have been so beautiful in the rain'!

Although conceived in response to very different cultural conditions, Ando's concrete was in tune with work elsewhere characterized by the extensive deployment of a single, and sometimes singular, material. Rafael Moneo's National Museum of Roman Art in Mérida,

Spain (1980-6), for example, was as emphatic in its use of brick. Although the repeated brick walls and arches were clearly intended to evoke memories of Ancient Rome, and as such reflected the all-pervasive 'rediscovery' of history in those years,[17] their insistent repetition and facture were entirely modern, and calculated to distance them by abstraction from too close an association with the past. The spacing of the walls was determined intuitively, in response to their physical presence as richly textured surfaces – in concrete, says Moneo, the dimensions would have had to be different[18] – and the bricks themselves are laid without mortar: 'A dry joint without mortar', explains Moneo, 'secures the *brickness* of the material, and allows the wall to remain as an almost abstract element … I believe the abstract use of materials depends on our attempts to keep their own identities alive, without dissolving them in the reality of the architectural element.'[19]

Despite sounding dangerously like the motto of some politically correct movement, 'keeping their identities alive' would be a good working definition of the now widely used – and equally widely misused – term 'materiality'.[20] As we noted in the discussion of Lewerentz's brick churches (see page 96), whilst the attitude to the 'nature of materials' emphasized what materials can *do*, materiality has been adopted as the password for an attitude that seeks to express what materials *are* – and as such is concerned more with their emotional effect upon the observer than with conventional structural uses.

Respecting and bringing out the 'essence' of materials has been the most widely pursued tactic in the recent search for 'reality' and 'authenticity' in architecture, but like earlier

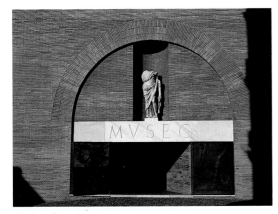

Above: Entrance, National Museum of Roman Art in Mérida by Rafael Moneo.

attempts to define their functional 'nature', the proposition that sensual qualities can be apprehended directly, independent of context or culture, is clearly fraught. All our perceptions, no matter how seemingly elementary, are inescapably culture- and time-bound, not universal and timeless. This need not, however, detract from the quality of much of the work inspired by paying close attention to the phenomena of the world – for which the writings of Heidegger, in particular, have provided numerous architects with stimulating, if sometimes rather weighty, intellectual baggage. Gazing at Lewerentz's brickwork or Ando's concrete we may feel that we are being granted a privileged glimpse into the essence of the material, but this is an effect of art, not a fact of perception.

Although particularly associated with the so-called 'Swiss School', which emerged in the late 1980s, promoting a heightened awareness of materials has been a key feature of otherwise disparate trends in recent architecture on both sides of the Atlantic. In part this can be seen as a reaction against the semantic/cerebral extremes of Post-Modernism and Deconstructivism, both of which, in their different ways, exemplified the tendency to reduce architecture to visual imagery. Equally, emphasizing the richness and specificity of the

direct, sensual experience of architecture offers a potent way of countering the all-pervasive anonymity of the 'non-places' – supermarkets, hotels, shopping malls, airports – which dominate so much of the public space of what the anthropologist Marc Augé has described as the 'supermodern world'.[21]

Many contemporary buildings are designed to impress more via the instant impact of printed photographs than through direct encounter, let alone the gradual familiarization of use and inhabitation; depressingly few are conceived with their users' five senses in mind,[22] still less Ruskin's 'golden stain of time'. Lamenting the consequent 'loss of plasticity' in this narrowly 'retinal art of the eye', the Finnish architect and theorist Juhani Pallasmaa advocates the use of natural materials that 'allow the gaze to penetrate their surfaces' and thereby convince us of 'the veracity of matter'. By contrast, he argues, the familiar materials of most contemporary architecture – 'sheets of glass, enamelled metal and synthetic materials' – merely 'present their unyielding surfaces to the eye without conveying anything of their material essence or age'.[23]

Key catalysts for the growing fascination with materials came from artists and art movements that had flourished two decades and more before. Both Peter Zumthor and Jacques Herzog, for example, have declared their debts to Joseph Beuys and the Arte Povera group. 'What impresses me', writes Zumthor, 'is the precise and sensuous way they use materials. It seems anchored in an ancient elemental knowledge about man's use of materials, and at the same time to expose the very essence of these materials which is beyond all culturally conveyed meaning.'[24] Beuys's discovery of elementary meanings in seemingly 'inartistic' materials was deeply personal, stemming as it did from the felt and fat used by the Tartars in the Crimea to save his life following a crash as a Stuka pilot during the War.[25] But what he extrapolated from this

'Unyielding surfaces' of Modernity: office tower in Chicago by KPF.

'Veracity of matter': Can Lis, Majorca, by Jørn Utzon.

experience was intended to be universal: conceptualized as 'reservoirs' of heat and energy, felt and fat became part of his therapeutic conception of art as a salve for society's ills.[26]

Although renowned as a pioneer of installations, Beuys also pursued more traditional artistic activities such as drawing, albeit in predictably unpredictable ways. According to Heiner Stachelhaus, he liked to work on 'stamped, creased, torn, written-on, ruled, squared, patched-together, discoloured sheets of paper' using 'blood, beef tea, whey, fruit juices, vegetable juices, herb juices, coffee, tea, stagnant water enriched with rust and dust, iodine, and wood stain'.[27] Architectural devotees of materiality may not enjoy such artistic freedom, but the love of conspicuously worked, worn and distressed surfaces and the determination to transgress the conventional uses of materials that we encounter in Beuys find direct echoes in recent architecture.

More widely canvassed as a source of inspiration is the fascination with Minimalism, a movement for which phenomenology also supplied the philosophical underpinnings, in this case primarily through the ideas of the Frenchman Maurice Merleau-Ponty.[28] Arguing that we can know ourselves only through our relationship with the environment, through what we see and touch, Merleau-Ponty saw our bodies and the world as inseparable parts of a system. Conceiving their art in an analogous way, exponents of Minimalist art viewed their works as perceptual systems, in which the work, the space and light of the gallery and the observer are interlocked. To encourage the viewer to focus on the complexity of such inter-relationships rather than on objects in isolation, the formal structure of Minimalist works frequently consisted of the repetition of simple geometric forms – of which Carl Andre's 'Tate Bricks' (officially, Equivalent VIII, 1966) became the *cause célèbre*.[29]

In Donald Judd's installation of his own work at Marfa, Texas, for example, 100 open-topped aluminium boxes, variously subdivided by orthogonally arranged aluminium plates, create an ever-changing interplay of reflections and shadows.[30] The work has no subject, no 'meaning', no cumulative 'form', no preferred viewpoint: its aesthetic effect is intended to flow from the viewer's unmediated experience of the visual 'facts'. In a 'Statement' written in 1968, Judd explained that his work challenged the 'traditional separation of means and structure', which rendered materials, and our experience of them, subservient to an idea of order that 'underlies, overlies, is within, above, below or beyond everything'.[31] As a consequence, 'a shape, a volume, a colour, a surface' should be treated as 'something itself' and not 'concealed as part of a fairly different whole. The shapes and materials shouldn't be altered by their context. One or four boxes in a row … is local order, just an arrangement, barely order at all.' It is difficult to imagine a better description of the motivations that underpin that reduction of buildings to 'boxes' that has been a hallmark of the Swiss School.

Top: Minimalist form: Herzog and de Meuron's Goetz Gallery in Munich.

Above: Repetition of identical elements can heighten our awareness of their material qualities: Beyeler Gallery, Basel, by Renzo Piano.

Reviewing the 'new monuments' of Judd, Robert Morris, Sol LeWitt, Dan Flavin and other American artists in 1966, the sculptor Robert Smithson suggested that 'instead of causing us to remember the past like the old monuments, the new monuments seem to cause us to forget the future. Instead of being made of natural materials, such as marble, granite or other kinds of rock, the new monuments are made of artificial materials, plastic, chrome and electric light.'[32] Smithson went on to interpret this as a response to the 'vapidity and dullness' of the everyday environments of post-war America, with their commercial interiors of sheet aluminium, leather-textured plastic and Formica-like wood. For the Minimalists, using 'neutral' forms and artificial materials, and having their pieces fabricated in a factory – or at least making them appear to have been industrially produced – was a way of attacking the tactility and emphasis on the artist's touch in Abstract Expressionism. Materials such as 'Formica, aluminum, cold-rolled steel, Plexiglas, red and common brass', explained Judd, were 'specific' and 'aggressive', whilst their 'obdurate identity' permitted an 'objectivity' that was not so easily achieved with more traditional ones.[33] And by shifting attention away from intrinsically interesting surfaces and any lingering traces of craftsmanship, this 'objectivity' enabled viewers better to concentrate on the interaction between the forms and their environment.

For architects, the attraction of 'cheap' industrial or apparently non-architectural materials was reinforced by the economies of construction. As the ever-rising costs of labour made traditionally 'precious' materials more widely affordable, works of artistic ambition could be distanced from the commercial mainstream by making expressive use of cheap, previously ignored ones. In this way, the longstanding Modernist tradition of finding unexpected uses for materials such as glass blocks and wire mesh acquired a new inflection, not dissimilar in its motivations to the Japanese Imperial family's decision, in the seventeenth century, to distance themselves from the vulgar taste of the wealthy shoguns by taking delight in refined versions of peasant buildings (see page 130). The need to find inventive responses to the pressure to build cheaply has been particularly acute in The Netherlands, forcing Dutch architects – with Rem Koolhaas, as ever, in the vanguard – to revel in the high-impact, low-cost effects that can result from making artful and unexpected uses of conspicuously cheap materials.[34]

A significant factor in facilitating the emphasis on material expression in architecture, if not directly in promoting its emergence, has been technical: the development of 'rainscreen cladding', to which we referred in the Introduction when discussing MVRDV's houses near The Hague. This began life, almost by default, as the 'upside down' flat roof,[35] and involves placing the insulation on the outside of a sealed structure. As a result, the building fabric conserves heat and, more importantly for our concerns, the cladding has merely to screen –

Multiplex cinema,
Schouwburgplein, Rotterdam,
by Koen van Velsen.

Corner, Kunsthal, Rotterdam,
by Rem Koolhaas/OMA.

In the Kunsthal, Koolhaas parodies the Miesian commitment to clear structure and fine materials.

not completely protect – the insulation from rain. To avoid condensation, a ventilated gap is generally left between insulation and cladding, so that when stone is used, air gaps replace mortar joints. The result is 'honestly' non-structural but also disconcerting: the detailing of Stirling and Wilford's extension to the Staatsgalerie in Stuttgart (which opened in 1984), with its 'graphic' arch and 'ruined' holes, was an early and witty commentary on the dilemmas of the appropriate expression of what appear to be, but are not quite, solid walls.

Compared with the more dramatic structural innovations in building over the last two centuries, rainscreen cladding sounds almost prosaic. But it represents a significant further stage in the replacement of monolithic construction by a layered building fabric, which began in earnest during the last quarter of the nineteenth century – with, as Otto Wagner (amongst others) realized, major implications for architectural expression.[36] By detaching the building's external finish more radically than ever before from the underlying construction, rainscreen cladding allows, even invites, exceptional freedom – some might say licence – in the choice of finishes. The variously coloured dream-coats of MVRDV's housing and the field-stone 'walls' of Edward Cullinan Architects' visitor centre at Fountains Abbey in Yorkshire,

England, for example, are both made possible by this development.[37]

Even more clearly than when Semper was writing in the mid nineteenth century, cladding can now be seen as a form of 'dressing', a fabric to be chosen at will and, potentially, changed with relative ease. Traditional cladding systems are typically designed with a life of a half or even a third of the structure that supports them, and buildings may soon be tailored with stylish but cheaper, short-life 'suits', intended to be replaced with something more fashionable after a few years. Another intriguing implication is that rainscreen cladding turns buildings inside out. Ephemeral 'decorative' exteriors could be complemented by permanent 'structural' interiors, offering the pleasures of working 'in the nature of materials' that high levels of insulation render problematic due to the cold bridges resulting from exposed structure.[38] An illustration of what this might encourage is offered by the ceiling of Jørn Utzon's Bagsværd Church near Copenhagen (1973-6), where the voluptuous reinforced-concrete ceiling supports a cheaply constructed roof. The result, observes Utzon, offers 'the reassurance of something above your head which is built, not just designed'.[39]

In Switzerland, in addition to these general cultural and technical factors, local conditions

Top: Staatsgalerie, Stuttgart by Stirling Wilford: non-structural 'arch' in rainscreen cladding.

Above: The only 'real' stones in the Staatsgalerie are found in this 'ruined' ventilation hole.

At Fountains Abbey visitor centre in Yorkshire, England, the rainscreen cladding echoes local stone walls.

also played a vital part. The Protestant, German-speaking region, which extends from Basel in the west, where Herzog and de Meuron are based, to Grison in the east, home to Peter Zumthor, escaped the direct effects of the two World Wars. The continuity this permitted enabled Modern architecture, or *Neues Bauen* as it was known locally, to be gradually assimilated as part of the culture. The general quality of building in Switzerland, and the level of craft skills, remain exceptionally high by European standards, and on small and medium-sized jobs architects retain a degree of control that has all but disappeared elsewhere, acting almost like traditional master-builders who both design and manage the construction. For architects of Herzog and de Meuron's generation, a rather surprising stimulus to involvement with the kind of peripheral environments that Smithson and Judd explored came from Aldo Rossi during his brief but influential time as a Professor at Switzerland's leading school of architecture, the ETH (Eidgenössische Technische Hochschule) in Zürich.[40] Encouraged to ground their work in an engagement with the city, Rossi's students became fascinated by the 'impressions of the incidental and seemingly unintentional' gleaned from the no-man's-land between cities, with their 'sometimes prismatic, often complexly

formed'[41] buildings made of cheap materials.

Choosing a cheap or unexpected material for a building of artistic pretension may be an obvious way of drawing attention to it, but regardless of the choice, expressing a material's identity also involves, as Herzog and de Meuron put it in an interview in 1993, pushing it 'to an extreme to show it dismantled from any other function than "being"'.[42] In an early house in Bottningen near Basel, for example, they used plywood on every surface to create an almost seamless volume, transforming the interior, as Ulrike Jehle has written, 'into a "resonance box", into an empty, resounding form'.[43] Visually, the house was unusual, but its distinctive sound made its impact even more singular. The widely published Frei photography studio, completed in 1981 in Weil am Rhein, Germany, also made extensive use of plywood – and, in response to the incoherent surroundings, paired it with even more 'humble' asphalt and other cheap materials drawn from the context.

To clad the iconic storage building for Ricola, completed in 1987 in Laufen, Switzerland, Herzog and de Meuron chose that familiar material of industrial estates, fibre-cement siding, and made it seem extraordinary by exquisite handling. Diminishing in size from top to bottom – the reverse of expectations grounded in traditional materials[44] – and crowned

In Utzon's Bagsværd Church, the ceiling is structural and supports a lightweight, insulated roof.

Ricola storage building in Laufen by Herzog and de Meuron: an early icon of materiality.

by a cantilevered 'cornice', the panels were intended to recall the stacked timbers in the area's numerous saw mills and to echo the strata of the rock faces of the quarry within which the building sits. The repetition with slight variation is mesmerizing, in much the same way as it is in the Minimalist music of Philip Glass or the sculptures of Sol LeWitt.

As they pursued the expression of materials, the Swiss architects developed a range of design strategies. Forms were simplified, leading to their works quickly being dubbed the 'Swiss Box' school, and, to make the buildings even more object-like, elements such as windows and doors were suppressed. Buildings were also frequently wrapped with a single material: as functional requirements dictated, this could be opaque or permeable – wooden or metal slats and perforated or woven metal sheets have been applied to buildings as diverse as houses, hotels, signal boxes and offices, as illustrated here in projects by Herzog and de Meuron, Burkhalter and Sumi, and Peter Zumthor. The porous outer layer may sometimes be opened up, like shutters, to reveal windows or balconies and, as an alternative to the suppression of openings, some – such as entrance doors or special windows – are emphasized by being boldly framed: projecting, box-like entrances, doubtless derived from Le

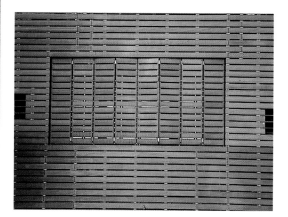

Top: Wood-slatted 'box' enclosing Roman remains at Chur, Switzerland, by Peter Zumthor.

Above and right: The wooden slats of Burkhalter and Sumi's extension to the Zürichberg Hotel open to reveal private balconies.

Copper-clad monolith: railway
signal box, Basel, by Herzog
and de Meuron.

The Migros Shop in Lucerne
by Diener and Diener is clad with
sheets of pre-patinated copper.

The glass planks of Gigon
Guyer's extension to Winterthur
Art Museum transform
the exterior into a shimmering,
luminescent box of light.

Industrial glass planks clad one wall of the Kunsthal in Rotterdam.

At Winterthur, matt-finished galvanized steel heightens awareness of the play of light on the glass.

Winterthur Art Museum: MDF-lined staircase linking the extension to the original museum.

Corbusier,[45] are a recurring feature.

The strategy of giving new life to familiar materials is well illustrated by the use of glass. On traditional curtain-walled buildings, glass may be used to cover opaque, insulated spandrel panels, as well as to provide a continuous ribbon of windows. But placing it directly over insulation as the skin of a solid wall, as Gigon Guyer did on the Kirchner Museum in Davos (1989-92), challenges most of our assumptions about the material – as does their use of crushed, recycled glass instead of gravel to ballast the roof covering. Cast as a veil over the wall, as Martin Steinmann has written, glass 'pretends to deny what it has to show, at the same time as pretending to show what it denies'.[46] Simultaneously, Rem Koolhaas did something similar with translucent glass planks: originally developed to give diffuse light in industrial buildings, Koolhaas used them to clad a long, blank wall of a top-lit gallery in the Kunsthal in Rotterdam (1987-92).

In Koolhaas's disjunctive composition the glass planks were just one of several wilfully chosen finishes, but three years later Gigon Guyer used the same product to wrap almost the entire exterior, as well as the ceiling of the ground floor car park, of a major extension to the Art Museum in Winterthur. Shimmering and almost uncannily luminescent, the aqueous green surface is broken only by three large, floor-to-ceiling windows. The extension is entered through an equally surprising, and totally contrasting, stair and link. There, the interior surfaces are lined with the generally maligned MDF – intended, according to the architects, as a contemporary echo of the deep wooden frames of the old building.

Clad with square stainless
steel plates, which overlap
like fish-scales at their corners,
the rainscreen cladding
of Gigon Guyer's Liner Museum
in Appenzell is perceived
as a skin with no direct
relationship to the spaces within.

At first sight, Gigon Guyer's Liner Museum in Appenzell (1996-8), clad all over in square stainless-steel plates externally and abstractly white internally, save for the pale grey floors, has many of the familiar features of the Swiss Box. But it also represents an effort to escape some of its limitations: mono-material boxes were a valuable purgative, but you quickly run out of 'novel' materials with which to animate them. The north-light roof section is directly expressed and cleverly exploited: the lights grow larger in response to the spaces within, but seen from the north, as you approach from the town centre, perspective diminution makes you read them as being of even height – expectation defeats perception. By being overlapped diagonally at their corners, the steel plates eliminate continuous horizontal and vertical lines, thereby detaching the skin from the underlying orthogonal configuration of the building and making it appear almost to float. The cladding has the material matter-of-factness we have come to expect, and offers magical optical phenomena as the light and your point of view change. But it is also calculated to evoke associations – of armour, perhaps, or snakeskin, or fish scales – which take it beyond the strict confines of the purely phenomenal.

Although the architects of the Swiss School have understandably been grouped together as a distinctive, even markedly regional, phenomenon, the formal similarities in their work cannot conceal a sharp divide between the cerebral, designerly approach exemplified by Herzog and de Meuron, and that of a builder such as Peter Zumthor. Apprenticed as a joiner before training as an architect, Zumthor's instincts are those of the craftsman and maker. An intuitive phenomenologist, he likes to begin from concrete experiences and memories: 'There was a time', he recalls, 'when I experienced architecture without thinking about it. Sometimes I can almost feel a particular door handle in my hand, a piece of metal shaped like the back of a spoon. I used to take hold of it when I went into my aunt's garden. That door handle still seems to me like a special sign of entry into a world of different moods and smells.'[47] Seeing his work as a search for the 'corporeal wholeness' found in the architecture of the master builders,[48] Zumthor has a deep respect for 'the art of joining, the ability of craftsmen and engineers'. As a consequence, he is 'tempted to think' that our appreciation of works of art arises in part from 'the effort and skill we put into them'[49] – a position, as he is well aware, that could be regarded as hopelessly *retardataire* by more sophisticated contemporaries. These interests place him at the opposite pole, intellectually as well as geographically, from Jacques Herzog, who argues that an intellectual approach to materials is the only one now open to architects.[50] Suspicious of the contemporary search for 'special form', Zumthor wonders why 'we have so little confidence in the basic things architecture is made from: material, structure, construction, bearing and being borne, earth and sky ... (and) in spaces whose enclosing walls and constituent materials, concavity, emptiness, light, air, odour, receptivity and resonance are handled with respect and care'.[51]

All the dimensions Zumthor describes are brought into play in the widely acclaimed Thermal Baths at Vals (1990-6),[52] but for me the tiny Sogn Benedetg chapel in the village

Building as stone cave: Thermal Baths, Vals, by Peter Zumthor.

of Sumvitg, Switzerland, completed in 1988 as the replacement for a stone church destroyed by an avalanche, remains his most moving project to date. Unlike Le Corbusier at Ronchamp, where stone from a similarly ruined chapel was incorporated into the new building, Zumthor chose to make his entirely of wood. The volume generated by the elliptical, boat-like plan – by turns wonderfully slender and generously broad – is clad with tiny strips of larch, like miniature shingles, and capped by a crisply detailed clerestorey, which hints at the delicate, exquisitely layered structure within. Despite its diminutive actual size, the space is enlarged acoustically by opening the volume to a store below and creating a longer reverberation time. Externally, the larch finish is weathering from rusty brown to silver-grey. Being dependent on the ultraviolet light of the sun, this process is both slower on the northern side and locally variable across the surface; the consequent multiplicity of colours is further enriched by the way they are affected by differences in lighting and weather. The combined effect of this changefulness – to borrow Ruskin's term – is both to emphasize the chapel's form and to render it figurative rather than abstract: standing tall on its Alpine meadow, it has a presence and grace out of all proportion to its size.

The effect of weathering is more self-consciously embraced as part of the architecture in Gigon Guyer's 1998 extension to the art patron and collector Oskar Reinhart's residence in Winterthur, known as the Römerholz. Determined not to make any conventional contextual responses to the imposing house, they opted to manipulate the surface of the cladding in response to the copper roofing of an earlier extension. The concrete of the pre-cast panels was modified by adding limestone and copper, which on oxidation rapidly gave the surface a green cast – a vivid example of Gigon Guyer's belief that 'making architecture is a kind of alchemist's recycling of materials, of the stuff and the things of this world'.[53] The effect was enhanced by allowing rainwater from the copper roof to run down the walls, so that 'the façades lend expression to the various conditions of the building: the particularities of the site, the construction, the climate and the budget.

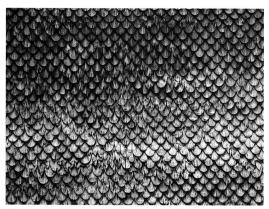

Top: Sogn Benedetg chapel, Sumvitg, by Peter Zumthor: varied weathering of the larch-strip cladding.

Above: Standing tall on its Alpine meadow, Sogn Benedetg has a presence that belies its size.

The apparent size of Sogn Benedetg is enlarged acoustically by opening the interior to a void below.

Weathering as art: copper-stained wall at the extension to the Römerholz, Winterthur, by Gigon Guyer.

In the new art gallery in Bregenz, Austria, Peter Zumthor juxtaposes buildings of metal and glass.

Moreover, the exterior is a reflection of its making – it reveals the principles governing its construction and the grammar of its materiality.'[54] Gigon Guyer's concrete is designed to change slowly, almost imperceptibly, whereas the translucent, etched-glass panels with which Zumthor clad the art museum in Bregenz (1990-7) are calculated to respond instantly to changes in weather and light. Depending on the cloud cover, the position of the sun and your angle of vision, this mysterious, ghostly apparition of a box offers itself as a shimmering light sculpture or a veiled half-revelation of the gallery's inner workings. Silver, pale grey or tinged with blue during the day, as the sun sets it becomes by turns dark and brooding, or a blaze of pale gold. In the presence of such manifold 'phenomenal' delights it is tempting to suppose that these pleasures are readily accessible to anyone with the time to pay attention to them. Tempting, but misguided, because the act of attention they require is inescapably a product of culture.

Knowledge of the magic Dan Flavin could work with fluorescent-tubes, or that James Turrell can extract from framing an experience as ordinary as looking at the sky, is helpful preparation for enjoying Bregenz. Similarly, familiarity with the Modernist fascination with drips, stains, random marks and graffiti – the subject of radical reinterpretation in the 1996 exhibition and book *Formless*[55] – is an invaluable aid to enjoying the more esoteric delights of Gigon Guyer's artful, copper-stained concrete. The 'Swiss Boxes', with their emphasis on the direct optical/haptic experience of materials, were a valuable cleansing after the semantic and formal excesses of the 1980s, but their appeal too often depended on downplaying – if not neglecting – some of the broader social and contextual challenges of architecture.

Although the specific features of the Swiss School can be explained in part as a function of local traditions, a surprisingly wide range of recent work reveals a similar preoccupation with reducing buildings to a singular formal

Above and right: Variously
translucent and reflective,
the glass carapace of the
Bregenz gallery responds
seductively to changing light.

The envelope of Caruso St John's Walsall Art Gallery, England, is expressed as a taut skin.

Alejandro de la Sota's Civil Government Headquarters in Tarragona, Spain, of 1954-57 is a key reference for a new generation of architects in the 1990s.

statement, and then heightening the impact by the surprising use of only one or two materials. Rodolfo Machado and Rodolphe el-Khoury have discussed this tendency under the rubric 'Monolithic Architecture',[56] whilst for Hans Ibelings it is a defining feature of architectural 'supermodernity'.[57] In addition to the Swiss, these authors' examples are as diverse as Dominique Perrault's grand and much maligned Bibliothèque Nationale in Paris; Rafael Moneo's Kursaal in San Sebastian; Simon Ungers' weathering-steel-clad T-house in Wilton, New York; Philippe Starck's Baron Vert office/apartment building in Osaka; and Foreign Office Architects' acclaimed Yokohama International Port Terminal.

In The Netherlands, Willem Neutelings sees the need for strong, forceful buildings as a response to the metropolitan way of life that is transforming the Dutch landscape by erasing the last vestiges of the traditional distinctions between settlements and countryside. A driver need now only travel for twenty minutes, he suggests, to see, strung out along the highway, 'sculptural oil refineries, colourful fields of flowers, intimate garden cities, medieval rings of canals, eight-lane highways … airports, marketplaces, plazas, and mosques'.[58] These disconnected fragments offer 'a rich variety of intense experiences', and, in response,

Neutelings' buildings, designed with partner Michiel Riedijk, frequently assume a bold, sign-like quality.

Utrecht University's Minnaert Building, which Neutelings Riedijk completed in 1997 to house the Earth Sciences department, for example, has its name spelt out in giant, storey-height letters at ground level – like the PSFS sign beloved of Roberti Venturi come down to earth – whilst above, the bulky, sculptural volume of rust-coloured concrete suggests an uplifted geological formation: made of sprayed-on concrete, it has thick wavy lines projecting from its surface intended to evoke ridges in a landscape. The result is reminiscent of Venturi's advocacy of the architecture of the commercial strip, but the interest in material expression and references to landscape make it very much a building of the 1990s.

The same, of course, can be said of two of the most celebrated and widely discussed

Rem Koolhaas's Congrexpo in Lille is a montage of crystalline glass, profiled metal cladding and concrete, richly textured to suggest elephant hide.

Minnaert Building, Utrecht, by Neutelings Riedijk: housing the university's Earth Sciences building, the sprayed-on concrete finish evokes ridges in a landscape.

The all-over zinc cladding and seemingly random diagonal gashes and openings transform Daniel Libeskind's Jewish Museum in Berlin into a continuous wrapped surface.

buildings of the decade: Frank Gehry's titanium-covered Guggenheim Museum in Bilbao and Daniel Libeskind's zinc-clad Jewish Museum in Berlin. Although Frank Gehry works out his initial ideas quite traditionally, using sketches and physical models, the complex three-dimensional forms of his recent buildings can be accurately drawn and engineered only using computer programmes developed in the aerospace industry.[59] Many younger architects prefer to work directly on the computer, using sophisticated new modelling tools that enable the computer to 'think' in terms of surfaces. Variously bent, folded and warped into three-dimensional shapes of extraordinary complexity, the surfaces of the digital architectures being pioneered by, amongst many others, the California-based Greg Lynn, are part of a burgeoning fascination for so-called 'organic' forms, which became evident across many fields of design during the 1990s.[60]

Jan Kaplicky, the Czech-born founder of the London-based Future Systems, has long been one of the most fervent advocates of such architecture, and in 1995 he and his partner Amanda Levete finally won the chance to build a substantial project – the Media Centre at Lord's, the world's most revered cricket-ground, in north London. This large, semi-monocoque structure was fabricated from aluminium in a boatyard and, despite its resemblance to a popular Sony bedside radio, quickly earned the soubriquet 'blob' from the typically sceptical British press.[61] Although intended as a term of abuse, 'blob' was already in widespread use as the most apt description of a worldwide fascination with projects for amorphous buildings – so much so that in 2002, Delft University founded a research department devoted to Blob Architecture.[62] Shortly after their Media Centre opened in 1999, Future Systems won a competition to design for a major new Selfridges Store in Birmingham, England. To be clad with 30,000 aluminium discs, it will be a prime, and still relatively rare, built example of the genre.

The complex curved surfaces of Foster and Partners' glazed roof over the British Museum's Great Court (above) and aluminium-clad North Greenwich Traffic Interchange (top) were made possible by computer-aided design and manufacturing systems.

The complex shapes of Frank
Gehry's Guggenheim Museum
in Bilbao were drawn using
digital data generated
by scanning models.

Reflective by day and translucent by night the undulating glass wall of Norman Foster's Willis Faber Dumas building in Ipswich, England (top and above) is suspended from the eaves and stiffened by glass fins.

The glass panels on Willis Faber Dumas are secured with steel patch fixings and sealed with silicon.

Although the buildings we have discussed represent a diverse range of attitudes to architecture, from boxes to blobs, their emphatic monolithic forms offer an effective way of making a mark amidst the bland or vulgarly strident commercial buildings that dominate modern cities. The self-containment and autonomy that characterize many of them can also be seen as a response to the era of the Internet, of the global flux of information, money and people. As daily life becomes less and less tied to particular places, more and more buildings are becoming could-be-anywhere enclosures, which pay scant regard to their local context. This is equally true of many recent explorations of those hallmarks of Modern architecture, transparency and translucency, which have been given new life by rapid developments in materials technology.

Consider, for example, Norman Foster's building for the insurance brokers Willis Faber Dumas, completed in Ipswich in the east of England in 1975. By hugging the boundaries of the sprawling, amorphous site, its plan recalls a low-rise version of Mies van der Rohe's 1923 Glass Tower, which the faceted glass elevations exploit to similar aesthetic ends. But whereas Mies could only dream of draping his structural skeleton with a continuous, mullion-free glass skin, Foster had at his disposal Pilkington's newly developed suspended glazing system. This enabled the three storeys of glass to be hung from the roof slab and stiffened by structural glass fins, with patch fixings at the corners of each sheet of glass and silicon joints to seal the narrow gaps between them. The dark, bronze-tinted anti-sun glass ensures that by day the exterior becomes an almost seamless surface across which the moving observer sees a complex, ever-changing tapestry of reflections – more figurative than the interplay of light and shade that Mies conjured up with charcoal, perhaps, but still beguiling. And at night, of course, the almost unbroken glass façade allows – to use the words of the prescient article of 1849 quoted in Chapter 3 – 'a magical splendour … to stream out'.[63]

Frameless glazing systems, such as that pioneered by Pilkington, are now part of the commercial vernacular, forcing innovative designers with a passion for technology, such as Norman Foster, to push the possibilities of the material to ever greater lengths – quite literally at the new Hong Kong airport, and metaphorically

The glass wall of the new Hong Kong Airport by Foster and Partners runs for five kilometres (three miles).

Glass-floored atrium of Norman
Foster's Hong Kong and
Shanghai Bank.

Top: Hong Kong and Shanghai
Bank: emblem of open
management or panopticon
of control?

Above: Bibliothèque Nationale,
Paris, by Dominique Perrault.

at Tower Place, an office building completed in the City of London in 2002, which features a vast suspended glass wall of remarkable delicacy. Earlier, at the Hong Kong and Shanghai Bank (1979-86), Foster chose to illuminate the atrium with sunlight reflected from a vast mirror, and then allow the sun to beam its way down through a glass floor onto the broad plaza/passage beneath the building's elevated lower floor – the resulting experience of being under a large building yet still in the sun is uncanny.

In common with many architects, Foster regards the open-plan spaces of buildings like the Hong Kong and Shanghai Bank as means to promote more 'democratic' ways of working. But in a corporate context, such openness frequently demands a high level of control over the occupants' work spaces, and even clothing, to project the efficient image expected in the business world.[64] As critics of modernity have frequently pointed out, the much-vaunted openness of such architecture can just as readily be a vehicle for panoptic control as an expression of the breakdown of social hierarchies. The correlation of transparency with the supposed 'openness' of democratic societies and processes is equally fraught, but that has not stopped it becoming something of a cliché of late twentieth-century government buildings such as Behnisch and Partners'

German Parliament in Bonn, Foster's spectacular glass dome at the Reichstag, or Richard Rogers' Law Courts in Bordeaux and competition-winning design for the new Welsh Assembly.

So far as I am aware, Jean Nouvel has made no claims other than 'architectural' ones for one of the most inventive and successful essays in transparency, the Cartier Foundation in Paris (1991-4). The building, if such it can be called, is conceived as a layered composition of glazed screens, some free-standing to define the site frontage, others extending past the enclosed space to capture the sky and surrounding garden. Whereas with many would-be transparent structures, the box-like form and far-from-transparent reflections still dominate, here the result has a landscape-like feeling of permeability. By helping to maintain the openness of the site – which used to be continuous with the adjacent garden – Nouvel's use of transparency made eminent sense. But when Dominique Perrault decided to house the books of the new French National Library in four L-shaped glass towers, the decision struck many critics as perverse. Not only did it mean consigning the readers and staff to the vast podium below – admittedly around an inviting sunken 'forest' – but protecting the books from sunlight necessitated a continuous screen of hinged timber panels. In practice, the result is beguiling: opening and closing like the covers of giant books, the shutters become public guardians of knowledge, describing seemingly random, ever-changing patterns like monumental bar codes.

Jean Nouvel's Cartier Foundation in Paris is a composition of layered glass screens.

Transparency in excelsis:
Ichthus Hogeschool, Rotterdam,
Erick van Egeraat.

A transparent material such as glass, especially one that can shatter if subject to unwelcome stresses, is not an obvious candidate to be used structurally. When glazing systems are referred to as 'structural', it means only that they are hung from the building structure without the necessity of additional framing. In point of material fact, however, glass is tremendously strong, and when toughened can take compressive forces comparable to many building stones. In principle, therefore, there is no reason why it might not be used to support roofs – even, conceivably, floors. The major glass companies that control the world supply have been reluctant to provide the detailed performance data required to use glass structurally,[65] but for many architects and engineers this has only added to the fascination of all-glass structures, or of the more limited ambition of glass floors – the final surface to resist dematerialization.

In 1986 the Dutch architects Benthem and Crouwel startled the world with a minimal, super-transparent sculpture pavilion at Sonsbeek, in which the glass walls supported the steel lattice beams, which in turn held the glass roof. In 1990, Bernard Tschumi made a similar impact with the Glass Video Pavilion in Groningen, but it fell to the London-based American architect Rick Mather, working with

the engineers Dewhurst Macfarlane, to complete the world's first genuinely all-glass structure two years later. The scale was modest – a conservatory added to a house in Hampstead – but the detailing was elegant and the construction involved no metal connectors or bolts of any kind – just glass and glue. Suddenly, Bruno Taut's Alpine homages to glass seemed a step nearer to reality.

In 1994, the hybrid structure of my own Radiant House, designed with the engineer Mark Lovell, was begun at Milton Keynes.[66] The 5.5 tonne stressed skin plywood roof is supported entirely by a wall and clerestorey of 15mm-thick sheets of toughened glass, yielding one of the world's most highly stressed glass structures – beyond the limits of a recent Code of Practice.[67] The south-facing glass wall, 3.6 metres (12 feet) high, is stiffened by a Vierendeel beam made of galvanized steel and hung horizontally to double as wind girder and sun-louvre. Suspended from the roof, it transmits wind-loads horizontally into reinforced-concrete piers at each end, whilst doubling as a sunshade for the lower section of glass.

Translucency, transparency's discreet cousin, has also been given new life by a range of developments in materials technology and manufacturing. Glass can be veiled by meshes and nets of perforated or woven metal; its surface can be made milky by etching with acid or blasting with sand – in this way, translucency feels like transparency made material; and it can be screen-printed with 'frits' of dots, lines or meshes – developed to help control solar heat gains, these are now being used to render even more elusive the interplay between surface, reflection and interior.

Various types of polycarbonate sheet, hitherto of dubious merit due to their tendency to discolour and turn increasingly opaque, are now far more stable and offer a reasonable life expectation at much less cost than glass. And they, like glass, can be screen-printed with images as well as geometric patterns.

Top: Glass-structured conservatory, Hampstead, London, by Rick Mather.

Middle: Roof of laminated glass arches, Cosham, England, by the author.

Above: At the author's Radiant House, Milton Keynes, 15mm-thick glass walls support a 5.5 tonne roof.

True to his love of conspicuously cheap materials, Rem Koolhaas has made extensive use of corrugated polycarbonate sheeting. At the Kunsthal in Rotterdam (completed in 1992), for example, it appears in the roof-lights in the galleries and as illuminated internal cladding and doors in the lecture hall. Following Koolhaas's lead, Koen van Velsen chose an opalescent polycarbonate to clad the entire complex of the multi-screen cinema that frames one side of the West 8-designed Schouwburgplein in Rotterdam. It is impressive by day but even more so, as Catherine Slessor describes it, at night: 'the entire building lights up like a huge, free-form Japanese paper lantern, glowing with a softly luminous intensity'.[68] A similar quality is produced, with altogether more refined, costly and durable means, by Rafael Moneo's Kursaal in San Sebastian, completed in 1995. The tilted glass 'boxes', which, like Utzon's 'shells' in Sydney, house the auditoria, are clad with subtly scalloped glass planks, transforming their crystalline forms into an interplay of texture and light in tune with the fugitive surfaces of sea and sky.

Herzog and de Meuron have made characteristically inventive use of screen-printing. The principal façade of their second building for Ricola, completed in 1993 in Mulhouse, France, is covered with a repeated image of a leaf taken from a photograph by Karl Blossfeldt, the Jugendstil teacher whose work was later championed by advocates of New Objectivity.[69] Such 'tattooing' of buildings – a piquant challenge to Adolf Loos's strictures about ornament and crime[70] – shows every sign of becoming increasingly popular[71] and can also be economically applied to opaque materials, as Herzog and de Meuron subsequently demonstrated with the new library for the Technical School at Eberswalde in Switzerland (1997-9). In an echo of all-over *sgraffito* – a traditional Swiss speciality – bands of newspaper photographs are wrapped around all the façades. Repeated 66 times, as if on a stationary newsreel, they were transferred to the concrete using a special 'serilith' process, and silkscreened across the high-level glazing – the small windows for view were spared. Although the surface is best described literally as a 'tattooed skin', the result is perceptually more like a translucent veil, which seems to float slightly in front of the 'real' materials, whilst seen from an acute angle, or in the rain, the images appear sharper, 'like lead-type newspaper printing plates'.[72]

Of the new translucent materials, the most intriguing, perhaps, is ETFE (Ethylene Tetra Fluoro Ethylene), a recyclable lightweight foil that admits a wide spectrum of light. Despite appearing milky in some conditions, ETFE

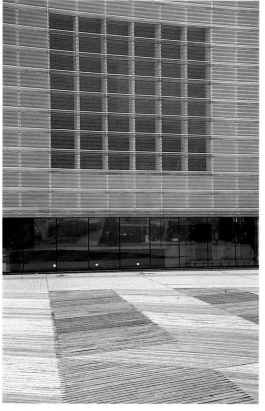

Polycarbonate cladding on multiplex cinema, Schouwburgplein, Rotterdam, by Koen van Velsen.

Rafael Moneo's Kursaal in San Sebastian, Spain, is clad with scalloped glass planks.

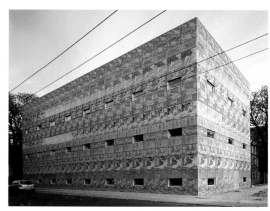

Eberswalde Library by Herzog and de Meuron.

Translucent front elevation
of Herzog and de Meuron's
building for Ricola in Mulhouse.

actually allows through more useful light for growing plants than glass: it was this that commended its use on the inter-linked geodesic domes of one of Britain's most successful Millennium projects, the Eden Centre by Nicholas Grimshaw and the engineer Tony Hunt, which opened in Cornwall, England, in 2001.

In Japan, the extensive use of clear glass runs contrary to the spirit of the tradition of admitting light through paper screens, and it was this aspect of Westernization to which Jun'ichiro Tanizaki alluded in the title of his celebrated lament, *In Praise of Shadows*.[73] Traditionally, Tanizaki nostalgically explains, 'the light from the garden steals in but dimly through paper-panelled doors, and it is precisely this indirect light that makes for us the charm of a room.'[74] Recently, Japanese architects as diverse in their approaches as Tadao Ando, Toyo Ito and Itsuko Hasegawa have begun to explore again the delights of filtered and indirect light. In the long, straight corridor that leads to the Chapel on Mount Rokko (1985-6), for example, Ando uses heavily etched glass in a manner that recalls the filtered light of *shoji* screens. Combined with the lack of strong textures or colours, the soft, even illumination makes for a slight feeling of levitation, whilst the lack of shadows helps to distance the ceremonial space from the quotidian world of the hotel it serves.[75]

Toyo Ito makes extensive use of both glass and transparency, but the effects he seeks are inflected by his interest in the qualities of traditional Japanese light. His ideal is spatial fluidity, and by this he means something more than the elimination of visual barriers between inside and out. Fluidity, for Ito, is exemplified above all by the Barcelona Pavilion, which, he suggests, exhibits 'not the lightness of flowing air but the thickness of molten liquid. … it makes us feel as if we are looking at things underwater, and would be better described as translucent. What we experience here is not the flow of air but the sense of wandering and drifting gently underwater.'[76] As so often with architects' readings of other people's work, this description – written in 1997 – was also a statement of Ito's aspirations for the building on which he began work that same year, the Sendai Mediathèque, which opened three years later.

In Sendai, the metaphor of being underwater is made almost palpable. Formally, the building could be described as a straightforward re-working of Le Corbusier's 'Five Points of a New Architecture',[77] complete with public roof garden. But the changes Ito makes to the Corbusian schema transform his building into something new. Most obvious is the dematerialization of the vertical pilotis into transparent bundles of steel tubes that resemble high-tech basketry. Swerving and swaying their way up through the floors, they provide both support and services – lifts, stairs and conditioned air. Ito thought of them as 'seaweed-like',[78] and the simile is reinforced by the feeling that they are held captive by glass, as if in a giant aquarium. This is, in fact, the presiding metaphor for the building, which Ito sees as a container for the random-seeming experiences of the metropolis and the ceaseless flows of digital data.[79]

A decade ago, as concerns about global warming became matters of general public concern, many commentators were predicting the end of the all-glass building. Now, layered façades and 'intelligent skins'[80], which combine

Tadao Ando's chapel on Mount Rokko is reached via a translucent, etched-glass colonnade.

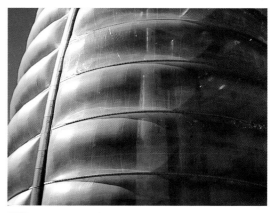

ETFE cladding, National Space Science Centre, Leicester, England, by Nicholas Grimshaw.

Building-as-aquarium: Sendai
Mediathèque by Toyo Ito.

Façade as layered environmental filter: GSW Building, Berlin, by Sauerbruch Hutton.

various types of high-performance glass, automatic blinds, solar shading and other devices to selectively admit or exclude sun, control the admission of daylight and retain thermal energy, are rapidly gaining ground as amongst the most energy-efficient forms of construction available for high-performance buildings. A good early example is provided by Foster & Partners' Business Promotion Centre in Duisburg (1988-93), flagship for the city's post-industrial Microelectronics Park. The building's proximity to a major road precluded the use of opening windows, and the sealed double-skin glass façade is supported by slender aluminium mullions suspended from a steel ring-beam at eaves level. Its cavity contains computer-controlled perforated metal blinds, which tilt automatically in response to heat and light sensors in each office: even when closed, the seven per cent density of perforations allows the occupants to enjoy a view out.

At first sight, the multi-coloured, pixellated west façade of Sauerbruch Hutton's 1999 headquarters office building for GSW – one of the largest providers of social housing in Berlin – might appear to be a large-scale essay in abstract art. In fact, the coloured panels are perforated shades, which pivot and slide to provide solar control whilst, as in Duisburg, still allowing a veiled view out. Here, they sit in the void of a convection-driven 'solar flue' formed by the outer, single-glazed layer and the inner, double-glazed skin of the offices. The latter includes opening windows, and the building is designed to be naturally ventilated for much of the year. When wind speeds are low, the solar flue helps to promote air movement; and when they are uncomfortably high, it is used to moderate airflows through the offices – as the system is based on cross-ventilation, it works for rooms on both sides of the building. Air movement through the solar flue is automatically controlled by dampers at top and bottom, whilst red and green indicator lights on the window transoms, controlled by the Building

Management System, provide individual occupants with an indication of whether or not they need to switch to mechanical ventilation.

For a new arts centre in Singapore, completed in 2002, architect Michael Wilford and London-based engineers Atelier One and Ten have developed a complex, three-dimensional glazed envelope, insulated and shaded by aluminium-clad panels. As the curvature of the skin increases, the panels are allowed to pop up to form an array of small 'beaks' to allow views out whilst cutting out even low-angle sun. As the engineer Neil Thomas observes, 'the modulated skin began to take on the combined qualities of the scales and gills of a fish, by either providing a protective, smooth, sealed skin, or by opening up to let it breathe'.[81]

The 'intelligent' façades of buildings such as the GSW Headquarters are giving new meaning to the word 'skin' in architecture, which has been used elsewhere in this book to denote a thin surface 'stretched' across a building. Now, as buildings become capable of responding to changes in temperature, light and other environmental factors, their surfaces are performing like skin in the biological sense of the word – layered, multi-purpose membranes designed to mediate the body's contact with the environment. And in the process, the familiar, fixed states of transparency, opacity and form are giving way to translucency and transformability. With the need to reduce human impacts on the global climate becoming a major concern, maximizing the use of natural light and solar energy, whilst minimizing dependence on mechanical systems, is an increasingly important objective of the design of building envelopes. Similarly, reducing embodied energy and designing with recycling, not demolition and disposal, in mind offers a challenging new agenda for future explorations of the expression of materials and form in architecture.

Business Promotion Centre, Duisburg, by Norman Foster.

Singapore Arts Centre by Michael Wilford and engineers Atelier One and Ten.

Conclusion

This book began with MVRDV's houses near The Hague, so contemporary in their surreal packaging, so knowing as a commentary on the housing market. It ends with the courtyard houses designed by Jørn Utzon for a site on the edge of Fredensborg in Denmark. Completed in 1963, they were built for professional people – civil servants and diplomats, consultants and military officers – returning home after careers abroad. Utzon valued the courtyard type as a means of accommodating people's varied lifestyles within a shared form, and the walls that contain the courts were individually designed on site as the houses neared completion, to take account of views, overlooking and exposure to sun and wind.

The balance between repetition and variety is finely struck, and reinforced by the variations that result from fitting the houses to the sloping land. The result, with its continuous bounding walls and sentinel-like chimneys, evokes memories of the organic cohesion of a medieval walled town. This feeling is reinforced by Utzon's choice of materials and, just as important, by his rigorous suppression of those secondary elements – the vent pipes and flues, which MVRDV celebrate – that might undermine the homogeneity of the built fabric. The bricks are minutely varied in texture and colour, and almost fuse with the yellow tiles, whose smoothness and colour have been softened by weathering: like a mud-brick-built Islamic city, you feel it might almost have been cast, rather than built, from clay. As for the inevitable pipes, they are accommodated in the chimneys, and they in turn, cubic in form and with tiny pitched roofs, are like miniatures of the houses.

Designed forty years apart, these two groups of houses sum up many of the issues and attitudes we have explored in this book. Although the Classicist Semper might be somewhat taken aback at the suggestion, the lineage of MVRDV's designs belongs to the theory of 'dressing', which he expounded with such ingenuity. Utzon's work, on the other hand, epitomizes not only that belief in 'truth to materials', which underpinned much Modernist architecture, but seems equally paradigmatic for more recent attempts to ground the discipline in what Juhani Pallasmaa has called 'the veracity of matter' (see page 194). Both projects could equally well be advanced as contrasting models for the future, the one eagerly – if somewhat ironically – embracing synthetic materials and unmistakably of the moment, the other a potential model for sustainable design, made of baked earth, designed to weather gracefully, and feeling both ancient and modern.

Despite frequent predictions about a brave new world of synthetic, purpose-designed materials just around the corner, and opposing, sometimes almost messianic prophecies of a radical, back-to-basics future to be lived out in buildings made largely of earth and (soft)wood, the history of the conservative business of building suggests that these, and many other futures, are likely to continue to live side by side. Much the same could be said of massive walls and multi-layered 'intelligent' skins, both of which have their fervent advocates as means towards low-energy buildings.

The renewed interest in materials and surfaces has done much to enrich the vocabulary of architecture, but like the easy formulae of the International Style – which Aalto dismissed in 1935 as 'a pleasing compote of chromed tubes, glass tops, cubistic forms, and astounding colour combinations' – it is already in danger of promoting an 'architecture' that amounts to little more than an ingratiating display of tastefully matched and contrasted textures and colours. The materials of our exemplary housing schemes result from far more than narrowly 'aesthetic' decisions, and they speak loud and clear about different attitudes to living, about the individual and society, and about community and privacy. All architecture worth the name embodies a vision of how we might live, and the architect's challenge, as ever, is to materialize that vision through construction.

Courtyard housing, Fredensborg, Denmark, by Jørn Utzon, completed in 1963.

Index

Notes

Chapter 1
Materials For Building

1. Quoted in Herman Hertzberger, Addie van Roijen-Wortmann and Francis Strauven, *Aldo van Eyck* (Amsterdam: Stichting Wonen/Van Loghum Slaterus, 1982), p47.
2. Sir Banister Fletcher, *A History of Architecture on the Comparative Method* (London: Batsford, 7th edn. 1924), p1.
3. See Joseph Rykwert, *On Adam's House in Paradise* (New York: Museum of Modern Art, 1981), pp62–3.
4. See ibid. for a detailed exploration of the 'primitive hut' in architectural history.
5. Ibid., p105.
6. Ibid., p39.
7. Marc-Antoine Laugier, tr. by Wolfgang and Anni Herrmann, *An Essay on Architecture* (Los Angeles: Hennessey & Ingalls, 1977). The original French edition appeared in 1753; the engraving was added to the second edition, published in 1755.
8. For a fascinating discussion of timber construction, see Klaus Zwerger, *Wood and Wood Joints. Building Traditions of Europe and Japan* (Basel: Birkhäuser, 2000), esp. p78ff.
9. Ibid., p80.
10. The illustration of the store on Gotland is taken from Erik Lundberg, *Arkitekturens Formspråk* (Stockholm: Nordisk Rotogravyr, 1945), p92.
11. Asano Kyoshi, foreword to M. N. Parent, *The Roof in Japanese Buddhist Architecture* (New York and Tokyo, 1985), p4.
12. For the Cimone and other bridges, see Andrea Palladio, tr. by Isaac Ware, *The Four Books of Architecture* (New York: Dover, 1965), pp65–73. The illustration is taken from p69.
13. John Harvey, quoted in Cecil A. Hewitt, *English Historic Carpentry* (London: Phillimore, 1980), p188.
14. See Lynne Elizabeth and Cassandra Adams, eds, *Alternative Construction. Contemporary Natural Building Methods* (New York: John Wiley, 2000), p88ff.
15. R. E. Wycherley, *The Stones of Athens* (Princeton: Princeton University Press, 1978), p267.
16. The classic source on English brickwork is Nathaniel Lloyd, *A History of English Brickwork* (London, 1928).
17. Andrew Plumridge and Wim Meulenkamp, *Brickwork: architecture and design* (New York: Abrams, 1993), p22.
18. Richard A. Goldthwaite, *The Building of Renaissance Florence* (Baltimore: Johns Hopkins University Press, 1982), p177.
19. Robert Atkins and Hope Bagenal, *Theory and Elements of Architecture*, Vol. I (London: Ernest Benn, 1926), p30.
20. Goldthwaite, op. cit., p223.
21. For building construction in Ancient Egypt see Dieter Arnold, *Building in Egypt* (Oxford: Oxford University Press, 1991).
22. Wycherley, op. cit., p267. The quotation is from Xenophon's *Poroi*, 1.4.
23. See Jole Leivick, *Carrara. The Marble Quarries of Tuscany* (Stanford: Stanford University Press, 1999).
24. Palladio, op. cit., p4.
25. Francis Horner is quoted by Samuel Smiles in his *Industrial Biography* (1863). Cited in Asa Briggs, *Iron Bridge to Crystal Palace* (London: Thames and Hudson, 1979), p137.
26. I am grateful to my colleague Mark Lovell, principal of the structural engineers MLDE, for this information.
27. J. E. Gordon, *The Science of Structures and Materials* (New York: Scientific American Library, 1988), p135.
28. See Dan Klein and Ward Lloyd, *The History of Glass* (London: Orbis, 1984), and Michael Wigginton, *Glass in Architecture* (London: Phaidon, 1996).
29. Briggs, op. cit., p168.
30. The ninth- or tenth-century treatise known as the *Mappa Clavicula* is mentioned in Raymond McGrath and A. C. Frost, *Glass in Architecture and Decoration* (London: The Architectural Press, 1937), p49.
31. The source of nickel sulphide in glass is sand, and the quantities vary significantly between different deposits. The nature and extent of this problem is still the subject of dispute amongst experts.
32. See Bjørn Berge, tr. by Filip Henley, *Ecology of Building Materials* (Oxford: Architectural Press, 2000).
33. See ibid. and Elizabeth and Adams, op. cit.
34. See Klaus Dunkelberg, *IL 31: Bambus – Bamboo* (Stuttgart: Institute for Lightweight Structures, 1985).
35. See Otto Kapfinger, *Martin Rauch. Rammed Earth* (Basel: Birkhäuser, 2001).
36. See Easton's contribution on rammed earth in Elizabeth and Adams, op. cit., pp151–73.

Chapter 2
Materials and Form

1. Gottfried Semper, *The Four Elements of Architecture and Other Writings* (Cambridge: Cambridge University Press, 1989), p269.
2. John Ruskin, *The Seven Lamps of Architecture*, Ch. V, I.
3. Quoted in James Hall, *The World as Sculpture* (London: Chatto and Windus, 1999), p62. In 1893, the sculptor Adolf Hildebrand explained that it was essential for the sculptor to conceive the final form as latent in the block, and that even after the figure has been 'freed', we still 'sense the block as a unity even though it has materially disappeared'. See Hildebrand's 'The Problem of Form in the Fine Arts' in *Empathy, Form and Space*, tr. by Harry Francis Mallgrave and Eleftherios Ikonomou (Santa Monica: Getty Center, 1994), pp227–79.
4. Quoted in Penelope Curtis, *Sculpture 1900–1945* (Oxford: Oxford University Press, 1999), p86.
5. In David Leatherbarrow, *The Roots of Architectural Invention* (Cambridge: Cambridge University Press, 1993), p210.
6. David Pye, *The Nature and Art of Workmanship* (Cambridge: Cambridge University Press, 1968), p46.
7. Leon Battista Alberti, *Ten Books on Architecture*, Book 7, Ch. 2.
8. John Ruskin, *Seven Lamps*, Ch. 3, XI.
9. Adrian Stokes, 'Stones of Rimini' in *The Critical Writings of Adrian Stokes* (London: Thames and Hudson, 1978), Vol. I, p197.
10. Martin Heidegger, tr. by Albert Hofstadter, 'The Origin of the Work of Art' in *Poetry, Language, Thought*, (New York: Harper and Row, 1971), p46.
11. Arthur Schopenhauer tr, by E. F. Payne, *The World as Will and Representation* (New York: Dover, 1969), Vol. I, p215.
12. Ibid., p224.
13. Le Corbusier, tr. by Frederick Etchells, *Towards a New Architecture* (London: Architectural Press, 1946), p192.
14. See the discussion in Eugène-Emmanuel Viollet-le-Duc, tr. by Benjamin Bucknall, *Discourses on Architecture* (New York: Grove Press, 1959), Vol. I, pp50–5.
15. Gottfried Semper, op. cit., p102
16. Quoted in Demetri Porphyrios, *Classical Architecture* (London: Academy Editions, 1991), p142.
17. Le Corbusier, op. cit., p193.
18. Kenneth Frampton, *Studies in Tectonic Culture* (Cambridge, Mass. and London: MIT Press, 1995).
19. For classic discussions of this theme, see Wilhelm Worringer, tr. by Sir Herbert Read. *Form in Gothic* (London: Alec Tiranti, 1964), and Otto von Simson, *The Gothic Cathedral* (Princeton: Princeton University Press, 1962, pb. 1974).

20 Frank Lloyd Wright, ed. Frederick Gutheim, *In the Cause of Architecture. Essays by Frank Lloyd Wright for Architectural Record* (New York: Architectural Record, 1975), p175 – original article pub. in 1928.

21 The ribs seem to have emerged as elaborations of the lines of intersection of the different surfaces of the vault and their actual contribution to the stability of the structure has been much debated. Visually, however, they contribute greatly to the legibility of the construction.

22 John Ruskin, *Seven Lamps*, Ch. II, XXIV.

23 See Heinrich Wölfflin, 'Prolegomena to a Psychology of Architecture' in *Empathy and Space*, op. cit., pp149–90.

24 This is a major theme of Italo Calvino, tr. by Patrick Creagh, *Six Memos for the Next Millennium* (Cambridge, Mass.: Harvard University Press, 1988), esp. 'Lightness'.

25 John Ruskin, *The Stones of Venice*, Vol. II, XVII.

26 Quoted in Marco Frascari, 'The Lume Materiale in the Architecture of Venice', *Perspecta 24*, pp135–45.

27 Ibid., p143.

28 For this and other fascinating information and interpretation, see Paul Hills, *Venetian Colour* (New Haven: Yale University Press, 1999).

29 Karsten Harries, *The Bavarian Rococo Church* (New Haven: Yale University Press, 1983), p73.

30 Ibid., p116.

31 For a fuller discussion see my *Alvar Aalto* (London: Phaidon Press, 1995), pp200–12.

32 For an introduction to these movements see my *Modernism* (London: Phaidon Press, 1996).

33 See Iain Boyd White, ed. and tr., *The Crystal Chain Letters* (Cambridge, Mass.: MIT Press, 1985).

34 Wassili Luckhardt quoted in ibid., p52.

35 Ibid., p91.

36 Mies van der Rohe, 'Skyscrapers' in Fritz Neumeyer, *The Artless Word* (Cambridge, Mass.: MIT Press), p240 (originally pub. in *Frühlicht*, 1, no.4, 1922).

37 Ibid., p183.

38 Theo van Doesburg, 'Towards a Plastic Architecture', *De Stijl*, VI, 6/7 (1924), pp78–83.

39 For a difficult but provocative discussion, see Indra Kagis McEwen, *Socrates' Ancestor. An Essay on Architectural Beginnings* (Cambridge, Mass.: MIT Press, 1993). McEwen concludes by arguing that far from architecture being a form of 'built metaphysics', Greek philosophy was initially modelled on architecture.

40 Vitruvius, tr. by Morris Hicky Morgan, *The Ten Books on Architecture* (New York: Dover, 1960), p6.

41 Orig. 'commoditie, firmeness and delight' in Sir Henry Wootton, *The Architectural Elements*, 1624.

42 Leon Battista Alberti, ed. and tr. by J. Rykwert, N. Leach and R. Tavernor, *On the Art of Building in Ten Books* (Cambridge, Mass.: MIT Press, 1988), VI, 2, p156.

43 See Alberto Pérez-Gómez, *Architecture and the Crisis of Modern Science* (Cambridge, Mass.: MIT Press, 1983), p64.

44 Rudolf Wittkower, *Architectural Principles in the Age of Humanism* (New York: John Wiley, 1971; orig. pub. 1949).

45 Quoted in Hellmut Wohl, *The Aesthetics of Italian Renaissance Art* (Cambridge: Cambridge University Press, 1999), p60.

46 For many examples of such colour prejudices, see David Batchelor, *Chromophobia* (London: Reaktion Books, 2000).

47 Quoted from Walter Pater's classic account of the Renaissance in Batchelor, op. cit., p17.

48 See Alex Potts, *Flesh and the Ideal: Winckelmann and the Origins of Art History* (New Haven: Yale University Press, 2000).

49 Wohl, op. cit., p7.

50 Ibid., p153.

51 Ibid., p184.

52 The most recent and vigorous advocacy of Alberti's authorship is by Liane Lefaivre in *Leon Battista Alberti's Hypnerotomachia Poliphili. Eros, Furore and Humanism in the Early Italian Renaissance* (Cambridge, Mass.: MIT Press, 1997).

53 Francesco Colonna, tr. by Joscelyn Godwin, *Hypnerotomachia Poliphili* (London: Thames and Hudson, 1999), pp94–8.

54 Wohl, op. cit., p179.

55 See, for example, Otto von Simson, op. cit.

56 For Cosmati pavements see Paloma Pajares-Ayuela, *Cosmatesque Ornament* (London: Thames and Hudson, 2002).

57 For the 'Polychrome War' see David van Zanten. *The Architectural Polychromy of the 1830s* (New York: Garland Publishing, 1977).

58 Frank Lloyd Wright, op. cit., p174.

59 John Ruskin, *The Seven Lamps of Architecture*, Ch. II, XVIII.

60 Semper, op. cit., pp45–73.

61 *Di Lucio Vitruvio Pollione de architectura libri decem* was translated and illustrated by Cesare Cesariano and published in Como in 1521. The illustration is folio XXXII recto.

62 Semper, op. cit., p104.

63 Ibid., p39.

64 Ibid., p61.

65 Leatherbarrow, op. cit., p178ff.

66 For a discussion see Wolfgang Herrmann's introduction to *In What Style Should We Build?* (Santa Monica: Getty Center, 1992).

67 Semper, op. cit., p55.

68 Otto Wagner, tr. by Harry Francis Mallgrave, *Modern Architecture* (Santa Monica: Getty Center, 1988), p96.

69 For an iconographic interpretation of the bank see Ákos Moravánszky, ' "Truth to Material" vs "The Principle of Cladding": the language of materials in architecture', AA Files 31, pp39–46.

70 John Ruskin, *The Stones of Venice*, Vol. II, XXV.

71 See 'The Principle of Cladding', in Adolf Loos, tr. by Jane O. Newman and John H. Smith, *Spoken into the Void. Collected Essays 1897–1900* (Cambridge, Mass.: MIT Press, 1982), pp66–9.

72 Paul Hills, *Venetian Colour*, op. cit., p79.

73 The best known early example is by the Vesnin Brothers, in their 1924 competition project for the Pravda Tower. A glass-fronted lift shaft still greets visits to Alvar Aalto's Paimio Sanatorium, completed in 1933.

74 See Benedetto Gravagnuolo, tr. by C. H. Evans, *Adolf Loos* (Milan: Idea Books, 1982), pp125–33.

75 Adolf Loos, 'Men's Fashion', in *Spoken into the Void*, op. cit., pp11–14.

76 Norman Shaw's New Zealand Chambers were a possible model.

77 See 'A Coat of Whitewash. The Law of Ripolin' in Le Corbusier, tr. by James I. Dunnett, *The Decorative Art of Today* (London: The Architectural Press, 1987), pp185–92.

78 Mark Wigley, *White Walls, Designer Dresses. The Fashioning of Modern Architecture* (Cambridge, Mass.: MIT Press, 1995), p31.

79 Le Corbusier, *Towards a New Architecture*, op. cit., p31.

80 August Schmarsow, 'The Essence of Architectural Creation' in *Empathy, Form and Space*, op. cit. pp281–97, emphases in the original.

Chapter 3
In the nature of materials

1 P. V. Jensen-Klint was a leading Danish architect, best known for the all-brick Grundtvig Church in Copenhagen. His words of advice for students were written in 1919 and are quoted by Steen Eiler Rasmussen in *Experiencing Architecture* (London: Chapman and Hall, 1964), p169.

2 Frank Lloyd Wright, ed. Frederick Gutheim, *In the Cause of Architecture. Essays by Frank Lloyd Wright for Architectural Record* (New York: Architectural Record, 1975), p198.

3 See Alexander Tzonis and Liane Lefaivre, 'The Mechanization of architecture and the birth of Functionalism' in *Via 7*, 1984, pp120–43.

4 Perrault's ideas are also discussed by Tzonis and Lefaivre in ibid.

5 See Alberto Pérez-Gómez, *Architecture and the Crisis of Modern Science* (Cambridge, Mass.: MIT Press, 1983), esp. pp197–201.

6 Joseph Rykwert, *On Adam's House in Paradise* (New York: Museum of Modern Art, 1981), p56.

7 Ibid., p57.

8 Heinrich Hübsch, 'In What Style Should We Build' in Wolfgang Herrmann, ed. and tr. *In What Style Should We Build?*, op. cit., pp63–101.

9 See Michael Snodin, ed., *Karl Friedrich Schinkel. A Universal Man* (New Haven: Yale University Press, 1991).

10 M. F. Hearn, ed., *The Architectural Theory of Eugène-Emmanuel Viollet-le-Duc* (Cambridge, Mass.: MIT Press, 1990), p57.

11 Ibid., p85.

12 Ibid., p116.

13 Ibid., p171.

14 See Frank Lloyd Wright, op. cit.

15 The *Dictionnaire* has not been translated into English. For key passages, see Eugène-Emmanuel Viollet-le-Duc, tr. by Kenneth D. Whitehead, *The Foundations of Architecture* (New York: George Braziller, 1990).

16 Frank Lloyd Wright, *An Autobiography* (New York: Duell, Sloan and Pierce, 1977), p97.

17 Ibid., p187.

18 Ibid., p73.

19 Kenneth Frampton and Yukio Futagawa, *Modern Architecture 1851–1919* (New York: Rizzoli, 1983), p98.

20 Quoted in Fritz Neumeyer, *The Artless Word* (Cambridge, Mass.: MIT Press), p66.

21 A. W. N. Pugin, *The True Principles of Pointed or Christian Architecture* (London: Academy Editions, 1973; orig. pub. in 1841), p47.

22 Ibid., p2. For a discussion of the role of different stones in the development of Gothic, see Robert Atkins and Hope Bagenal, *Theory and Elements of Architecture*, Vol. I (London: Ernest Benn, 1926).

23 Ruskin, a Protestant, could never forgive Pugin his conversion to Roman Catholicism.

24 John Ruskin, *The Seven Lamps of Architecture*, Ch. I, I.

25 Ibid., Ch. II, XIX.

26 Ibid., Ch. V, XXI.

27 Ibid., Ch. II, X.

28 David Pye, *The Nature and Art of Workmanship* (Cambridge: Cambridge University Press, 1968), p59.

29 John Ruskin, *The Stones of Venice*, Vol. II, Ch. VI, XXIII.

30 Ibid., VI, XXXI.

31 Ibid., VI, LXXVIII.

32 Ibid., VI, LXXVIII.

33 Le Corbusier, tr. by James I. Dunnett, *The Decorative Art of Today* (London: The Architectural Press, 1987), p132. For Ruskin's influence on Le Corbusier's drawings, see M. P. M. Sekler, *The Early Drawings of Charles-Edouard Jeanneret (Le Corbusier), 1902–1908* (New York: Garland, 1977).

34 William Morris, 'On the external coverings of roofs', lecture, in May Morris, ed. *The Collected Works of William Morris* (London: Longmans Green, 1910–15), Vol. XXII, p429.

35 Quoted in Peter Davey, *Arts and Crafts Architecture* (London: The Architectural Press, 1980), p25.

36 Quoted in Asa Briggs. *Iron Bridge to Crystal Palace* (London: Thames and Hudson, 1979), p169.

37 Viollet-le-Duc, *The Foundations of Architecture*, op. cit., p186.
38 Quoted by Sokratis Georgiadis in his Introduction to Sigfried Giedion, *Building in France, Building in Iron, Building in Ferroconcrete* (Santa Monica: Getty Center, 1995), p10, emphasis in original.
39 See the editors' Introduction to *Empathy, Form and Space*, tr. and ed. by Harry Francis Mallgrave and Eleftherios Ikonomou (Santa Monica: Getty Center, 1994).
40 Ibid., p53.
41 For a detailed discussion of these ideas, see Sokratis Georgiadis's introduction to *Building in France. . .* op. cit.
42 Ibid., p6.
43 Ibid., p102.
44 See my *Modernism* (London: Phaidon Press, 1996), p27.
45 See David van Zanten. *The Architectural Polychromy of the 1830s* (New York: Garland Publishing, 1977), p34.
46 Mrs Merrifield, 'The Harmony of Colours', in *The Crystal Palace Exhibition Illustration Catalogue* (1851; reprinted New York: Dover Publications, 1970), p1.
47 It remained open to the public until it was destroyed by fire in 1936.
48 The lower piers were originally painted a deep red-brown, and the colour was progressively lightened towards the top. See Joseph Harriss, *The Tallest Tower: Eiffel and the Belle Epoque* (Boston: Houghton Miffin, 1975), p100.
49 The tiny painting (24x16cm/9.5x6in) is in the collection of the Fine Arts Museum of San Francisco and is reproduced in John Rewald, *Seurat* (London: Thames and Hudson, 1990), p168.
50 *Building in France. . .*, op. cit., p24.
51 Hermann Muthesius, tr. by Stanford Anderson, *Style-Architecture and Building-Art* (Santa Monica: Getty Center, 1994), p74.
52 Ibid., p85.
53 The *Neue Sachlichkeit* movement of the 1920s in Germany is generally translated as 'New Objectivity'.
54 *Building in France. . .* op. cit., p26.
55 Ibid., p27.
56 Ibid., pp31–2. Josef-August Lux's *Ingenieur-Aesthetik* was published in Munich in 1910.
57 Meyer identified four features of the new aesthetic. A 'new spatial value' which was 'limitless' and 'bright', and created a 'sculptured atmosphere'. 'New width', made possible by the massive spans which lightweight construction could offer. The 'decisive power of the line', which he linked to the verticality of the Eiffel Tower, although he found this offered 'the charm of the stupendous' rather than beauty. And finally, 'new lines', typified by the structural contours of bridges. Reluctant to sacrifice the ideal of beauty, Meyer could not quite make the leap to embrace the sublime – 'powerful force in simple form' – as the appropriate aesthetic category to describe the vertiginous experience of looking down through the framework of the Eiffel Tower.
58 *Building in France. . .* op. cit., and *Space, Time and Architecture* (Cambridge, Mass.: Harvard University Press, 1941).
59 Quoted in Detlef Mertins, 'The Enticing and Threatening Face of Prehistory: Walter Benjamin and the Utopia of Glass', *Assemblage* 29, pp6–23.
60 *Building in France. . .* op. cit., p101.
61 Ibid., p142, capitals and emphasis in original.
62 Johannes Itten, *Design and Form. The Basic Course at the Bauhaus* (London: Thames and Hudson, 1975), p34.
63 Sigfried Giedion, 'Bauhaus und Bauhauswoche zu Weimar', *Das Werk*, no. 9, 1923, p233.
64 For a comprehensive introduction to László Moholy-Nagy, see Krisztina Passuth, *Moholy-Nagy* (London: Thames and Hudson, 1985).
65 Quoted in Neumeyer, op. cit., p317.
66 The remark is in Le Corbusier, tr. by Francis E. Hyslop, *When*

the Cathedrals were White (London: Routledge, 1947), p208. I have quoted the more fluent translation by Margaret Guiton in *The Ideas of Le Corbusier* (New York: George Braziller, 1981), p73.
67 Quoted in Penelope Curtis, *Sculpture 1900–1945* (Oxford: Oxford University Press, 1999), p78.
68 Radu Varia, *Brancusi* (New York: Rizzoli, 1986), p134.
69 Quoted in Penelope Curtis, *Sculpture 1900–1945*, op. cit., p85–6.
70 In Neumeyer, op. cit., p246.
71 Le Corbusier, tr. by Frederick Etchells, *Towards a New Architecture* (London: Architectural Press, 1946), p214.
72 Arthur Korn, *Glass in Modern Architecture* (London: Barrie and Rockliff, 1967; 1st, German edn. 1926), pp6–7.
73 Henry-Russell Hitchcock and Philip Johnson, *The International Style: Architecture Since 1922* (New York: W. W. Norton, 1932; reissued 1966).
74 These quotations are from Chapters 1 and 111 – the first and the last – of *Glasarchitektur*. Paul Scheerbart and Bruno Taut, ed. by Denis Sharp, *Glass Architecture and Alpine Architecture* (London: November Books, 1971).
75 See Rosemarie Haag Bletter, 'The Interpretation of the Glass Dream – Expressionist Architecture and the History of the Crystal Metaphor', *Journal of the Society of Architectural Historians*, 1981, vol. 40, no. 1, pp20–43.
76 Quoted in Neumeyer, op. cit., p314.
77 Ibid., p317.
78 Quoted in ibid., from an article published in *Kunstgewerbeblatt*, N.S. XXVII, October 1915.
79 Quoted in Rosemarie Haag Bletter, 'Paul Scheerbart's Architectural Fantasies', *Journal of the Society of Architectural Historians*, 1975, vol. 34, no. 2, pp83–97.
80 Bruno Taut, *Alpine Architecture*, op. cit.
81 Walter Gropius, 'Glasbau', *Die Bauzeitung* 23, 1926, pp159–62.
82 Quoted by Nancy Troy, *The De Stijl Environment* (Cambridge, Mass.: MIT Press, 1983), p106.
83 Paul Scheerbart, 'Ch. 4: Double glass walls, light, heating and cooling', in *Glass Architecture*, op. cit., p42.
84 Frank Lloyd Wright, 'The Meaning of Materials – Glass', in *In the Cause of Architecture*, op. cit., pp197–204.
85 Frank Lloyd Wright delivering the Kahn lectures at Princeton University in 1930, quoted in Michael Wigginton, *Glass in Architecture* (London: Phaidon, 1996), p59.
86 See ibid. for a discussion of the structural use of glass.
87 Frank Lloyd Wright, op. cit., p205.
88 Pier Luigi Nervi, tr. by Giuseppina and Mario Salvadori, *Structures* (New York: F. W. Dodge, 1956), p29.
89 Quoted in Mario Manieri Elia, *Louis Henry Sullivan* (Princeton: Princeton Architectural Press, 1996), p116.
90 Adrian Stokes, 'Stones of Rimini' in *The Critical Writings of Adrian Stokes* (London: Thames and Hudson, 1978), Vol. I, pp244 and 248.
91 For a discussion of carving and modelling see ibid. and Stephen Kite's 'Introduction to *Stones of Rimini*' in Adrian Stokes, *The Quattro Cento and Stones of Rimini* (University Park: The Pennsylvania State University Press, 2002), pp1–18. Kite's as yet unpublished doctoral thesis on Stokes (Newcastle University, 2002), is a major contribution to the small but growing body of scholarship on Stokes.
92 Frank Lloyd Wright, 'IV. The Architect and the Machine', in *In the Cause of Architecture*, op. cit., pp145–8.
93 Louis Kahn quoted in Jan C. Rowan, 'Wanting to Be: The Philadelphia School', *Progressive Architecture*, April 1961.
94 Le Corbusier, *Towards a New Architecture*, op. cit., pp215–6.
95 Le Corbusier, *Oeuvre Complète*, Vol I, pp78–88, and Sigfried Giedion, *Building in France. . .*, op. cit., pp167–180.

96 See discussion at the end of Ch. 2 above.
97 Sigfried Giedion, *Building in France. . .*, p169.
98 See Reyner Banham, *The New Brutalism* (London: Architectural Press, 1966).
99 See, for example, Udo Kultermann, *New Architecture in the World* (London: Thames and Hudson, 1966).
100 Richard Saul Wurman, *What Will Be Has Always Been. The Words of Louis I. Kahn* (New York: Rizzoli, 1986), p30.
101 Ibid., p174.
102 Ibid., p125.
103 Pier Luigi Nervi, op. cit., p17.
104 Frank Lloyd Wright, *In the Cause of Architecture*, op. cit., p142.
105 The cantilevers at Fallingwater defied analysis by the statical means available at the time they were built; they have recently undergone substantial structural work to stabilize them.
106 See Frank Lloyd Wright, *In the Cause of Architecture*, op. cit., p208.
107 For pictures of the column test see Robert McCarter, *Frank Lloyd Wright* (London: Phaidon Press, 1997), p288.
108 Neumeyer, op. cit., p316.
109 *Louis Kahn in His Own Words*, op. cit., p152.
110 Ibid., p127.
111 Alessandra Latour, ed., *Louis I. Kahn: Writings, Lectures, Interviews* (New York: Rizzoli, 1991), p227.
112 See Carlos Vallhonrat, 'Tectonics Considered. Between the Presence and the Absence of Artifice', *Perspecta 24*, pp122–35.
113 Latour, op. cit., p323.
114 See my *Town Hall, Säynätsalo* (London: Phaidon Press, 1993).
115 Paul Thompson, *William Butterfield* (London: Routledge and Kegan Paul, 1971), p226.
116 For Lewerentz's churches see Claes Caldenby, Adam Caruso and Sven Ivar Lind, *Sigurd Lewerentz. Two Churches* (Stockholm: Arkitektur Förlag, 1997).

Chapter 4
Place

1 Marcel Proust, quoted in Stephen Bann, 'The Case for Stokes (and Pater)', in *PN Review 9*, vol. 6, no. 1, p8.
2 Steven Feld and Keith H. Basso, ed's., *Senses of Place* (Santa Fe: School of American Research Press, 1996), p84.
3 See, for example, Christian Norberg-Schulz, *Genius Loci. Towards a Phenomenology of Architecture* (London: Academy Editions, 1980).
4 For a critical discussion of this topic, see Kathryn Moore, 'Genius loci', paper at given at the conference 'Constructing Place' held at Newcastle University in April 2002.
5 Alexander Pope in *Epistle to the Right Honourable Richard Earl of Burlington*, 1731, reprinted in John Dixon Hunt and Peter Willis, *The Genius of the Place: The English Landscape Garden 1620–1820* (Cambridge, Mass.: MIT Press, 1988).
6 Christian Norberg-Schulz, op. cit., exemplifies this attitude.
7 *Book of British Villages* (London: Drive Publications, 1980), p57.
8 William Morris, 'On the external coverings of roofs', lecture, in May Morris, ed., *The Collected Works of William Morris* (London: Longmans Green, 1910–15), Vol. XXII, p429.
9 Quoted by John Piper in 'Colour and Texture', *The Architectural Review*, Vol. 95, Feb. 1944, pp51–2.
10 Frank Lloyd Wright, *An American Architecture* (New York: Horizon Press, 1955), p24.
11 Myron Goldfinger. *Villages in the Sun. Mediterranean Community Architecture* (London: Lund Humphries, 1969); the rev. colour edition (New York: Rizzoli, 1993) covers the same ground but is aesthetically less pleasing than the original.

12 See Arthur Rüegg, ed., *Polychromie architecturale. Le Corbusier's Colour Keyboards from 1931 and 1959* (Zurich: Birkhäuser, 1997).

13 See Hanne Raabyemagle and Claus M. Smidt, eds, *Classicism in Copenhagen* (Copenhagen: Gyldendal, 1998).

14 See Paul Hills, *Venetian Colour* (New Haven: Yale University Press, 1999), p44.

15 The phrase is from ibid., p40.

16 John Ruskin, *The Stones of Venice*, Vol. II, Ch.1, I.

17 Ibid., XXXVII.

18 Lawrence Gowing, ed. *The Critical Writings of Adrian Stokes Vol. II* (London: Thames and Hudson, 1978), p108.

19 For a discussion of the problem see Richard Foster, *Patterns of Thought. The Hidden Meaning of the Great Pavement of Westminster Abbey* (London: Jonathan Cape, 1992).

20 For a discussion of pattern, see Ernst Gombrich, *The Sense of Order* (London: Phaidon Press, 1979).

21 Tudy Sammartini, *Decorative Floors of Venice* (London: Merrell, 2000), p163.

22 These details are summarized from an interview with Carlo Scarpa by Marco Frascari, in 'Notes of a Theory of Making in a Time of Necessity', *Perspecta 24*, pp2–23.

23 Text of lecture by Alvaro Siza in Kenneth Frampton, ed., *Technology, Place and Architecture. The Jerusalem Seminar in Architecture* (New York: Rizzoli, 1998), pp138–57.

24 See, for example, the special issue on The Netherlands of *The Architectural Review*, January 1985.

25 Richard Neutra, 'House in the Colorado Desert', *Architects' Year Book: 3*, ed. by Jane Drew and Trevor Dannatt (London: Paul Elek, 1949).

26 The Taliesin Fellowship attempted to combine the roles of office and school of architecture.

27 Neil Levine, *The Architecture of Frank Lloyd Wright* (Princeton: Princeton University Press, 1996), pp254–97.

28 Semper's ideas were much discussed in late nineteenth-century Chicago where Wright served his apprenticeship.

29 Neil Levine, op. cit., pp269–70.

30 Frank Lloyd Wright, *An Autobiography* (New York: Duell, Sloan and Pierce, 1977), p335.

31 See Neil Levine, op. cit., pp216–53.

32 Frank Lloyd Wright, ed. Frederick Gutheim, *In the Cause of Architecture. Essays by Frank Lloyd Wright for Architectural Record* (New York: Architectural Record, 1975), pp179–88.

33 See my *Utzon. Inspiration, Vision, Architecture* (Hellerup: Edition Bløndal, 2002), pp368–403.

34 For Can Lis, see Christian Norberg-Schulz, 'Jørn Utzon and the Primordial', in *Utzon Mallorca* (Copenhagen: Arkitektens Forlag, 1996).

35 An influential early example of the architectural analysis of place is Gordon Cullen, *Townscape* (London: Architectural Press, 1962).

36 Lucy R. Lippard, *The Lure of the Local. Senses of place in a multicentered society* (New York: The New Press, 1997), p54.

37 Jackson was a prolific essay-writer; see, for example, John Brinckerhoff Jackson, *A Sense of Place, A Sense of Time* (New Haven: Yale University Press, 1996).

38 The article was published in 1967 and is reproduced in full in Jack Flam, ed. *Robert Smithson: The Collected Writings* (Berkeley and Los Angeles: University of California Press, 1996).

39 John Dixon Hunt and Peter Willis, op. cit., p337.

40 Quoted in Lippard, op. cit., p183.

41 The original is in the form of a question, '… is not Main Street almost all right?' in Robert Venturi, *Complexity and Contradiction in Architecture* (New York: The Museum of Modern Art, 1966), p102.

42 See Kenneth Frampton, 'The Work of Tadao Ando' in Yukio Futagawa, ed., *Tadao Ando* (Tokyo: A.D.A. Edita, 1987).

43 Colin Rowe and Fred Koetter, *Collage City* (Cambridge, Mass.: MIT Press, 1978).

Chapter 5
Time

1 Italo Calvino, *Invisible Cities* (London: Pan Books, 1979), p104.

2 Nikolaus Pevsner, 'Time and Le Corbusier', *The Architectural Review*, March 1959, pp159–65.

3 This process was confirmed by the completion in 1935 of the House at Mathes and the Small Week-End House near Paris.

4 For Pessac see Philippe Boudon, *Lived-in Architecture. Le Corbusier's Pessac revisited* (London: Lund Humphries, 1972).

5 Richard Meier, 'Essay', *Perspecta 24*, pp104–5.

6 Sophie Trelcat, 'Materials and their Ageing. As Time Goes By', *L'Architecture d'Aujourd'hui*, 331, Nov–Dec 2000, pp44–6.

7 Andrea Palladio, tr. by Isaac Ware, *The Four Books of Architecture* (New York: Dover, 1965), First Book, Chap. II.

8 Ibid., Chap. III.

9 John Ruskin, *The Seven Lamps of Architecture*, Ch. VI, XVI.

10 Ibid., Ch. VI, X.

11 'Daguerrotype' was the first practicable photographic process, announced to the public in 1839 by Louis Jacques Mandé Daguerre.

12 Sarah Quill, *Ruskin's Venice: The Stones Revisited* (London: Ashgate, 2000) p33.

13 Quoted by John Piper in 'Colour and Texture', *The Architectural Review*, Vol. 95, Feb. 1944, pp51–2.

14 Quoted by Christopher Woodward, *In Ruins* (London: Chatto and Windus, 2001), p123.

15 Sir Joshua Reynolds, quoted in 'Price on Picturesque Planning', *The Architectural Review*, Feb. 1944, pp47–50.

16 Leonardo wrote: 'When you look at a wall spotted with stains…you may discover a resemblance to various landscapes, beautified with mountains, rivers, rocks, trees, or again you may see battles and figures in action or strange faces and costumes and an endless variety of objects which you could reduce to complete and well-drawn forms. And these appear on such walls confusedly, like the sound of bells in whose jangle you may find any name or word you choose to imagine.' In his *Treatise on Painting* (Princeton: Princeton University Press, 1956).

17 Preface to the 1880 edition of *The Seven Lamps of Architecture*.

18 John Ruskin, *The Seven Lamps of Architecture*, Ch. VI, XVIII.

19 Quoted by Richard Murphy, *Carlo Scarpa and the Castelvecchio* (London: Butterworth Architecture, 1990), p4.

20 James Curl, *Oxford Dictionary of Architecture* (Oxford: Oxford University Press, 1999), entry on 'Conservation', p162.

21 See Richard Murphy, op. cit., for a comprehensive study.

22 See Christian Norberg-Schulz and Gennaro Postiglione, *Sverre Fehn* (New York: The Monacelli Press, 1997), pp129–44.

23 See Christopher Woodward, op. cit., p29.

24 Quoted by Ludwig Goldscheider, *Ghiberti* (London: Phaidon Press, 1949), p18.

25 For the fruits of his time there see Jan Hochstim, *The Paintings and Sketches of Louis I. Kahn* (New York: Rizzoli, 1991).

26 Alessandra Latour, ed., *Louis I. Kahn: Writings, Lectures, Interviews* (New York: Rizzoli, 1991), p123.

27 Aldo Rossi, *A Scientific Autobiography* (Cambridge, Mass.: MIT Press, 1981), p2.

28 For one explanation, see the letter 'Metallic taste' in *The Architectural Review*, August 2002, pp23–4.

29 For Serra, see Hal Foster and David Sylvester, *Richard Serra: Sculpture 1985–98* (Frankfurt: Steidl Verlag, 1999).

30 See Mohsen Mostafavi and David Leatherbarrow, *On Weathering* (Cambridge, Mass.: MIT Press, 1993), p42.

31 Aldo Rossi, loc. cit.

32 Bruno Taut, *Houses and People of Japan* (London: John Gifford, 1938), pp143–4.

33 I quote from memory: Wright's remark was placed next to a photograph of an icicle hanging from the eaves of Taliesin East, but the source eludes me.

34 Aalto engaged in an extended – and ultimately unsuccessful – dispute with the tax authorities, arguing that his house was a 'professional experiment'.

35 Alvar Aalto in a 1954 article for *Casabella*, cited in Göran Schildt, *Alvar Aalto. The Mature Years* (New York: Rizzoli, 1991), p214.

36 See my *Alvar Aalto* (London: Phaidon Press, 1995), esp. p121.

Chapter 6
Use

1 Octavio Paz, *Contemporary Crafts in the World* (Greenwich, Conn.: New York Graphic Society, 1974), p17.

2 James Hall, *The World as Sculpture* (London: Chatto and Windus, 1999), p81.

3 Peter Rice, *An Engineer Imagines* (London: Artemis/Ellipsis, 1993), p76.

4 See my *Alvar Aalto* (London: Phaidon Press, 1995), p102.

5 Juhani Pallasmaa, *The Eyes of the Skin. Architecture and the Senses* (London: Academy Editions, 1996), p40.

6 See my *Alvar Aalto*, op. cit., pp80–97.

7 George Baird, *Alvar Aalto* (London: Thames and Hudson, 1970), p16.

8 Theodor Adorno, tr. by E. F. N. Jephcott, *Minima Moralia* (London: Verso Editions, 1978), p40.

9 I heard van Eyck discuss this theme in lectures at the universities of Cambridge and Pennsylvania, and it is explored, sometimes rather self-consciously, in much of his work.

10 Herman Hertzberger, *Lessons for Students in Architecture* (Rotterdam: 010 Publishers, 1993).

11 Cited in Christoph Bignens, 'Plywood as Determinant of Form', *Daidalos*, 56, 1995, pp74–9.

12 Ibid.

13 Hellmut Wohl, *The Aesthetics of Italian Renaissance Art* (Cambridge: Cambridge University Press, 1999), p233.

14 See my *Utzon. Inspiration, Vision, Architecture* (Hellerup: Edition Bløndal, 2002), pp164–73.

15 Ibid., pp225–9.

16 John O'Regan, ed., *Aldo Rossi* (London: Architectural Design, 1983), p56.

17 See 'The Principle of Cladding', in Adolf Loos, tr. by Jane O. Newman and John H. Smith, *Spoken into the Void. Collected Essays 1897–1900* (Cambridge, Mass.: MIT Press, 1982), pp66–9.

18 Roberto Schezen, *Adolf Loos. Architecture 1903–1932* (New York: Monacelli Press, 1996), p17.

19 Loos's essay 'Ornament and Crime' (*Ornament und Verbrechen*) was written in 1908 and influentially re-published by the journal *Der Sturm* in 1912, and later by Amedée Ozenfant and Le Corbusier in *L'Esprit Nouveau*. It is reprinted in *The Architecture of Adolf Loos* (London: Arts Council of Great Britain, 1985), p100.

20 For an introduction to Loos and the *Raumplan*, see my *The House in the Twentieth Century* (London: Laurence King, 2002), pp36–40.

21 Michael Snodin and Elisabet Stavenov-Hidemark, eds, *Carl and Karin Larsson. Creators of the Swedish Style* (London: V&A Publications, 1997).

Chapter 7
Junctions

1 Peter Rice, *An Engineer Imagines* (London: Ellipsis, 1994), p26.
2 Flaubert said the same of literary composition, and the phrase is a 'truism that might equally well apply to all the arts.
3 A 'Full-sizing table' was an essential feature of many architects' offices in the first half of the twentieth century.
4 David Pye, *The Nature and Art of Workmanship* (Cambridge: Cambridge University Press, 1968).
5 See Peter Blundell Jones, *Günter Behnisch* (Basel: Birkhäuser, 2000).
6 M. F. Hearn, ed., *The Architectural Theory of Eugène-Emmanuel Viollet-le-Duc* (Cambridge, Mass.: MIT Press, 1990), p175.
7 James Gowan, lecture at the Welsh School of Architecture, Cardiff University, January 1985.
8 After a heated debate about whether to use granite or marble, a colleague in Helsinki tells me that the replacement marble cladding is again showing signs of bowing.
9 See my *Utzon. Inspiration, Vision, Architecture* (Hellerup: Edition Bløndal, 2002), pp152–3.
10 Daywork joints can now by eliminated by using synthetic renders applied as a thin coating, but these raise other issues about long-term stability.
11 Ákos Moravánszky, *Competing Visions* (Cambridge, Mass.: MIT Press, 1998), p183.
12 Engineer-colleagues whose judgements I trust assure me that this is the case.
13 See Richard Murphy, *Carlo Scarpa and the Castelvecchio* (London: Butterworth Architecture, 1990).
14 I recall reading this observation in a text by Alison and Peter Smithson, but the reference eludes me.
15 John Ruskin, *The Stones of Venice*, Vol. 1, Ch. IV, III.
16 I quote from memory – the reference eludes me.
17 Frank Lloyd Wright, *An American Architecture* (New York: Horizon Press, 1995), p61.

Chapter 8
Surfaces

1 Friedrich Nietzsche, Preface to 2nd ed. of *Die Fröhliche Wissenschaft* (The Gay Science), 1886.
2 For an interesting discussion of this and other textural effects see Carl Petersen 'Textures', a 1919 essay re-published in Simo Paavilainen, ed., *Nordic Classicism 1910–1930* (Helsinki: Museum of Finnish Architecture, 1982), pp35–8, and David Pye, *The Nature and Art of Workmanship* (Cambridge: Cambridge University Press, 1968), pp45–58.
3 Berlage cited in Ákos Moravánszky, *Competing Visions* (Cambridge, Mass.: MIT Press, 1998), p205.
4 Henry-Russell Hitchcock and Philip Johnson, *The International Style: Architecture Since 1922* (New York: W. W. Norton, 1932; reissued 1966), p41.
5 See Robert Venturi, *Complexity and Contradiction in Architecture* (New York: Museum of Modern Art, 1966), p37.
6 Otto Wagner, tr. by Harry Francis Mallgrave, *Modern Architecture* (Santa Monica: Getty Center, 1988), p124.
7 See *Nordic Classicism 1910–1930*, op. cit.
8 Paul Mebes, *Um 1800* (Munich: F. Bruckmann, 1920).
9 I quote from memory from a lecture by Simo Paavilainen given at Cardiff University in 1986.
10 See Josep Quetglas, *Fear of Glass. Mies van der Rohe's Barcelona Pavilion* (Basel: Birkhäuser, 2001).

11 John Ruskin, *The Stones of Venice*, Vol. I, Ch. XXVI, I.
12 Ibid., Ch. IV, V.
13 John Ruskin, *The Seven Lamps of Architecture*, Ch. IV, XXXVI.
14 James Gowan, lecture at the Welsh School of Architecture, Cardiff University, January 1985.

Chapter 9
Meaning

1 Frank Lloyd Wright, ed. Frederick Gutheim, *In the Cause of Architecture. Essays by Frank Lloyd Wright for Architectural Record* (New York: Architectural Record, 1975), p171.
2 Marc-Antoine Laugier, tr. by Wolfgang and Anni Herrmann, *An Essay on Architecture* (Los Angeles: Hennessey & Ingalls, 1977), p60.
3 Gage, *Colour and Culture* (London: Thames and Hudson, 1993), p155.
4 See ibid., pp129–31.
5 On a visit to the school I was told that this was one of Aalto's 'functional' justifications for the luxury!
6 Gottfried Semper, *The Four Elements of Architecture and Other Writings* (Cambridge: Cambridge University Press, 1989), p138.
7 Ibid.
8 Michael Barry, *Colour and Symbolism in Islamic Architecture. Eight Centuries of the Tile-maker's Art* (London: Thames and Hudson, 1996), p11.
9 Hellmut Wohl, *The Aesthetics of Italian Renaissance Art* (Cambridge: Cambridge University Press, 1999), pp73 and 156.
10 R. M. Titford, ed., *The Golden Age of Concrete* (London: Dorothy Henry Publications, 1964).
11 Cited in Gernot Böhme, 'Staged Materiality', *Daidalos* 56, 1995, pp36–43.
12 See, for example, Fu-Tung Cheng and Eric Olsen, *Concrete Countertops: Designs, Forms, and Finishes for the New Kitchen & Bath* (The Taunton Press, 2002).
13 Cited in Helmut Lethen, 'On the Coldness of Materials in the Twenties', *Daidalos 56*, 1995, pp50–55.
14 Ibid.
15 See Barbara Miller Lane, *National Romanticism and Modern Architecture in Germany and the Scandinavian Countries* (Cambridge: Cambridge University Press, 2000).
16 The quotation is from a report written by the architect Hugo Lindberg in 1897, cited in Sixten Ringbom, *Stone, Style and Truth* (Helsinki: Suomen Minaismuistoyhdistyksen Aikakauskirja, 1987), p50.
17 See Peter B. MacKeith and Kerstin Smeds, *The Finland Pavilions* (Helsinki: Kustannus, 1992).
18 See my *Alvar Aalto*, (London: Phaidon Press, 1995), pp81–97.
19 Ibid., p84.
20 Damjan Prelovšek, *Jože Plečnik 1872–1957* (New Haven: Yale University Press, 1997), pp226–7.
21 Ákos Moravánszky, *Competing Visions* (Cambridge, Mass.: MIT Press, 1998), p.392.

Chapter 10
Materiality and translucency

1 Peter Zumthor. *Thinking Architecture* (Basel: Birkhäuser, 1999), p58, elision in original.
2 See Hajime Yatsuka, 'Arata Isozaki after 1980: From Mannerism to the Picturesque', in *Arata Isozaki: Architecture 1960–1990* (New York: Rizzoli, 1991), pp18–23.
3 Charles Jencks, *The Language of Post Modern Architecture*

(London: Academy Editions, 1977).
4 See Anthony Giddens, *The Consequences of Modernity* (Stanford: Stanford University Press, 1990).
5 See, for example, the special project of The Columbia Architectural Journal *Precis* entitled *Architecture and Body* (New York: Rizzoli, 1987).
6 Kenneth Frampton, 'Towards a Critical Regionalism: Six Points for an Architecture of Resistance' in Hal Foster, ed., *Postmodern Culture* (London: Pluto Press, 1985) and *Studies in Tectonic Culture* (Cambridge, Mass. and London: MIT Press, 1995).
7 Michael Benedikt, *For an Architecture of Reality* (New York: Lumen Press, 1988).
8 A diverse range of influential historians, theorists and critics, including Christian Norberg-Schulz, Kenneth Frampton and Juhani Pallasmaa, have drawn widely on the literature of phenomenology.
9 The best record of Ando's early work remains Yukio Futagawa, ed., *Tadao Ando* (Tokyo: A.D.A. Edita, 1987).
10 When Ando lectured for the first time in London, at the Royal Institute of British Architects in 1985, the immediate response from several leading British practitioners was to question how people could live in such houses!
11 I was told this by a member of Ando's staff during a visit to Japan in 1986.
12 See Kenneth Frampton's introduction to Futagawa, op. cit.
13 Jun'ichiro Tanizaki, *In Praise of Shadows* (New Haven: Leete's Island Books, 1977), p4.
14 The influence was pervasive, especially in Northern Europe and Scandinavia, but to the best of my knowledge remains to be explored in depth.
15 Mirko Zardini, ed., *Tadao Ando. Rokko Housing* (Milan: Electa/Casabella, 1986), p61.
16 Ibid.
17 See Paolo Portoghesi, *Architecture 1980. The Presence of the Past. Venice Biennale* (New York: Rizzoli, 1980).
18 See 'The Idea of Lasting. A Conversation with Rafael Moneo', *Perspecta 24*, 1988, pp146–57.
19 Ibid.
20 In popular architectural usage 'materiality' is becoming all but interchangeable with 'materials'.
21 Marc Augé, tr. by John Howe, *Non-places. Introduction to an anthropology of supermodernity* (London: Verso, 1995).
22 Juhani Pallasmaa, *The Eyes of the Skin. Architecture and the Senses* (London: Academy Editions, 1996).
23 Juhani Pallasmaa, 'An Architecture of the Seven Senses', in *Questions of Perception*, special issue of *Architecture and Urbanism*, July 1994, pp27–37.
24 Peter Zumthor, *Thinking Architecture* (Basel: Birkhäuser, 1999), p10.
25 For Beuys, see Heiner Stachelhaus, tr. by David Britt, *Joseph Beuys* (New York: Abbeville, 1991).
26 Ibid., esp. pp61–78.
27 Ibid., p150.
28 See James Meyer, 'The Uses of Merleau Ponty', in *Minimalism* (Ostfildern: Cantz Verlag, 1988), pp178–89.
29 Illustrated in James Meyer, *Minimalism* (London: Phaidon Press, 2000), p96.
30 For a vivid account of a visit to Marfa, see Andrew Mead, 'Installed in Texas', *The Architects' Journal*, 2.10.97, pp32–7.
31 Donald Judd, 'Statement' in *Donald Judd, Complete Writings 1959–1975* (Halifax: Nova Scotia College of Art and Design, 1975), p196: orig. pub. in 'Portfolio: 4 Sculptors', *Perspecta*, March/May 1968.
32 Robert Smithson, 'Entropy and the New Monuments' (1966), in Jack Flam, ed. *Robert Smithson: The Collected Writings* (Berkeley and Los Angeles: University of California Press, 1996), pp10–23.

33 Donald Judd, 'Specific Objects' (1965), in Donald Judd, op. cit., pp181–9.
34 The Dutch construction industry is renowned for building 'economically': Foster and Partners' tower on the Wilhelminapier, for example, was completed in the mid 1990s for around 65 per cent of the cost of a similar building in the UK.
35 The 'upside down roof' was developed as a means of reducing thermal stresses on the roofing membrane.
36 Discussed in the 'Epilogue' to Kenneth Frampton, *Studies in Tectonic Culture*, op. cit., pp377–87.
37 The field-stone cladding at the Fountains Abbey building leans against the structure, making its construction much less demanding than with a freestanding wall.
38 The expression of structure in 'Classic' modern architecture – as, for example, in much of the work of Mies and Kahn – relied on columns and beams that were continuous between inside and out.
39 See my *Utzon. Inspiration, Vision, Architecture* (Hellerup: Editon Bløndal, 2002), p298.
40 See Martin Tschanz, 'Gentle Perversion', in *Daidalos* 56, June 1995, pp88–95.
41 Ibid.
42 See Alejandro Zaera, 'Continuities. Interview with Herzog and de Meuron', *El Croquis*, 60, 1993, pp6–23.
43 Quoted by Christoph Bignens in 'Plywood as Determinant of Form', *Daidalos* 56, June 1995, pp74–9.
44 As, for example, with the grading of natural slates, from broad at the eaves to narrow at the ridge.
45 I have in mind, for example, the entrance at the top of the external stair on the Millowners' Building in Ahmedabad of 1954 (*Œuvre complète*, Vol. VI, p145); close perusal of the *Œuvre complète* would doubtless yield other examples.
46 Martin Steinmann, 'The Presence of Things', in *Construction, Intention, Detail. Five Projects from Swiss Architects* (Zurich: Artemis, 1994), pp8–25.
47 Peter Zumthor. *Thinking Architecture*, op. cit., p9.
48 Ibid., p30
49 Ibid., p12.
50 For the contrast with Herzog, see the interview in *El Croquis* cited in n42.
51 Zumthor, op. cit., p32.
52 On visiting the building I felt that the interiors of the baths had a slightly 'stage-set' quality at odds with the critical claims for them as models of 'authenticity'.
53 Gigon Guyer, 'Concept into Matter', in Brian Carter and Annette W. LeCuyer, ed's., *Gigon/Guyer: The 2000 Charles and Ray Eames Lecture* (Ann Arbor: University of Michigan, 2000), pp58–9.
54 Ibid., p55.
55 Yve-Alain Bois and Rosalind Krauss, *Formless. A User's Guide* (New York: Zone Books, 1997).
56 Rodolfo Machado and Rodolphe el-Khoury, *Monolithic Architecture* (Munich: Prestel, 1995).
57 Hans Ibelings, *Supermodernism. Architecture in the Age of Globalization* (Rotterdam: NAi Publishers, 1998).
58 Cited in Hans Ibelings, ed., *The Artificial Landscape* (Rotterdam: NAi Publishers, 2000) p272.
59 The software used by Frank Gehry was developed by Dassault, the French manufacturers of the Mirage jet.
60 See Ellen Lupton, *Skin. Surface, Substance + Design* (New York: Princeton Architectural Press and London: Laurence King, 2002).
61 Jan Kaplicky, *Confessions* (London: Wiley/Academy, 2002), p128.
62 See *www.bk.tudelft.nl/users/veltkamp*
63 Sokratis Georgiadis in his Introduction to Sigfried Giedion, *Building in France, Building in Iron, Building in Ferroconcrete* (Santa Monica: Getty Center, 1995), p102.
64 When I visited shortly after the building opened, I was told that to ensure an image of efficiency, staff had been told to remove much of the material brought in to 'personalize' their workspaces.
65 For a brief history of the structural uses of glass, see Michael Wigginton, *Glass in Architecture* (London: Phaidon, 1996), p102–5.
66 I say 'begun' advisedly: the structure was designed and built in eleven weeks, but due to the unexpected closure of the new school of architecture at which I was due to teach the house was not fully completed and sold until November 2002.
67 At the time the house was designed the engineer was free to push the material to its limits: see the comments by Pier Luigi Nervi quoted above on p90.
68 Catherine Slessor, 'Light Box' in *The Architectural Review*, May 1998, pp56–7.
69 The classic books of Blossfeldt's photographs (*Urformen der Kunst*, 1928, *Wundergarten der Natur*, 1932, and *Wunder in der Natur*, 1942) have recently been reissued, but sadly the reproductions are a poor substitute for the original photogravures: Hans Christian Adam, *Karl Blossfeldt 1865–1932* (Cologne: Taschen, 1999).
70 Loos attacks tattooing as a feature of primitive or degenerate cultures in 'Ornament and Crime', in *The Architecture of Adolf Loos* (London: The Arts Council of Great Britain, 1985), p100.
71 See, for example the special issue of *L'Architecture d'Aujourd'hui* on 'Ornament' (no. 333, March–April, 2001).
72 Gerhard Mack, 'Building with Images' in *Eberswalde Library* (London: Architectural Association, 2000).
73 Jun'ichiro Tanizaki, *In Praise of Shadows* (New Haven: Leete's Island Books, 1977).
74 Ibid., p18.
75 With the exception of the 'Chapel with the Light', to the best of my knowledge Ando's chapels are designed primarily for wedding ceremonies.
76 Toyo Ito, 'Tarzans in the Media Forest' in Andrea Maffei, ed., *Toyo Ito. Works, Projects, Writings* (Milan: Electa, 2001), p343–5.
77 Le Corbusier, *Œuvre Complète*, Vol. I, pp128–9.
78 Toyo Ito, loc. cit.
79 Andrea Maffei, 'Toyo Ito, the Works' in Maffei, op. cit., p17.
80 See, for example, Michael Wigginton and Jude Harris, *Intelligent Skins* (Oxford: Butterworth-Heinemann, 2002).
81 'Diamond Pleaser', in *Building Design*, 23.8.02, pp16–7.

Picture Credits

The majority of the photographs in this book were taken by the author. Others are credited by page number and position on the page.

2 (centre right, above) Jordi Cuxart
  (centre right, below) C. Malcolm Parry
  (bottom right) Peter Cook/View/Architect: Eric Owen Moss
  (bottom left and centre left, below) Jeremy Lowe
6 Nicholas Kane/Architect: MVRDV
8 (right) Bryan Avery
9 Bryan Avery
10–11 Jeremy Lowe
13 (bottom) B. Norman/Ancient Art and Architecture
14 (centre right) Stephen Kite
17 (top right) Corbis
18 Peter Cook/View/Architect: Eric Owen Moss
19 (left, top and bottom) Jeremy Lowe
  (right) David Else/Christine Osborne Pictures
20 (left) Richard Parnaby
  (right) Will Dimond
21 (top) Jeremy Lowe
  (bottom left) Stephen Kite
22 (left and bottom right) Bryan Avery
  (centre and top right) Jeremy Lowe
23 Jeremy Lowe
24 (left, top and bottom, and right) Jeremy Lowe
25 (right) Andrea Mantegna 'La Madonna delle cave' (detail)/ Galleria degli Uffizi, Firenze/Scala
27 (bottom left) Jeremy Lowe
28 (right) Adrian Scholefield
31 (top) J. M. Tardy/Laurence King/Bridgeman Art Library
  (bottom) Martin Charles
34 (left) Mike Fitchett
36–7 Jordi Cuxart
40 Jordi Cuxart
41 (centre) Jeremy Lowe
42 (left) Scala
43 (bottom, left and right) Jeremy Lowe
44 Jeremy Lowe
46 J. C. Martel/Archipress
47 (left, top and bottom) Jeremy Lowe
49 (top, and bottom left) Jeremy Lowe
50 (left and centre) Jeremy Lowe
51 (bottom left, centre and right) Jeremy Lowe
52 (bottom left) Jeremy Lowe
54 (centre) Jeremy Lowe
59 (top) Théodore Labrouste *Temple d'Hercule à Cora restaure Elévation et plan*/ Ecole nationale supérieure des Beaux-arts, Paris
65 © FLC/ADAGP, Paris and DACS, London 2003
66 © FLC/ADAGP, Paris and DACS, London 2003
67 © FLC/ADAGP, Paris and DACS, London 2003 (photographer: Paul Harries)
71 (bottom) Jeremy Lowe
74 (right) John Carter
75 (top) Hiroyuki Hirai/Architect: Shigeru Ban
76 (top) Hulton Archive
77 Nigel Young/Architect: Foster and Partners
80 (top) © ADAGP, Paris and DACS, London 2003
  (bottom left and right) © FLC/ADAGP, Paris and DACS, London 2003

81 © FLC/ADAGP, Paris and DACS, London 2003
82 (right) Foster and Partners
86 (bottom left) C. Malcolm Parry
87 © FLC/ADAGP, Paris and DACS, London 2003
90 (left) Peter Cook/Archipress/Architect: Louis Kahn
93 © FLC/ADAGP, Paris and DACS, London 2003
94 (bottom left) Shinkenchiku Sha/Architect: Louis Kahn
96 (centre) Emlyn Cullen
97 Emlyn Cullen
102 (left) Bryan Avery
104 (centre) David Jenkins
110 Bryan Avery
115 (bottom) Tim Street-Porter/Esto/Architect: Frank Gehry
116–7 Jeremy Lowe
119 © FLC/ADAGP, Paris and DACS, London 2003
121 (bottom right) Bayerische Schlösserverwaltung
142 Mogens Prip-Buus
144 Pavel Stecha & Radovan Bocek/Architect: Adolf Loos
145 Pavel Stecha & Radovan Bocek/Architect: Adolf Loos
146–7 Tom Bonner/Architect: Eric Owen Moss
151 (left) Jeremy Lowe
161 (bottom right) © FLC/ADAGP, Paris and DACS, London 2003
162 (top) © FLC/ADAGP, Paris and DACS, London 2003 (photographer: Paul Harries)
166 (top right) Bryan Avery
175 (top) Stephen Kite
175 (bottom left) Adrian Mayer/Edifice
176 © FLC/ADAGP, Paris and DACS, London 2003
178 Finnish Museum of Architecture
179 (bottom right) Dezsö Eckler
187 (bottom) Margherita Spiluttini/Architect: Herzog de Meuron
188–9 Paul Warchol/Architect: Steven Holl
192 Lluís Casals/Architect: Rafael Moneo
193 (bottom) Jonathan Vining
199 (right) Margherita Spiluttini/Architect: Herzog de Meuron
201 (left) Margherita Spiluttini/Architect: Herzog de Meuron
  (right) Gaston Wicki/Architect: Diener and Diener
205 David Dernie
206 (bottom left) Hélène Binet/Architect: Peter Zumthor
210 Paul McMullen
211 (top) Jordi Bernadó/Architect: Alejandro de la Soto
  (bottom left) Christian Richters/Architect: Rem Koolhaas
  (bottom right) Christian Richters/Architect: Neutelings Riedijk
212–3 Stefan Müller/Architect: Daniel Libeskind
214 Nigel Young/Architect: Foster and Partners
215 Tim Hursley/Architect: Frank Gehry
216 (bottom left and right) Nigel Young/Architect: Foster and Partners
217 Dennis Gilbert/View/Architect: Foster and Partners
220 Christian Richters/Architect: Erik Van Egeraat
221 (top) Chris Gascoigne/Architect: Rick Mather Architects
222 (centre) Duccio Malagamba/Architect: Rafael Moneo
  (right) Margherita Spiluttini/Architect: Herzog de Meuron
223 Margherita Spiluttini/Architect: Herzog de Meuron
225 Hiro Sakaguchi/Architect: Toyo Ito
226 Bitter Bredt/Architect: Sauerbruch and Hutton
227 (left) Dennis Gilbert/View/Architect: Foster and Partners
  (right) Neal Thomas
228 Keld Helmer-Petersen

Author's Acknowledgments

Books, like buildings, are collaborative projects and I would like to thank the staff at Laurence King, and in particular Liz Faber, for their customary care and attention. Special thanks are due to the freelance project editor, Anne McDowall, whose attention to detail and design, and sympathy with long sentences, were exemplary. My father, Don Weston, and John Pardey commented helpfully on several chapters, and Stephen Kite kindly gave access to his unpublished doctoral thesis on Adrian Stokes.

Although the majority of pictures are my own, there would have been many conspicuous gaps without the help of numerous friends and colleagues in supplying colours slides. Jeremy Lowe, whose fine pictures delighted and informed many generations of students at the Welsh School of Architecture, requires especial thanks for the range of his contributions, and I am also enormously grateful to Bryan Avery, John Carter, Emlyn Cullen, David Dernie, Will Dimond, Foster and Partners, Paul Harries, David Jenkins, Stephen Kite, Richard Parnaby, C. Malcolm Parry, Mogens Prip-Buus, Adrian Scholefield, Neal Thomas and Jonathan Vining.